Sense &
Respond

Sense &
Respond

*Capturing Value
in the Network Era*

Edited by
Stephen P. Bradley and Richard L. Nolan

Harvard Business School Press
Boston, Massachusetts

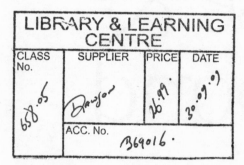
Copyright © 1998 by the President and Fellows of Harvard College
All rights reserved
Printed in the United States of America
02 01 00   5 4

Library of Congress Cataloging-in-Publication Data
Sense and respond: capturing value in the network era / edited by Stephen P. Bradley and
    Richard L. Nolan.
       p. cm.
    Includes index.
    ISBN 0-87584-835-4 (alk. paper)
    1. Business enterprises—Computer networks. 2. Client/server computing.
  I. Bradley, Stephen P., 1941–   . II Nolan, Richard L.
  HD30.37.S46   1998   97-39970
  658'.05—DC21   CIP

The paper used in this publication meets the requirements of the American National
Standard for Permanence of Paper for Printed Library Materials Z39 49-1984

Contents

Preface

Sense and Respond: Capturing Value in the Network Era is the outgrowth of research presented at the third Harvard Business School colloquium on the information technology revolution. The Network Era, the third major phase in the transition of the economy from the industrial age to the information age, is by far the most important of the three. Some observers, like the *Economist*, have suggested that the client/server technology that makes networking on the Internet possible is a more important advance than radio or television, or perhaps even the printing press.[1]

We began our research on the Network Era with a colloquium held in 1987 three years after the breakup of AT&T, ordered by Judge Harold Greene of the Federal District Court of the District of Columbia in the now infamous Modified Final Judgment.[2] At that time, we judged the effort to establish competition in telecommunications in the United States only a partial success. Nevertheless, the ability it conferred to freely integrate telecommunications and computers was key to triggering the Network Era. With the power of computers doubling (and cost halving) every eighteen months, networking for both business and pleasure became commonplace.

In 1991, enough had happened to warrant a second colloquium on the form of the emerging Network Era.[3] By that time, the Network Era had become a global phenomenon. Both the United Kingdom and Japan had privatized their formerly government-run telephone companies, and both were permitting competition in the provision of long-distance service. Even though some key restrictions on competition in the provision of long-distance service still exist in some countries (e.g., France and Germany), many countries now allow competition in the provision of data services, equipment, and cellular service. Today, the Network Era is in full swing, and virtually every nation is concerned with the development of its information infrastructure and with participation in the global information infrastructure. Indeed, some countries, like Singapore, consider the development of their information infrastructure to be pivotal in their ability to compete in the twenty-first century. Information exchange is now a competitive necessity.

Our 1995 colloquium, *Multimedia and the Boundaryless World*, continued our research on the form and impact of the Network Era, specifically the emerging enabling technologies of multimedia. Before the World Wide Web, the Internet was largely a provider of e-mail to the academic community. But the rich graphical interface of the Web laid on top of the robust open architecture of the Net, changed the stodgy network overnight. Virtual shopping, virtual manufacturing, and virtual organizations exploded. This important phenomenon and its implications for the manager, entrepreneur, and policymaker, are the subject of this book.

Research Approach

The approach we used to investigate the Network Era was the same in all three colloquia. First, we used the stages framework based on organizational learning to track the penetration of new technologies in three distinct eras: the Data Processing Era, the Microcomputer Era, and the Network Era. In each era, the organizational learning about the technologies progressed from the awareness stage to the mastery and use stage, in which the information technologies are effectively managed to capture value for the firm. Just as the Data Processing Era involved mastery of mainframe technologies and automation of transaction processing, and the Microcomputer Era involved mastery of the microcomputer technology and "informating" (leveraging the activities of the organization's employees), the new Network Era involves mastery and use of client/server and networking technologies.

Through the stages framework, we developed our views about the ways that the era's information technologies were impacting on various organizations. At this point, we have observed that companies are evolving from physically contiguous fixed functions to flexible functions free of the constraints of physical contiguity. Consequently, we see today's businesses moving toward a boundaryless, or "virtual," type of organization. Multimedia technologies are playing an important role in this transformation by making computers accessible to all workers, not just those who have mastered the rather sophisticated skills required to negotiate through mainframe and personal computer operating systems and networks.

The second step in our approach was to refine our ideas about the impact of emerging information technologies using the network of academics and practicing managers we had developed through our earlier colloquia and research. After the leading technologies and concepts had been identified, our third step was to build a general framework for thinking about the technologies, identifying pertinent managerial issues, and structuring a body of knowledge helpful to managers and academicians seeking to learn about emerging technologies and their impact. Based on this framework, we then worked with academics and practitioners to develop working titles and outlines for the papers.

In this third colloquium, we were able to go beyond the limitations of the usual research papers. Before the colloquium was held we worked with the authors to develop a CD-ROM that would include not only background readings and abstracts of the papers, but also video clips and graphics showing the new technologies in action. The purpose was to demonstrate the importance of the issues to be addressed by providing an experience in actually using the multimedia technology in preparation for the colloquium. The project was extremely successful and gave us a head start in discussing the ideas that would later be considered at the colloquium.

At the colloquium, our objective was to discuss both the ideas in the papers and the usefulness of our framework for thinking about managerial issues and the impact of technology. About eighty participants were invited, including academics, managers who were developing information technologies, and managers who were using those technologies. All the discussions held over the two-and-a-half days were videotaped, so key ideas could be captured for inclusion in this book and use in our classrooms.

The colloquium discussions, papers, video clips, and graphics provided the starting point for this book.

Organization of This Book

Although we began work on this book with the organizing theme of "Multimedia and the Boundaryless World," gradually the idea of a boundaryless world evolved into the notion of a "virtual" world—virtual teams, virtual offices, virtual shopping, and manufacturing. We sought to discover how companies were using the emerging Network Era technologies to capture economic value in new ways. As we investigated this question more deeply, we found that companies were shifting from the traditional "make and sell" strategies to quicker, more responsive "sense and respond" strategies. That is, they were connecting with customers electronically in order to sense their needs, and then developing new capabilities using Network Era technologies to respond to those needs in real time.

The resulting new framework is reflected in the title *Sense and Respond: Capturing Value in the Network Era*. To develop the framework in depth, the book is organized into four main parts. Part One, "Creating and Capturing Value," describes how the revolution going on in the information technology industry provides the capabilities to develop "sense and respond" strategies for creating and capturing value in the information age. This part also includes chapters on the potential winners and losers in the restructuring of the information technology/multimedia industry, and the nature of the competitive environment for major network players.

The next two parts concentrate on the "sense and respond" strategies as they are being developed in the business world today. Separating the two components of sense and respond is difficult—indeed, there is substantial conceptual overlap in both parts. Nevertheless, we concluded that in most firms, the sensing capabilities were significantly less developed than the response capabilities.

Part Two, "Sensing the Customer," focuses on sensing customers' needs through the process of connecting with customers electronically, using the emerging network infrastructures. Then in Part Three, "Responding with Capabilities," we consider developing capabilities to respond to customer needs more effectively, taking advantage of our improved ability to sense these needs.

Part Four, "Transforming the Organization," focuses on the evolution of the emerging "sense and respond" organization. The distinguishing characteristic of this type of organization is the shift from a physical place or places to virtual offices, teams, factories, markets, and stores. The old "command and control" hierarchical organizations of the industrial age are being replaced by the flatter, more responsive, electronically networked organizations of the information age.

Acknowledgments

We would like to express our thanks to the hundreds of managers, technologists, and academics who have collaborated with us on this book. Starting with the colloquium and ending with the book, so many gave freely of their time and ideas that we cannot begin to list them. Without the help of hundreds of such contributors, this work would not have been possible. The Division of Research of the Harvard Business School and our HBO Associates funded our colloquium and research. We would like especially to thank the Director of Research, Professor F. Warren McFarlan for his encouragement. Warren was very supportive of our experimentation with the CD-ROM as a medium for facilitating preliminary work for the colloquium. We would especially like to thank our research associate, Elise Martin, who helped organize the *Multimedia and the Boundaryless World* colloquium and was the project manager for the development of the innovative CD-ROM. We would also like to thank our research associates, James Leonard and Takia Mahmood, who successively managed the development of the book and Betty Morgan who edited the book manuscript. Finally, both of our administrative assistants, Mary Kennedy and Martha Laisne, contributed in many ways throughout the project, for which we are most appreciative.

S. P. B.

R. L. N.

Endnotes

1. *Economist,* July 1, 1995.
2. See Stephen P. Bradley and Jerry A. Hausman (eds.), *Future Competition in Telecommunications* (Boston, MA: Harvard Business School Press, 1989).
3. See Bradley, Hausman, and Richard L. Nolan, *Globalization, Technology and Competition* (Boston, MA: Harvard Business School Press, 1993).

PART ONE

Creating and Capturing Value

1 Capturing Value in the Network Era

Stephen P. Bradley and Richard L. Nolan

FUELED BY THE INTERNET, the Network Era is exploding, bringing about change more sweeping than did the advent of minicomputers or even personal computers (PCs). And this is just the beginning. Inside companies, intranets begotten by the Internet are growing at a faster pace than the Internet itself. These revolutionary changes will transform not only the information technology (IT) industry, but almost every other industry as well.

The unprecedented explosion of Internet technologies is creating enormous opportunities for companies to capture value. Microsoft continues to dominate the IT industry, capturing additional value through its nearly overnight shift to a new strategy of embracing and extending Internet technologies. With less than $10 billion in revenue but more than $9 billion of accumulated cash reserves, Microsoft is riding the cutting edge, realizing gross margins exceeding ninety percent. Though its revenues are just one sixth those of IBM, Microsoft's market value now exceeds that of the once dominant competitor. A new entrant, Netscape, has come out of nowhere to become the fastest growing software company in the world. Netscape rather than

IBM is the company that is mounting a challenge to Microsoft's dominance and industry leadership. The rapid pace of change in the IT industry is unlike anything ever seen before.

Sense and Respond

Driven by this revolutionary change in information technology, a paradigm shift is taking place in the way companies compete and are managed. Traditional "make and sell" strategies, tied to the annual budget cycle, are being replaced by radically faster, real-time, "sense and respond" strategies. Rather than competing by forecasting customers' needs and then planning the year's production using inventories to match supply and demand, firms are relying on real-time sensors to continuously discover what each customer needs, sometimes even anticipating unspecified needs, and then quickly fulfilling those needs with customized products and services delivered with heretofore unavailable capabilities and speed. The result is an almost immediate response to consumers' demand through dynamic resource allocation and execution.

All kinds of innovations are being driven by this paradigm shift to "sense and respond" management. Whole industries are restructuring, moving from lumbering vertical integration structures to more responsive disaggregated horizontal structures. The rapid development and adoption of technological standards is facilitating this structural shift. Industry consolidation occurs rapidly as key technologies merge, allowing firms to pursue ever greater market opportunities. Strategic alliances form to share the costs and benefits of the new technologies. Today, all industries are under pressure to move toward the "sense and respond" paradigm.

"Sense and respond" is steadily replacing the "make and sell" paradigm that has been institutionalized by the highly successful organizations of the 1950s right up to the 1990s. These familiar organizations are highly complex pyramid structures tightly integrated through disciplined functions and rigorous annual budgeting systems. Detailed line-item general ledger codes provide the basis for control, enabling factories to produce a plethora of equally complex products like cars, trucks, ships, airplanes, and computers. The global automotive industry, topping $1 trillion of revenue a year, is unparalleled in economic history in size and number of workers employed. Not only are the industries and companies of the late industrial era unequaled in size and achievements, they have operated at a high level of success for over 40 years.

This extraordinary record is the reason it is so hard to challenge this established paradigm with a fledgling new one. However, the new approach of "sense and respond" has some extremely desirable virtues not found in the old "make and sell" approach. For example, the "sense and respond" management approach, as practiced by leading firms in the IT industry, such as Microsoft, Sun, Trilogy, Cisco, and Netscape, is creating products of unparalleled complexity and functionality in ever decreasing cycle times. Windows 95 and now Windows NT are cases in point. These operating systems were developed on the foundation of an earlier Windows Operating System, but with an entirely new underlying technical architecture.

In contrast to the approach of its arch rival, IBM, as early as a working version of the Windows 95 vision could be cobbled together, Microsoft made a beta version available to thousands of its customers. Those customers formed a community that helped the Microsoft developers create an operating system that had maximal value to them. Windows 95 and Windows NT are now released products, but the customer community continues to enable a "win-win" situation—customers maximize their value-added from Microsoft, while Microsoft maximizes revenue by providing customers what they most need and want. There is no way that the traditional "make and sell" paradigm, with people confined within company walls trying to figure out what customers want and are willing to pay for, can effectively compete with this "sense and respond" paradigm in terms of:

- reducing cycle-time for developing extremely complex products,
- efficiently delivering value to customers,
- yielding high levels of innovation,
- providing highly challenging work for knowledge workers, and
- achieving high levels of financial results.

But, of course, this paradigm has shortcomings. One of the severest has to do with fatal errors—a shortcoming that was brought into focus by a question from a bright Harvard MBA to a world-class professional who was advocating the new paradigm. The question was: Do you think Microsoft (or Sun) could build a Boeing 777 jet aircraft, and if so, would you fly on it?

The ensuing class discussion highlighted a number of key issues. Microsoft's "sense and respond" approach could undoubtedly build a 777 jet aircraft, but even more importantly, could probably build a passenger spaceship to the moon. However, most people would want to wait for "Version #3" as advocated by Paul Saffo of the Institute of the Future, to fly on any product built by "sense and respond" organizations in the software industry.

Turning the question around also raises some interesting points. Could Boeing (or perhaps IBM) be as successful building Windows 95? Undoubtedly not! The "make and sell" paradigm copes with complexity through disciplined control, operating in a slower time frame governed by the annual budget cycle. Although these "make and sell" companies have certainly used computers to speed things up, such as collapsing the product cycle for bringing out new car models from seven years to one and one-half years, and achieved more efficient resource use through monthly budget reviews, the governing heartbeat of the organization still revolves around annual planning and budgeting. In order to operate in this manner, the "responding" organization is buffered from outside stimuli through inventories, separate sales organizations, and distributors. Product designs are frozen relatively early in the process and engineering changes during production are minimized.

In direct contrast, the "sense and respond" organization installs customer sensors (e.g., direct e-mail from beta users of Windows 95 to the developers) as a basis for determining what to design, when, and what features to include. Figure 1-1 contrasts some of the key differences between the "make and sell" and "sense and respond" paradigms.

While this juxtapositioning of extremes, contrasting "make and sell" with "sense and respond," is constructive for driving home the differences between the two approaches, there are far more practical impli-

FIGURE 1-1   "Make and Sell" vs. "Sense and Respond"

"Make and Sell" versus	"Sense and Respond"
Annual budget resource allocation is the "heartbeat"	Dynamic, real-time resource allocation is the "heartbeat"
Glacial change	Real-time change
Design, build, sell	Sell, build, redesign
Plan	Act
Market share	Mind share
Build to inventory	Build to customer
Build reliable, complex products and services	Create unimaginably complex products and services

cations which are extremely important to senior managers' success in the new competitive landscape. While we believe that the "sense and respond" paradigm will prove superior to the "make and sell" paradigm over the long run, a number of problems and issues need to be resolved in the short run. For example, the "make and sell" paradigm focuses on making versus sensing. Because most businesses are not very effective at sensing their customers' needs, a great deal of faddish rhetoric has developed: being "customer-driven," or ensuring that "the customer is #1," and the like. However, much less is known about how to actually sense customer needs than about how to develop new capabilities to respond to them more effectively. Thus, we believe that the current rhetoric on sensing may delay important initiatives to fully understand the requirements for "sensing," and develop appropriate capabilities.

In contrast, "make and sell" organizations have gotten quite good at "making." Thus, we believe that they will take more substantive actions to effectively respond to unique customer needs. Nevertheless, their ability to do so effectively will be highly constrained by the robustness of their sensing capabilities. Ultimately, however, the situation is likely to be reversed, and refinements in sensing customers' needs will for the most part exceed a firm's ability to effectively respond. Thus, a new wave of innovation, this one devoted to developing capabilities to respond, will be initiated.

Within this context of "sense and respond," a new competitive standard is emerging. Being able to respond to the new standard, and thus avoid strategic jeopardy, is highly dependent on a firm's expertise with the technologies required to create the new IT-enabled organizations.

Creating and Capturing Value

New technologies continue to enable new strategies. What we call the technologies of the Network Era are enabling the shift to "sense and respond" strategies, which will be key to creating and capturing value in the Network Era.

THE ENABLING TECHNOLOGIES OF THE NETWORK ERA

The evolution of IT can be viewed as three overlapping organizational learning curves representing the introduction and maturation of three dominant technologies: centralized mainframe computers (the Data Processing Era), decentralized personal computers (the Microcomputer Era), and now interlinked networks of computers (the Network Era).

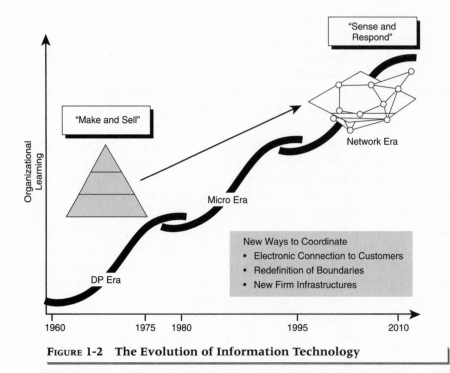

FIGURE 1-2   The Evolution of Information Technology

The rapid deployment of computer networking and the addition of broadband capability is at the heart of the transition from the traditional functional hierarchy, still the organizational construct of most companies today, to the broadband IT-enabled network organizational structure of the future.

As Figure 1-2 illustrates, information technology has been used in the firm for almost 40 years. During that time, the technology has become simultaneously cheaper and more powerful. By the 1980s, mainframe computers that cost $10 million in the 1960s could be bought for less than $3,000. Today the same amount of computational power can be bought for less than $5 in the form of a "computer on a chip." Of course, few of us buy computers for less than $5; the ones we buy cost thousands of dollars and include all kinds of capabilities, from word processing and graphics to multimedia encyclopedias on a CD-ROM and browsing on the World Wide Web. At the same time, broader bandwidth for multimedia applications is becoming available at lower and lower costs. The combination of technological evolution and organizational learning about how to incorporate information technology into the firm's operations provides some unique strategic opportunities.

Building on the organizational learning developed during the Data Processing and Microcomputer Eras, firms are using emerging Network technologies to gain flexibility and responsiveness in meeting customer demands. The old functional hierarchy was designed as a command and control structure for the manufacture and sale of products and services in an industrial economy. Companies forecast demand for their products and services, scheduled manufacturing to meet demand over time, and used inventory to fill both customer needs and manufacturing requirements. Information technologies during the Data Processing and Microcomputer Eras were used primarily as support to the internal functions of the firm.

In the new "sense and respond" business model, companies use the emerging Network Era technologies to go beyond the walls of their organizations to monitor their customers continuously, not merely sensing their needs but actually anticipating their unrecognized needs, developing new capabilities to meet those needs, customizing their offerings to micro-market segments, and competing with each other on speed in delivering products and services. To operate in a "sense and respond" world, they create new partnerships and alliances, new interorganizational networking capabilities, and new business processes. Some organizations are fortunate enough to start from scratch in building structures appropriate for competing in this new world. But most must completely transform their historical "make and sell" structures and technologies into "sense and respond" structures and technologies.

New technologies create new opportunities to capture economic value. In this sense, information technologies are the most significant technologies since the advent of the steam engine—some say since the advent of the printing press. For over a decade, more than fifty percent of new capital investment in the United States has been dedicated to technologies that in some way involve computers. Multimedia and networking technologies are establishing new frontiers for creating and capturing value in entirely new industries and are rapidly restructuring many existing industries by creating new sources of competitive advantage and devaluing existing ones. The very concept of industry is being challenged as the boundaries between industries begin to blur, and in some cases, to disappear altogether.

The challenges of creating and capturing value in the Network Era have raised a number of strategic issues for every company. What can companies do with this new capability for collaboration and knowledge sharing? Where are the opportunities for investment and the extraction of high returns? How should companies organize to effectively implement sense and respond strategies? What are the new business processes, and how should those processes be engineered (or their functions reengineered)? How will employees' work change? How can companies network more effectively with other organizations, to create and capture value? How can companies both compete and cooperate to provide value? How will they compete to develop the technological solutions of the future?

Some have likened the explosion of the Internet to the California gold rush of 1849. While many clamored in vain to find gold, the few who provided implements for the search—picks, shovels, and Levi's—wound up the real winners of that movement. Today, a number of companies are basing their strategies on the belief that the way to capture the value of the new technologies is to control the content—the creative content of movie making, existing databases, and major works of art and science. Other companies are investing in the development of transmission infrastructures or hardware components. Still other companies, like Microsoft, are simultaneously investing in content, online information services, and Internet gateway control.

Capturing Value by Creating New Businesses

Whenever new technologies emerge, new businesses are likely to be created. The knowledge about a new technology and the core competencies needed to capitalize on it are not widely dispersed, but there are clear economies of scale or scope for new supplier industries to capture. Thus, the advent of networked computing has spawned a variety of new industries. Online information service providers like America Online (AOL), Microsoft Network (MSN), and Prodigy are the most visible examples of the creation of a new business spawned by a new technology.

In many of these new businesses, some distinct advantages accrue to early movers. In some instances the early movers actually gain the advantage, but in others they merely bear the pioneering costs, while the advantages go to those who manage to learn from their early mistakes. Thus, though AOL was not the first online information service, it has outperformed Prodigy and CompuServe, but may in turn lose to Microsoft's Internet-based MSN service or even to AT&T, with its huge customer base and brand identity. In the long run all may lose to the pure Internet access providers. Again quoting Paul Saffo of the Institute for the Future, "The information services providers will be the first casualties on the information highway."

However, in the context of this new management paradigm of "sense and respond," one should not be too quick to predict that a company like AOL will be among the losers. AOL typifies the fierce determination and agility of a company scrambling to be a winner, defying competitors' efforts in making inroads. It has aggressively pursued new customers by giving away starter disks for its services, including them with new modems and in newspapers, and distributing them widely via direct mail. AOL has added new content, striking creative deals with substantially larger companies; up-sized and down-sized resources based upon productivity and competitive needs; matched competitive pricing levels; and embraced the Internet through a gateway access, blunting the threat of the Internet access companies enticing its customers away. And despite very serious service problems encountered when they shifted to flat rate pricing, their customer base and stock price continue to increase.

Another example of a Network Era value-added service is the financial information services industry. Companies like Bloomberg, Dow-Jones, Reuters, and Quote.com provide real-time financial information to financial professionals and consumers alike. Bloomberg has captured value not only through its proprietary network, but by committing to the Internet while expanding its business to include broadcast stations that focus on financial news. News retrieval services like Dow-Jones, Lexis-Nexis, Desktop Data, and Oxford Analytica are another form of value-added information service, which came into existence because of an available infrastructure and the increasing comfort level of users with computer networking in general and the Internet in particular.

Many new businesses have resulted from the outsourcing of business processes through networking technology. American Transtech, a subsidiary of AT&T, provides support for telephone-intensive business processes, which they refer to as "customer and employee care." Examples of the services the firm provides include Kraft General Foods' consumer hot line and administration of General Electric's employee benefits program. The consumer who uses the service or calls for information, or the employee who wishes to borrow against his retirement account, is completely unaware that another firm is involved. Another example is GE Capital, which manages a portfolio of private credit card businesses for a number of companies, such as Montgomery Ward. Outsourcing of the credit card business helps both companies, because GE can run the credit card operation more efficiently than Montgomery Ward due to its economies of scale, and Montgomery Ward can free up fixed capital, reduce operating expenses, and lower noncash working capital by factoring its receivables.

In the information technology industry itself, many new businesses have been created by successful outsourcing of key business processes and critical activities. EDS is in the business of managing data centers and private networks for a host of companies. In a well-publicized $3.2 billion deal with Xerox, EDS recently took over the management of Xerox's legacy systems, including 1,900 employees, for a decade, leaving Xerox in a position to pursue its strategy of being the world's leading document management company. Internal management of its legacy systems and associated staff would have locked Xerox into an obsolete Data Processing Era infrastructure and a culture not likely to produce the cutting-edge thinking needed to compete in the Network Era.

The theme of creating and capturing value in a multimedia world is developed further in Chapter 2, "The Converging Worlds of Telecommunication, Computing, and Entertainment," by P. William Bane, Stephen P. Bradley, and David J. Collis. The authors describe the convergence of the three historically vertically integrated industries into the IT/multimedia industry of tomorrow, in which competition will take place not among traditional vertically integrated players but among focused competitors in five horizontal segments: content, packaging, transmission, manipulation, and terminal devices. They then speculate about structure of competition in each emerging segment and about which firms are best positioned to create and capture value.

CAPTURING VALUE BY RESTRUCTURING INDUSTRIES

Publishing is an industry that will be radically restructured by multimedia and networking technologies. The publisher of the *Encyclopedia Britannica* is a now infamous example of a firm that did not understand how technology would affect its industry. Managers thought they were in the business of selling beautiful books containing a vast store of the world's information. Because they considered CD-ROMs to be a fad or a minor new market, they sold the electronic rights to the encyclopedia, and very soon thereafter the firm went bankrupt. Clearly, a CD-ROM that describes the political situation leading up to the dropping of the atomic bomb, provides multicolor maps of the bomb site, plays video clips of survivors and audio clips of President Truman's speech on the event, and is cross-linked to articles on the medical treatment for radiation sickness provides an enormously richer experience than the traditional book. And an encyclopedia that can be easily updated and distributed on the World Wide Web is even better. The new *Encyclopedia Britannica* has in fact reemerged on the web.

The new technology is, of course, not only a threat to the publishing industry, but an enormous opportunity to create new value. *Becoming a Manager,* a book written by Linda Hill of the Harvard Business School, deals with the problems encountered by an individual employee in an organization when he or she becomes a manager. It provides some sound advice and a rich set of examples that help the reader to understand some of the problems one may encounter in becoming a manager. But consider how much more valuable the book becomes when accompanied by a CD-ROM illustrating real problems and situations involving real people and personalities. With this new technology, Hill becomes a personal trainer, helping readers through the complexities of the case and providing practical advice on how to respond to similar situations. In the long run, this type of experience can be delivered over the Internet as well.

A less obvious example of an industry that may be facing complete restructuring is the used car business, three times the size of the new car market. CarMax, a subsidiary of Circuit City, is using multimedia and networking technology to radically change the way Americans shop for used cars. The basic idea is to replace the difficult-to-access used car market with an efficient, information-intensive market. CarMax purchases used cars at wholesale auctions, then uses multimedia technology to provide customers with complete and reliable information on them. The vehicles are resold at CarMax locations. The keys to the success of this new business are the availability and reliability of its information, the large selection of cars, the convenient locations, and the customer-friendly buying process. Traditional dealers of used cars are likely to be forced to follow suit to survive.

One of the more hotly debated questions of the Network Era is what will be the impact of broadband technologies on the video rental business. As movies become available on a pay-per-view basis from cable and direct satellite broadcasters, many consumers will choose to avoid the inconvenience of a trip to the video store. Soon the eight-fold compression of signals over ISDN lines or the arrival of ADSL technology will allow telephone companies to compete in this lucrative segment as well. Though the market is still a long way from true video on demand, a change in consumer buying habits is already evident.

These are but a few examples of the industries that will be substantially restructured by Network Era technologies, and in these restructurings there are enormous opportunities to create and capture value. The questions of how much value can potentially be created from new multimedia information services and who will capture value by investing in infrastructure are discussed in some detail in Chapter 3, "Telecommunications: Building the Infrastructure for Value Creation," by Jerry A. Hausman.

Hausman has estimated the consumer value that is created by the new services. He argues persuasively against regulatory delay of innovative offerings and makes some predictions about the ultimate beneficiaries of the changes that are sweeping the telecommunications industry.

Capturing Value by Blurring Industry Boundaries

Network Era technologies are also blurring the boundaries between industries. One of the major strategic initiatives in retail financial services today is OneSource from Charles Schwab. This service allows Schwab's customers to choose from over 620 no-load mutual funds reported on a single statement at no additional fee. Although OneSource is not strictly a technological initiative, it is marketed and supported through network technology. In its first four years of operation, OneSource collected over $39 billion of mutual fund assets becoming the third largest distributor of mutual funds in the United States.

What is the impact of the OneSource initiative? First, it provides customers access to a vast array of funds, lowering the barriers to entry into the mutual fund business and increasing competition among funds. Second, it shifts customer control to Schwab and away from the mutual funds. Third, it undermines the concept of the mutual fund family since, when customers transfer their assets from a particular fund into a money market account, they must move then into Schwab's money market account. Finally, OneSource increases Schwab's knowledge of an important set of customers, to which it can then offer other products and services.

What are Schwab's next moves likely to be? One is to sell other products and services, such as insurance, to its mutual fund customers, which Schwab is already doing. This company that began as a discount broker now offers mutual funds, insurance, and trust and advisory services and will soon offer expanded banking services. Undoubtedly, the biggest threat to the banking and insurance industries is the brokerage business. The cost structure of the leading brokerage businesses—Fidelity, Schwab, and even Merrill Lynch—will be difficult for the retail banking and insurance industries to compete against. Furthermore, the brokerage industry will concentrate largely on the wealthiest customers, leaving the smaller, more-costly-to-serve customers to the banks and insurance companies. In a sense, the banks and insurance companies face a "winner's curse," in that they may win a substantial market share based on number of customers, but a modest market share based on total assets.

In another blurring of boundaries involving financial institutions, Fidelity Group announced its entry into total benefits administration. Instead of simply managing the 401k assets in corporate retirement accounts, Fidelity will bundle that service with the outsourcing of their clients' human resources' management functions. Retirement, health, and welfare benefits—all are managed by Fidelity with administrative help—networking, telephone support, and desktop systems—from partners. For clients who are trying to focus on their core businesses, without distraction from noncore businesses, this is a very attractive opportunity. Since few other firms in the 401k and investment market are positioned to offer this scope of support, for Fidelity it is an opportunity to expand its control of the 401k market.

Finally, the healthcare industry is just beginning to confront the impact of the Network Era through a variety of applications of telemedicine thus blurring the traditional geographic boundaries. In diagnostic imaging, for example, magnetic resonance imaging and ultrasound output are now captured digitally at the point of creation. Images can be stored, retrieved, and archived digitally. Given broadband transmission capability, these images can also be read at a distance almost instantaneously, enabling remote diagnosis by some of the best experts in the world. In more radical experiments, surgeons have operated using computer-controlled "hands." Thus, the patient no longer needs to be in the same room as the doctor. In the future, much consultation and diagnosis will be done from afar, and in some cases, even routine care giving will be supervised remotely.

As these examples all suggest, "sense and respond" strategies enabled by Network Era technologies are the key to creating and capturing value in the new competitive environment.

Sensing the Customer

Sensing the customers' needs in new ways in real time is the key challenge to implementing innovative "sense and respond" strategies. As a result many companies have initiated a variety of experiments to better understand their customers. Customer satisfaction ratings are now an integral part of the balanced scorecard by which many companies measure their performance. However, actually sensing customers' needs in real time is exceedingly difficult and is probably best done at present by the software companies through their communities of beta version users.

However, Caterpillar Tractor has attempted to apply the same basic idea to the manufacture of hard goods, including customers in the design process by letting them test drive vehicles in virtual reality. The approach can be thought of as the logical extension of the beta testing that is prevalent in the software industry. Just as Microsoft assembled thousands of beta testers during development of Windows 95, testing and modifying the program continuously, right up until its release, Caterpillar hopes to freeze the design of its products as late as possible and with as much "hands-on" customer feedback as possible.

One insurance company has built an entirely new franchise by correctly sensing the needs of its customers. USAA began as a standard property and casualty insurance company, except that its customer base was restricted to military personnel and their offspring. The firm became a model of efficiency by taking advantage of technology at an early stage in its development. It invested in technology to automate basic business processes, capturing data electronically as early as possible and using imaging technology to ensure that data was never entered more than once. Having attained a leadership position in technology, USAA then turned to using its technology to better understand customers. Managers discovered that they could offer a variety of products and services of substantial value to customers, from finance packages for the purchase of boats or airplanes to actual replacement of insured goods (in lieu of the traditional check to cover losses). This convenience to customers led to the creation of a major purchasing operation. Today, USAA is one of the largest direct merchandisers in the United States, based on its commitment to sensing customers' needs.

One way to visualize the dimensions through which we can sense our customers' needs is to think of our potential links to our customers in terms of the virtual value chain.[1] The critical idea behind the concept is a recognition of the underlying information flows that support the physical value chain, enabling a firm to do business in the marketplace. The virtual value chain (see Figure 1-3) illustrates the critical information flows in any business. At any point in the design, sourcing, manufacture, marketing, sale, or servicing of a product or service, there is a supporting information structure. At each stage information is gathered, organized, selected, synthesized, and distributed. That information can be the basis for a new business or a new competitive advantage in an existing business.

Many firms enhance their understanding of their customers by linking to them through the virtual value chain. FedEx is an example of a firm that is always on the leading edge in using technology to link to its customers in order to gain or enhance its competitive advantage in the overnight package delivery business. FedEx pioneered real-time

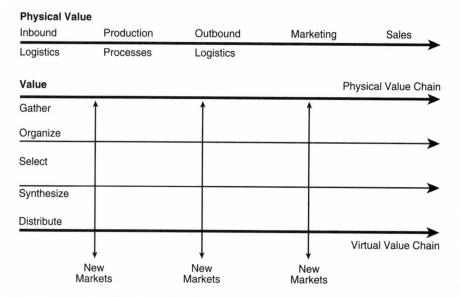

Physical Value

| Inbound Logistics | Production Processes | Outbound Logistics | Marketing | Sales |

FIGURE 1-3   The Virtual Value Chain
Adapted and reprinted by permission of *Harvard Business Review*. From "Exploiting the Virtual Value Chain" by Jeffrey Rayport and John J. Sviokla, November–December 1995. Copyright 1995 by the President and Fellows of Harvard University; all rights reserved.

tracking of packages with its now famous COSMOS information system. At first, the firm used the technology to track packages internally, then to respond to telephone inquiries from customers. Then, recognizing the time and people intensity of the firm's service, its key differentiator, FedEx began to distribute software to customers, so they could answer their own inquiries. Today the same service is available over the Internet at the FedEx web site, an advance that has eliminated the need to distribute software upgrades to users, solved most user problems, and provided excellent customer access.

DEALING WITH UNCERTAINTY

Researchers report that seventy percent of the significant shifts in market share that have been observed over time, in fact, were caused by major technological innovations.[2] The Network Era is driven by successive technological innovations that will not only restructure the information technology industry but will radically restructure most of the other industries in the economy as well. However, there is enormous uncertainty over the form and implications of these innovations and particularly how consumers will react and behave as the traditional industries are restructured.

The challenges companies face in dealing with the strategic uncertainties that result from technological change are discussed in Chapter 4, "Strategic Uncertainty and the Future of Online Consumer Interaction," by Eric K. Clemons and Stephen P. Bradley. The chapter begins with an examination of six strategic uncertainties in online consumer interaction, many of which concern consumer response to the new medium. Understanding and being able to sense changing consumer preferences will be a great advantage to those retailers that get it right. The authors then use scenario analysis to explore the possibilities for the future. Recognizing that most companies do not have the resources to prepare for all eventualities, the authors suggest alternative strategic responses that may be appropriate when faced with such uncertainty.

EMBRACING NEW DISTRIBUTION CHANNELS

Some firms use their sales and marketing activities to experiment with the virtual value chain. One interesting example is MusicNet, which distributes a CD-ROM sampler of various music and/or video CDs. The idea is to provide a way for consumers to shop for music that does not involve going to the music store. Users of MusicNet simply listen to excerpts from albums they might be interested in and decide whether they want to make a purchase. If they do, they can place their orders over the Internet or by phone using a toll-free number.

Can such a service survive and prosper in the marketspace? The obvious problem with the MusicNet business is that the CD-ROM sampler must be produced, packaged, and distributed. Those activities are so costly that at least for now, in order to prosper, MusicNet will have to focus on the affluent, convenience-driven segment of the market. Imagine, however, how the service would work if the sampler were distributed through a web server rather than a CD-ROM. Production costs would not disappear, but the packaging and distribution costs would be negligible. In the future, MusicNet's success will depend on the existence of a ubiquitous broadband infrastructure, which will allow consumers to easily download clips from video CDs. This method of distribution could prove attractive to the broader market, putting great pressure on music stores in the marketplace.

Today, mail order catalog operations are faced with deciding how and when to do business over the World Wide Web. In Chapter 5, "Delivering

Customer Value Through the World Wide Web," Kathy Biro describes how
L.L. Bean is experimenting with this new channel, to avoid losing its customers to marketspace imitators. Whenever a business is challenged by a
substitute, it faces the strategic choice of whether to enter the new format,
defend against the new format, perhaps with an enhanced approach, or
harvest its business using its existing approach. In Bean's case, managers
recognized the need to experiment early with web-based delivery in order to avoid being overtaken by the new form of distribution.

Bean has created a new web site which can be thought of as value
added. At the web site browsers can receive information on the national parks, including activities that can be pursued there, such as hik-
ing, kayaking, cross-country skiing, and snowmobiling. Thus, potential
customers have reason to visit Bean's web site, whether or not they
intend to purchase anything. In addition, they can obtain access to an
enhanced electronic version of Bean's catalog, as well as interesting
background information about the firm. Assuming that users identify
themselves, Bean can track which sections of the catalog they browsed,
what information they requested, and which purchases they ultimately
made. This begins a very sophisticated system for customer tracking,
with the objective of understanding each customer's individual needs,
and eventually micromarketing to meet those needs.

Although Bean does not yet do so, with the addition of a geographic
information database, its tracking system could include a good estimate
of each customer's income and the value of his or her primary residence. (As described in Chapter 6, the software and the geographical
databases from public sources needed for this to become economically
feasible are all in place.) The key to a successful web site of this type is
to engage the user and, if at all possible, execute some type of transaction. Bean seems to have been successful in doing exactly that. While
the average age of Bean's customer base has been in the mid-fifties,
since the web site opened the firm has attracted an entirely new set of
customers, primarily in their mid-thirties.

"Hearing" Customers in New Ways

Companies are just beginning to realize the potential of geographic information systems (GIS). In Chapter 6, "Using Geographic Information
Systems to Sense and Respond to Customers," Brian E. Mennecke, Jack
Dangermond, PJ Santoro, and Mark W. Darling describe how firms
such as American Isuzu and Levi Strauss are using GIS to improve their

ability to sense customer needs. Isuzu first used its GIS to locate new dealerships near potential customers, then applied it to selecting the most promising markets for new product launches. Soon thereafter Isuzu sales representatives were using the system to help dealers analyze sales trends. This chapter ends with a survey of current functions and future directions in GIS, including nationwide systems like the Realtor Information Network.

A uniquely creative approach to understanding customers' deeper impressions and subjective feelings has been developed by Professor Gerald Zaltman of the Harvard Business School. Zaltman uses multimedia techniques to elicit customers' underlying impressions of companies, their products and services, and even their management—subtle understandings that would otherwise be difficult to elicit, and perhaps even more difficult to articulate. Zaltman's technique is described in detail in Chapter 7, "Seeing Through the Customer's Eyes with Computer Imaging," by Gerald Zaltman and Linda J. Schuck. The chapter is illustrated with collages prepared by customers of Pacific Gas and Electric during interviews with technicians trained in using Zaltman's techniques. The results of that research, and the uses PG&E found for them, are also described.

Responding with Capabilities

The advanced networking and multimedia technologies of the Network Era are enabling companies to shift from narrow business strategies, highly constrained by physical boundaries and oriented toward manufacture and sales to more robust business strategies, unconstrained by physical boundaries and oriented toward customer satisfaction. These advanced technologies enable companies to connect with customers in real time, and thus to take advantage of the strategic opportunity to learn customers' needs and their perception of the firm's products and services. But electronic connections can run two ways. Thus, the second strategic opportunity of the Network Era is to develop the capability to respond to customer needs through enhanced fulfillment.

Of course, fulfillment can be tailored to the individual customer using modern information technologies, an approach that is often referred to as mass customization of products and services. Everyone is familiar with the high impact of beepers that workers like physicians and computer technicians carry when they are on call. However, the ramifications of the extended use of these technologies for real-time management of physical, human, and information resources are just beginning to become clear. For instance, new technologies can also permit customer involvement with the product, such as enabling a child to become a character in a televised cartoon show.

LINKING CUSTOMERS DIRECTLY WITH SUPPLIERS

Through the use of advanced technologies such as geographic information systems (GIS) and global positioning systems (GPS), companies can now maintain real-time inventories of their resources, regardless of location. The technology is already being used in the railroad and trucking industries for scheduling and redeployment of railcars and trailers. GPS is being used in the electric utility industry, to locate electrical transformers so that outages can be traced and reversed more rapidly. Using a special hand-held GPS device, a utility worker drives by telephone poles and other scattered plants of a utility company and "shoots" them with the device. Later, the information in the device is transferred to another computer, and an inventory is developed of the various plant components and their locations.

Real-time resource management can also be used to respond to customers in extraordinary ways. A relative early use of technology to sense and respond to customer needs was developed by the National Bicycle Company of Japan. When potential customers enter a National Bicycle retail store to purchase custom-made bicycles, they sit at a CAD/CAM machine that looks like part of an actual bicycle. The sales consultant then adjusts the height of the seat, the type and drop of the handlebars, the length of the leg extension, and the type and position of the gear shifts, among other measurements. As he is doing so, the consultant asks about the type of material for the frame, the brand and quality of the components, the color scheme, the location of the customer's nameplate, and other items. Because the CAD/CAM machine is linked directly to the factory, by the time the session is over, the complete specifications for the customer's custom-made bicycle have been transferred to the factory. Though the bicycle can be shipped within 48 hours, National holds it for a week so customers can "enjoy the anticipation of receiving their new bicycles."

This approach to custom manufacture has been applied to automobiles in Saturn showrooms in the United States. When a customer decides to purchase a Saturn, the order is sent to the factory electronically and entered directly into the production scheduling system. Simultaneously, the information system at the retail store prints the invoice. Adding some multimedia and networking technologies to this system would allow customers to select their options on a PC connected to the Internet. Manufacturing response time might be cut from the current eight weeks to two weeks. What would be the impact of this kind of technology on the auto industry? The large inventories of automobiles on dealers' lots might be replaced by a few demonstrators and virtual reality facilities. Both the customer and manufacturer would win, while the dealers and the companies that finance the dealers' floor plans would lose as full information became more readily available to customers.

Airline reservation systems are moving in the same direction. Both American Airline's Sabre reservation system and United's Covia reservation system now feature front-end technology that enables travelers to access information on plane routes and prices and enter their own reservations over the Internet. While the vast majority of travelers still prefer to use travel agents, as the new technology becomes cheaper, more user-friendly, and more convenient, more and more travelers may opt to eliminate the intermediaries in the airline business.

LINKING DESIGN WITH OPERATIONS

Multimedia technology could have an even more dramatic impact on the retail fashion industry, cutting time-to-market by seventy-five percent. One example that has gained a high profile recently is custom-made Levi's for women. Presumably everyone—women and men—would prefer custom-fitted clothes to the mass-produced garments currently available. Levi Strauss has introduced electronic kiosks in some of its stores that allow customers to order custom-made Levi's. The customer is measured, and an appropriate body style is selected from over one hundred different styles. The order is placed, and within ten days the jeans are shipped via FedEx. The premium for this service is only twenty-five percent more than the standard price: customers who have been surveyed are extremely satisfied with their purchases. The challenge, of course, is to adapt Levi's manufacturing strategy so that it will remain responsive even if its new service becomes very popular.

Companies like Benetton, the Limited, and Nike have used new technologies to improve market sensing, make design changes that reflect changing customer preferences, and alter manufacturing and sourcing procedures to postpone commitment to specific styles and colors to a point later in the manufacturing process. But that is only the beginning. With multimedia technology, teams of designers in remote locations can collaborate on designs and transfer them immediately to factories with available capacity. In such a system, a garment could be designed, the fabric produced, cut, and assembled, and the finished product shipped in a few days or weeks at most. Overlaying technology similar to that used by Levi Strauss could result in an increasing percentage of the output being custom made.

Most of the large retail fashion firms prefer to contract for manufacturing capacity rather than own it, an approach that allows them to focus on capturing profitable fashion trends and getting garments into the stores quickly, while fashions are still hot. One retailer has fashion experts roam the world with digital cameras, taking photos of promising new styles. The digital pictures can be transferred via network to the retailer's headquarters, where CAD/CAM technology is used to design and produce the garments. Colors and designs are printed directly onto fabrics using a high-end laser printer. Within hours, a model can show the garment to key decision makers, and a decision can be made to produce it using contracted manufacturing capacity.

A similar approach to product development is being pioneered in the personal computer software and Internet service industries. Firms in this industry are developing radically new capabilities that allow them to compete on the leading edge in rapidly changing markets. The key idea, referred to as "technological integration," is for customers to become part of the development process, affording programmers rapid feedback on software performance and customer needs. Software components are developed in parallel rather than successive stages to capture rapidly evolving technological and customer trends. The objective is to delay finalization of product specifications to the last possible moment in order to incorporate the very latest technologies.

Marco Iansiti and Alan MacCormack, both of the Harvard Business School, describe this revolutionary new approach in Chapter 8, "Product Development on the Internet." The chapter begins with a description of the cumbersome and frustrating development process of Word for Windows 1.0, and the changes Microsoft made as a result of that experience. The authors then describe the much more streamlined development process at Netscape, Yahoo!, and NetDynamics. These firms developed their software products on the Internet, which allows them to receive almost instantaneous feedback from potential customers. The authors stress the proactive nature of this approach to a chaotic, rapidly changing market.

More conventional manufacturers, such as those engaged in aerospace production, have also begun to take advantage of increases in bandwidth and advances in multimedia technology. The application of advanced technologies to engineering, design, and manufacturing activities is, in most cases, just a matter of updating the traditional "make and sell" strategy. Innovative manufacturers are already using advanced design tools to communicate with suppliers and customers during product development. For instance, Boeing designed the Boeing 777 without constructing multiple mockups in order to experiment with different design alternatives. Instead, a team of designers working in multiple locations used computer simulations to replace the traditional physical testing of models. Similarly, New Zealand's America's Cup team used Silicon Graphics' computers to design the hull and sails of their yacht, simulating air and water flow in virtual reality.

Chapter 9, "The Emergence of Internetworked Manufacturing," by David M. Upton and Andrew P. McAfee, examines currently used internetworking technologies—Electronic Data Interchange (EDI), groupware, and wide area networks (WANs). The wave of the future in networked manufacturing is the Internet. The chapter presents a case study of Aerotech Service Group, a Net-based network that integrates McDonnell Douglas Aerospace with many of its customers, suppliers, and subcontractors. This pioneering effort allows McDonnell Douglas to remain competitive by sharing information seamlessly with its partners.

Shopping in a Virtual World

Network Era technologies enable a company almost anywhere in the world to efficiently tap into the global market without the necessity of maintaining a physical presence in each local market. The Internet provides the capability to serve global markets in real time. The CD-ROM has also been used as an economical way to create highly visual, interactive electronic markets, whether for catalog sales in the United States or used-car auctions in Japan.

In Chapter 10, "Virtual Value and the Birth of Virtual Markets," John J. Sviokla explores some successes and failures in creating and facilitating electronic markets. As discussed in the chapter, multimedia technology has completely changed the wholesale used-car market in Japan. Cars are no longer shipped to a central marketplace for auction. Instead, a company called AUCNET produces a CD-ROM containing pictures and text on each vehicle, including mileage, detailed specifications, any dents, service history, tire condition, and any other information relevant to the vehicle's value. The auction then takes place over a computer network. In just four years, AUCNET has become the largest wholesale dealer in Japan.

In the United States, virtual shopping for groceries is gaining favor. One of the first companies to enter the market was Peapod, which takes orders online, selects from the shelves, bags groceries for customers, and delivers to their homes. Peapod's approach to online retailing is clearly a high-priced convenience offering for the well-to-do, however. If virtual grocery shopping is to capture a wide market share, it must become truly cost competitive. That can happen only if demand for the service is large enough to justify special warehouses in which orders can be picked electronically. Delivery would also need to be revamped to be cost-effective, perhaps through the opening of convenient pickup locations. Kroger, Hannaford Brothers, and Stop and Shop are all experimenting with virtual shopping, so the efficiency of the approach is likely to improve in the near future.

A great deal of debate has occurred as to how shopping will be done on the Internet. Most analysts tend to apply traditional marketing models to online shopping. For example, the Internet Shopping Network (ISN) uses a traditional broadcast-advertising approach to attract potential customers. At numerous locations on the Internet, ISN runs ads imploring potential customers to visit ISN's web site. The first page of the web site carries several advertised specials, genuine bargains on computers, peripheral devices, and software.

Compare ISN's broadcast approach with that of CUC International, a fee-based membership organization. CUC is similar to a buying cooperative in that its profit is derived entirely from membership fees. CUC holds no inventory; instead, it devotes intelligent agents to search for the best prices on products of interest to its members. If a customer wants product information on a specific camera model, CUC can link the customer to the manufacturer's web page, where detailed product information is available. With specific guidelines provided by members, CUC's intelligent agents can search whole product categories. Currently, the search is limited to a group of products that CUC "carries," but it is easy to see how this service can be extended to intelligent searches over the entire Internet.

Which is the best model for virtual shopping? ISN's or CUC's? Most online retailers are currently offering the traditional broadcast-advertising model, though the use of intelligent agents to do searches for the customer appears to have a great deal of merit. In fact, it appears such a threat that many organizations have attempted to ban intelligent agents from their web sites. In Chapter 11, "Real Shopping in a Virtual Store," Raymond R. Burke first looks at virtual shopping from the consumer's point of view. Then he examines the design of the virtual store, comparing text-based versus graphic interfaces and considers ways to enhance them. Burke provides a comprehensive description of virtual shopping, including both its history and prospects for the future.

Transforming the Organization

In order to implement "sense and respond" strategies, firms will need to develop entirely new sets of capabilities enabled by Network Era technologies. To do so effectively will often require transforming the entire organization. In the past the firm's value proposition has been seen in terms of the choice between performing functions internally or purchasing them on the market. This traditional business model breaks down when new technologies are used to connect with customers electronically. Once connected, firms have the opportunity to go far beyond the production of high-quality goods and services to the customization of those goods and services to individual customer needs.

COORDINATING IN THE EXTENDED ORGANIZATION

Network Era technologies enable new methods of value creation, particularly through strategic alliances, joint ventures, long-term contracts, and outsourcing. Outsourcing agreements—long-term arrangements (often more than a decade) that include not only unique technological capabilities but innovative business processes—are emerging in a form more complex than traditional contracting. An example is the outsourcing of all of Laura Ashley's logistics, including not only IT systems but warehousing, surface transportation, and employees, to FedEx. Another example of value creation is the development of communities of interest over the Internet, from sports groups (e.g., golf) to groups of people with shared situations (e.g., cancer patients) and groups of aeronautical engineers (e.g., Aerotech Service Group). These virtual communities represent an opportunity to access customers with unique needs, as well as labor resources with unique skills. Indeed, these communities often come together first as providers and consumers of services. Thus, network technologies offer an opportunity to flatten the organizational hierarchy and expand beyond conventional contracting to new virtual connections.

Advanced multimedia technologies are changing the way we think about and organize our work. Our concept of the organization's limits is changing from that of a narrow physical boundary, often defined by gates and badges, to that of a more fluid and organic boundary that encompasses dynamic work groups and strategic alliances. For instance, groupware like Lotus Notes, an emerging Network Era technology, is enabling teams to work together in ways that were once limited by geographical constraints.

In financial services, networking technologies are making bank branches and traditional insurance agencies obsolete as electronic distribution takes over many of their functions. Various experiments in branchless banking, such as First Direct in the United Kingdom, may siphon off some of the best customers, leaving traditional branch banks with their high-cost structure to serve a lower-balance, less-sophisticated customer group. Mutual life insurance companies, with their large traditional salesforces, may find it increasingly difficult to justify the cost of those salesforces, since few agents have a close working relationship with their customers.

In Chapter 12, "Inventing the Organizations of the Twenty-first Century: Control, Empowerment, and Information Technology," Thomas W. Malone addresses the challenges of managing these new ways of organizing work. Malone sees a trend toward decentralization of decision making, which can be seen in Wal*Mart's local pricing policy and in the management of Visa International, a partially decentralized organization. He concludes with a forward thinking description of the radically decentralized organization of the Internet itself.

DRIVING TOWARD VIRTUAL ORGANIZATIONS

Traditional organizations were designed to carry out work in centralized places such as plants and offices, with the individual worker as the primary focus of the design. Both concepts are being challenged in the Network Era by the emerging focus on teams of workers sharing knowledge. With the emphasis on knowledge work versus manual work, tapping into knowledge workers wherever they are is becoming a competitive necessity.

Having network technologies in place, the physical proximity of workers is no longer a constraint. Applications such as groupware, video conferencing, and video on demand enable virtual teams to move information and knowledge from place to place. Through cheaper and cheaper processing power, computers can now economically access large databases, culling out the information knowledge workers need. As storage continues downward in cost, the databases grow in content and accessibility. Plunging costs of bandwidth and new networking technologies are enabling the interconnection of millions of computers, databases, and search engines—both within and outside the company. Moreover, multimedia technologies are making those capabilities accessible by ever-increasing numbers of workers—that is, not just the ones proficient in negotiating through the rather complex suite of desktop applications such as spreadsheet, word processing, and graphics.

Professional service firms are among the first to embrace the new Network technologies to enable their professionals to work in virtual teams across the globe. In Chapter 13, "Virtual Teams: Using Communications Technology to Manage Geographically Dispersed Development Groups," Dorothy A. Leonard, Paul A. Brands, Amy Edmondson, and Justine Fenwick show how Network Era technologies enable effective long-distance coordination of widely dispersed development teams. The chapter presents a case study of American Management Systems, an international consulting firm that develops custom software and integrated systems. It confronts the problems in long-distance management of virtual teams and concludes with practical suggestions for minimizing the problems.

As organizations master the Network Era technologies of working in teams anywhere that they might be (at the office, at home, with the customer, in transit), the concept of "physical place of work" shifts to "virtual spaces," or the idea that work can be anyplace, anytime. Indeed, this concept of physical place to virtual space does not happen overnight. New ways of working, relating, and just getting things done must be learned and institutionalized. As illustrated in Figure 1-4, the evolution toward virtual usually starts with the virtual office and grows from there.

Some organizations, such as VeriFone, have aggressively embraced the concept of working in a virtual context and have evolved it into a manifestation of the virtual organization. Richard L. Nolan and Hossam Galal, both at the Harvard Business School, describe the benefits of the movement toward virtual organizations in Chapter 14, "Virtual Offices: Redefining Organizational Boundaries." Their chapter presents a typology of organizational boundaries and a discussion of IBM's experience with virtual offices.

During the transformation of companies, it is important to recognize the importance of the role of different types of boundaries. While the term "boundaryless" is rather catchy and draws attention to the breaking down of the importance of the traditional physical boundaries of organizations, other types of boundaries take on increasing importance. Chapter 14 concludes with a discussion of the various types of boundary changes—economic, social, legal, and political—and the way that these set of boundaries play a role in "sense and respond" organizations.

Virtual Offices	Virtual Functions	Virtual Organizations
Examples:	*Examples:*	*Examples:*
• GE medical sales force: Laptops CD-ROMs • Bristol-Myers sales force: Laptops • IBM customer service: Marketing reps' desks	• Ford — engineering • Boeing — design of 777 (virtual design) • Whirlpool — global design and manufacturing	• Calyx and Corolla — Uses AOL, CompuServe, and Internet to sell flowers direct from growers • VeriFone — $300 million credit authorization systems. No corporate headquarters, distributed functions and virtual offices • Rosenbluth International — global travel alliance

FIGURE 1-4   **From Virtual Offices to Virtual Organizations**

The Future

Present-day businesses are operating in a time of unprecedented technological change. The speed with which advances are being made, not just in information technology, but in business applications of that technology, is breath-taking. Indeed, the ramifications of those changes on companies, industries, and business and society as a whole are just beginning to become clear to those who study them. However, what is becoming increasingly clear is that creating and capturing value in the Network Era will require a paradigm shift from the traditional relatively slow "make and sell" strategies and supporting hierarchical organizations to the quicker more responsive "sense and respond" strategies with their leaner supporting networked organizations. And having made the decision to shift to "sense and respond" firms are then faced with the daunting tasks of building new capabilities and transforming their organizations.

Endnotes

1. Jeffrey F. Rayport and John J. Sviokla, "Exploiting the Virtual Value Chain," *Harvard Business Review* 73, 6 (1975) 75–85.
2. Pankaj Ghemawat, *Commitment: The Dynamic of Strategy* (New York: Free Press, 1991).

2 | The Converging Worlds of Telecommunication, Computing, and Entertainment

P. William Bane, Stephen P. Bradley, and David J. Collis

THE EMERGING MULTIMEDIA INDUSTRY will include some of the largest business opportunities of the next two decades. Formed from the convergence of the telecommunication, computer, and entertainment industries, and facilitated by the digital revolution, it holds the promise of creating and capitalizing on an interactive "information superhighway." Yet there is no clear picture of how this futuristic industry will evolve.[1] In the presence of such uncertainty, players who articulate a consistent strategy to exploit the opportunities and address the risks will shape the evolution of industry structure.[2]

Much has been written about the strategic implications of the multimedia industry's evolution.[3] This chapter builds on existing literature, incorporating insights from "industry analysis,"[4] the "resource based view of the firm,"[5] and economic analyses. It also reflects the authors' experience in working for, and researching, the industry.[6]

Note: This chapter extends results introduced by the authors in David B. Yoffie (ed.), *Competing in an Age of Digital Convergence* (Boston: Harvard Business School Press, 1997), chapter 4.

In the first section, we argue that the structure of the consumer multimedia industry is changing from that of three discrete vertical businesses (telephone, television, and computer) to that of five largely independent "horizontal" industry segments (content, packaging, manipulation, transmission, and terminals). In the second section, we suggest what the structure of these five new industry segments might look like, and who will be the likely participants. In the third section, we identify the key success factors in each industry segment and match them to current participants' capabilities. In the final section, we discuss the implications of these fundamental changes in the multimedia industry and offer some conclusions about what can be expected in the near future.

The Emerging Structure of the Multimedia Industry

Today, the multimedia industry is being formed by the convergence of three industries: the telephone industry, which originated in the 1890s; television, which originated in the late 1930s; and personal computing, which arose in the 1980s. Originally, the product content and technologies of these industries were as distinct as those of the airline and pipeline industries. Their convergence was precipitated by the rapid increase in computer processing speed and the dramatic decline in the cost of processing and memory capacity, together with parallel advances in transmission technology—notably, radio technologies and the vast improvements in bandwidth made possible by fiber optics and compression capabilities.[7]

At the same time, digitization has rendered the analog signals transmitted by telephone and television indistinguishable from the digital signals generated by personal computers, enabling their infrastructure to accommodate the manipulation and transmission—if not yet the input and display—of voice, video, and data. All three types of information can now be distributed on the same network. Even input and display are converging in video conferencing, which combines voice and video in one transmission.

The importance of the digital revolution is that it alters, in fundamental ways, the availability of information in time and place, and the cost of that information. The potential now exists to make information available at any time the consumer desires (rather than when it is convenient for the producer to distribute it). Consider, for example, the difference between a continually updated online news service (e.g., "push" technologies like PointCast Network), and traditional home delivery of daily newspapers. Through the use of improved wireline and, particularly, wireless satellite networks, information can be made available in any and every place the consumer desires.[8] Digitization also promises to reduce the cost of information transmission as companies exploit steep learning curves in the design and production of standardized electronic components, as well as economies of scale in network systems.

If the effects of digitization were limited to voice, video, and data, it would represent a powerful enough revolution. But it has the potential as well to transform an array of other businesses and industries. In effect, the forces of digitization are acting like the gravity of a "wormhole" in *Star Trek*, pulling recognizable industries through the wormhole and transforming them into something difficult to imagine (Figure 2-1). In fact, just as entertainment and shopping have already been pulled into the wormhole, publishing, education, gambling, and advertising, among other businesses, are just beginning to be pulled into its gravitational field.

To determine which markets and products are most likely to enter the "brave new world" of multimedia, then, we can start by examining the markets that are already being affected by the convergence of the telephone, television, and personal computing industries.

PRODUCT EVOLUTION

Figure 2-2 shows the average U.S. household expenditures in the product categories currently undergoing transformation. It indicates first that content and transmission have been more important to households than hardware and software. More important, the share of household income available to new multimedia markets may be largely limited to the share already expended on existing multimedia activities. At seven percent of household income, or $1,850 per annum, not much more discretionary income is available. This latter observation is supported by research on discretionary time, which shows that the average household already watches seven hours of television per day,[9] and spends more than one hour on the telephone. Clearly, new multimedia investments will have to be supported at the outset by the substitution of existing users, not by new markets.

Looking ahead, we can forecast the rate of substitution of multimedia for other products, such as on-demand video programming for

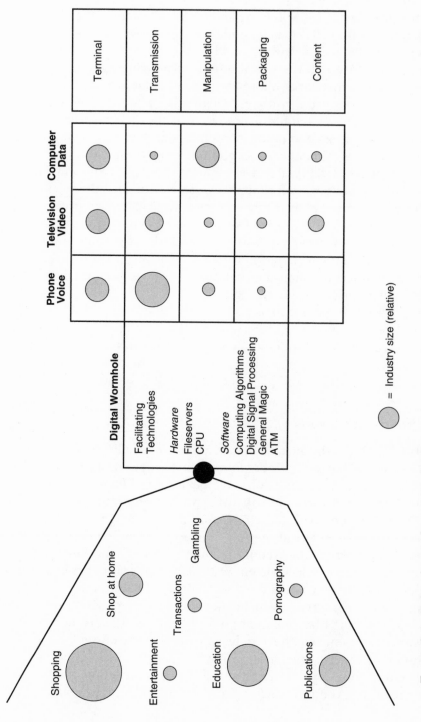

FIGURE 2-1 **Emerging Industry Structure**

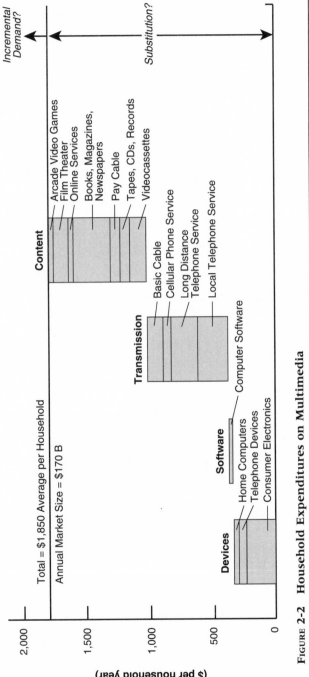

FIGURE 2-2 **Household Expenditures on Multimedia**

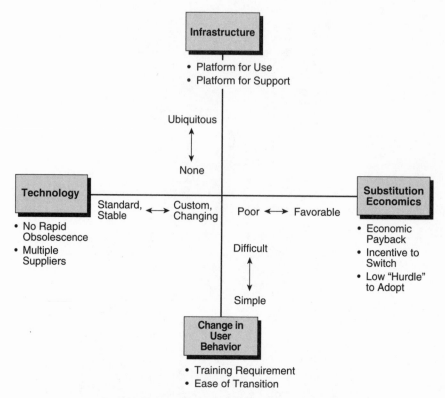

FIGURE 2-3   Factors Determining Industry Substitution
Adapted with permission from Mercer Management Consulting.

videocassette rentals, by considering the four key variables shown in Figure 2-3.

Substitution economics (right-hand side of the figure) refers to the economic benefit of multimedia over current distribution (e.g., the difference between an on-demand programming charge and a per-night movie rental fee). *Changes in user behavior* (bottom of the figure) depend on the relative ease of use of alternative distribution mechanisms (e.g., using a hand-held remote or telephone to order a movie versus a trip to the video store). *Technological criteria* (left-hand side of the figure) will affect speed of substitution. The existence of a stable standard that will minimize consumer investment risk will maximize the speed of substitution. Finally, the *required infrastructure* (top of the figure) must be in place. The closer a new technology is to the outer limits of the figure, that is, the more favorable the four key dimensions, the more likely the new technology will be substituted for the old.

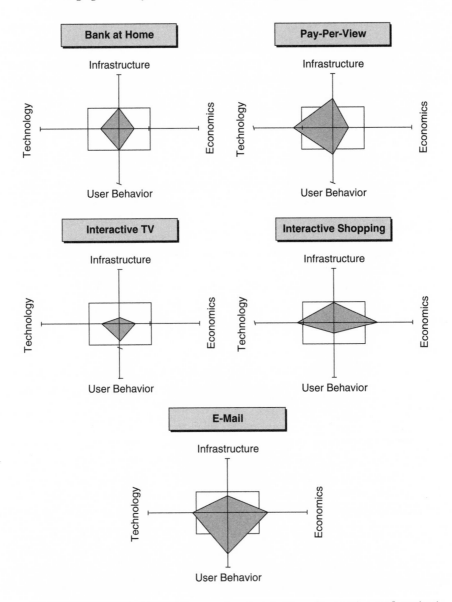

FIGURE 2-4   Feasibility of Conversion to Multimedia in Five Industries
Adapted with permission from Mercer Management Consulting.

Figure 2-4 arrays five common business applications along these four dimensions, to assess the feasibility of their conversion to multimedia. The larger the shaded area is, the greater the likelihood of conversion to multimedia. The results show that the first large markets for new multimedia products will be e-mail, on-demand movies, and interactive shopping—all now emerging or booming in some form on the Internet. The early emergence of these markets will facilitate the substitution of other new products by improving the technological infrastructure and changing consumer behavior. Newer multimedia product categories, such as wireless e-mail, will certainly follow, but after current products gain significant market penetration.

BUSINESS STRUCTURE

Whatever the rate of substitution or the specific products developed, the essence of the transformation of the multimedia industry is that content-specific distribution, through unique technologies, hardware, and methods, is being replaced by content-independent distribution through a common infrastructure. Thus, the multimedia industry is moving from a set of three vertical businesses to a collection of five largely independent, horizontal industry segments, namely:

- *Content.* Products and services transmitted by the medium. Disney, *The Wall Street Journal,* Lexis-Nexis, and Dun & Bradstreet belong to this segment.

- *Packaging.* The bundling of, or selecting from among, massive arrays of available content, and the addition of integrative and presentational functionality to create a finished product for consumers. America Online, Bloomberg, Disney, PointCast, and Time Warner, are packagers of content.

- *Transmission network.* The physical infrastructure that supports the transport of information. AT&T, CableVision, Direct Broadcast Satellite (DBS), MCI, and MediaOne, are part of the network, as are Internet access providers.

- *Manipulation infrastructure.* That which provides intelligence to the distribution system. Historically this segment has included the processing and storage hardware and various types of software in computer and telecommunications systems. In the Internet world, it includes manipulation software that performs the required interactive network tasks. AT&T, Digital, IBM, Microsoft, Novell, Oracle, and Sun are part of the infrastructure.

- *Terminals.* Any of a variety of local devices employed to capture and display information. Apple, Lucent Technologies, Motorola, Panasonic, Sega, Sharp, and Sony, for example, produce terminals.

The Evolving Structure of Industry Segments

Although these industry segments are increasingly independent and "horizontal" at present, some vertical linkages remain, and others are likely to re-emerge. However, those linkages will depend much less on discrete technologies than on the marketing and distribution packages that successful players (or alliances of players) install to serve distinct sets of customers. In the following sections, we assess the business patterns that are likely to develop in each segment.

CONTENT

The content segment will probably remain as fragmented and specialized as it is today but may gain more economic leverage. Today, the unique requirements of each type of content produce minimal economies of scope. Television news reporting requires fundamentally different logistics from those of jewelry retailing or stock market quoting. Thus, even though the three forms of content—voice, video, and data—may be provided to the home or office along the same pipeline, actual content production will remain specialized and relatively fragmented.

Content producers can today, and will even more in the future, sell content to multiple markets. For instance, Disney merchandises *Aladdin* as a movie, video game, soft toy, and home video on its cable channel. In the future, such broad distribution will be facilitated by the convergence of previously discrete distribution channels. Content providers will continue to control markets into which their products are sold. Indeed, because access to high-quality content will have unusual value to other industry participants during the transition period, content providers will be positioned to earn abnormally high returns.

PACKAGING

Two types of packagers will dominate the consumer multimedia industry. The first will be systems integrators who install systems or assist end users in entering, navigating, and creating web sites in cyberspace (e.g., @Home, a California-based firm, provides tools, technologies, and services to extend corporate LANs to the Internet and to develop interactive content and applications that exploit the broadband capabilities of @Home's network). Today, systems integrators are less important in the home consumer market than in the business arena, but they will be able to create a viable niche in the short- and medium-term by exploiting customer uncertainty and the lack of industry standards. Longer term, they will gradually disappear as standards are set, and as the manipulation infrastructure becomes more self-evident, self-configuring, and adaptive.

The other type of packager will deliver content to businesses or households, just as television networks, cable channels, and America Online do today. These packagers (we will refer to them as "distribution packagers") will exploit economies of scope in marketing by bundling various types of content—from AOL's Digital Cities to sports, movies, comic books, shopping, information, and advertising—into a single package. These packagers will be a force behind the partial reverticalization of the industry, because they will contract for, or otherwise provide access to, transmission, processing, and manipulation in order to deliver a complete package of content to specific user segments. Because intermediaries that provide these services will be invisible to consumers, packagers could end up "owning the customer," at least for a while.

Initially, distribution packagers will include a profusion of players, both existing competitors and new entrants. Opportunities will arise for competitors with new skills. Hollywood players, such as Steven Spielberg, Jeffrey Katzenberg, and David Geffen of DreamWorks SKG, and "Edutainment" software companies, such as Davidson, Electronic Arts, and Learning Associates, will bring the creative capabilities needed to develop new packaging forms that fully exploit the potential of multimedia and cyberspace. Initially, these entrants will merely adapt existing content to new distribution channels. Over time, they will become more sophisticated and separate from pure content providers. The industry will then consolidate to a greater or lesser extent as leading players exploit economies of scope.

The future structure of this industry segment could range from monopolistic to fragmented. It will be monopolistic if one player gains control of the gateway function (the Graphical User Interface that allows access to the information superhighway), and sets monopolistic standards. This could occur if, for example, America Online or Microsoft—through its integrated Windows 98/Internet Explorer interface—or Netscape through its browser—became the dominant entry ramp onto the information superhighway. As a bottleneck provider, such a monopolist could extract a toll from users and possibly even squeeze content providers.[10]

At the other end of the spectrum, we might see a widely differentiated set of distribution packagers, each specializing in a particular vertical market accessed through a common open network such as the Internet or the 800- and 900- telephone numbers. In this scenario, any distribution packager could freely access the network to make its services directly available to consumers, bypassing the need for intermediaries.

Which of these scenarios will actually come to pass will depend on three issues. The first is the extent to which consumers value simplicity and one-stop shopping—that is, receiving one invoice for all their multimedia activities, using one gateway onto the information highway, and so on. If substantial economies of scope exist across all services, then a concentrated packaging industry is likely to emerge, with a few firms competing to provide access to a huge range of products and services. But if significant differences in demand emerge—for example, between shopping for shoes and booking a vacation—we will likely see concentration only within segments. Today's cable network industry with only three music networks, three sports networks, and the like, exemplifies such a concentration within segments. As a whole, the cable industry is quite fragmented: there are more than one hundred cable networks. Players such as Microsoft may still make substantial royalties from a single gateway, but a profusion of packagers would license it.

The second issue that will shape the structure of the packaging segment will be whether or not a superpackager can preemptively establish a dominant reputation for quality and a large installed customer base. To gain such an advantage, a packager would have to become the exclusive distributor for much of today's most sought after content, which is unlikely. AOL, the currently leading superpackager, is continuing to boost its offering to critical mass but is finding the going difficult, especially against Microsoft Network (MSN). The jury is still out on how much power AOL's or MSN's brand name and customer base will have in their drive to reach superpackager status. Content providers will want to prevent a single superpackager from becoming too powerful by limiting the exclusivity of their distribution deals. Finally, players in the transmission infrastructure still have considerable control over access to multimedia. As they roll out their new services, they may influence the choice of a packager.

The third issue that will shape the future structure of the packaging segment is technology. In the emerging multimedia industry, consumer needs will be continuously redefined by new product innovations. Virtually any segment of the industry chain, therefore, has the potential to develop a "bottleneck technology"—unique displays, terminals, algorithms, or codes—that could be leveraged to temporary advantage. Thus, technical instability is likely to prevent any particular superpackager from dominating the industry.

Overall, we expect the same industry structure to emerge in packaging as in other channels of distribution—three or four broad super-packagers and a host of specialized vertical packagers. Whether these players endure long term will depend on developments elsewhere in the industry, because the manipulation segment may one day produce software that performs the same function as packagers.

TRANSMISSION

The transmission infrastructure will remain a shared function—a public network. That is not to say that there will be only one monopolistic transmission network, but rather that each network will be able to carry any content once it has been digitized. These networks will enjoy inherent economies of scope and unlimited, or at least very low cost, incremental capacity.[11]

The two most important questions concerning the future structure of this segment are: (1) how many local networks, of what type, will emerge; and (2) how competition between formerly local and long-distance providers will evolve. We will address the question of local networks first.

Local Networks At the local level, the multimedia industry might evolve to operate with only one broadband provider (one local loop), an arrangement that will probably be common in Western Europe. In the United States, following the groundbreaking Rochester approach, a single broadband loop could be made available (by a regulated entity) to any and all firms wishing to provide telephone and other multimedia services—including the regulated entity's own unregulated subsidiary.[12] The Telecommunications Act of 1996 attempts to direct all local "incumbent" telephone companies ("I-LECS") to open and freely sell access and usage of its network to competitors ("C-LECS"). Clear legal interpretations of this act are not yet in; however, its intention is to speed the movement to a multivendor local network environment. Consequently, single-loop solutions are unlikely to be widely adopted in the United States.

Based on this assumption, and on current economics of system investment, operating, and maintenance costs, we can assess the likelihood that each type of player—wireless, cable, and wireline telephone—will upgrade to some form of broadband network.

Wireless Wireless transmission already has a more or less saturated geographic coverage for narrow-band (limited digital transmission) dial-tone voice and data services. AT&T McCaw offers close to national coverage.[13] Air Touch, Bell Atlantic, NYNEX, and US West have aligned their cellular operations; and other such partnerships are likely. A new generation of licenses, for personal computer services (PCS), has recently been auctioned to encourage competition and provide national service.[14] Sprint and several cable TV companies have bid for and won very close to a national footprint. And more wireless spectrum is in the offing, both in the United States and abroad.

As competition increases and usage costs decline, wireless transmission will penetrate the mass consumer market. In 1993, the wireless penetration rate per person was about six percent, versus roughly fifty-six percent for wireline. As of 1997, penetration has grown to about fifteen percent. Our original 1993 analysis projected wireless prices would drop from the 1994 level of sixty to seventy cents per minute to ten to twenty cents per minute,[15] and penetration would rise to the thirty to forty percent range by approximately the year 2000. These projections continue to be accurate. Hence, wireless will become a very competitive domestic telephone service.

Even with increased penetration, however, wireless companies are unlikely to upgrade to broadband, because the technology lacks the capacity to economically convey more than trivial amounts of high-volume data (such as moving pictures and large files). There is some emerging but embryonic research activity on wireless multimedia. Therefore, in the foreseeable future, we expect the structure and profits of the wireless industry to be driven by the economics of stand-alone, dial-tone-only service.

Cable Broadband technology that enables interactive telephone service is currently available to cable television systems. The current coaxial networks would have to be upgraded to hybrid fiber/coaxial networks, however. The issue is whether the economics of such an investment are favorable.[16] On the demand side, evidence from the United Kingdom suggests that cable television providers of telephone service can capture over twenty percent of the market, at prices twenty percent below those of incumbent monopolist providers.[17] On the investment cost side, estimates for building interactive multichannel systems switched to offer telephone services vary from $500 to $1,500 per subscriber.[18] Considering the maintenance cost savings using fiberoptic technology, the new revenues from Internet access with cable modems and telephone services, and the incremental income from offering the promised eight hundred channels and interactive entertainment, cable companies are likely to upgrade. This scenario is further advanced by the "Prisoner's Dilemma," whereby the cable companies may need additional revenues just to stay even.[19]

Wireline Local telephone Exchange Companies (LECs) face similar decisions regarding upgrading to broadband capabilities. The economics of these decisions vary according to the assumptions made about how near to a residence the new fiber cable must be laid. Unfortunately, LECs may be forced to make the investment for defensive purposes. High-volume telephone users (over $50 per month) are the LECs' most profitable customers; in effect, they subsidize low-volume, high-cost customers that LECs are mandated to serve.[20] As LEC monopolies of local loops are challenged by new infrastructure competitors, the first targets will be high-profit, high-volume users. (In some downtown business districts, competitors have already compelled LECs to invest in fiber loops, to prevent erosion of their most profitable high volume business customers.[21]) Thus, it appears that LECs will have to upgrade their residential networks to protect their revenue base and market share.

In sum, we expect most cable and wireline players will upgrade so that competitive and complementary networks will proliferate. Most neighborhoods will have at least four local service providers: two wireless, one wireline broadband local loop, and one cable broadband local loop. Densely populated areas could have as many as nine. This degree of competition, combined with the considerable capacity of any one of these networks, suggests that there will be overcapacity in the local loop for a long time—and that many players who rush to participate in this business will become substantial losers.

The Local/Long-distance Dichotomy There is essentially no difference between local and long-distance transmission. In fact, under some circumstances sending a digital signal across the nation may be more economical than sending it across a state. Recognizing this, regulators have allowed LECs and Inter Exchange Carriers to compete[22]—which will erase current artificial geographic restrictions on competition.

But the end of the artificial divide between these markets will not necessarily mean the end of either type of competitor; both can in principle survive (see Key Success Factors and Capabilities later in this chapter). Nor will it necessarily mean the end of the local/long-distance dichotomy. Local service providers may well use other providers for long-distance transmission. With the possible exception of satellite-based systems, almost all such long-distance traffic is likely to be routed over trunk lines because of their economies of scale. LECs will almost certainly prefer not to create their own long-distance networks outside their own territory, but will enter into alliances with each other or with existing long-distance providers.[23] This will bring the aforementioned four to nine local-loop competitors into direct competition with the considerable transmission capacities of long-distance providers.

Unfortunately for current long-distance service providers, this new competition will most likely substantially reduce profitability. With only three major participants at the moment, overcapacity may not lead to poor industry returns but it almost inevitably will when the number of competitors increases to five or six.[24]

As the long-distance vendors come under attack, their responses will include adding local service offerings either utilizing assets mandatorily required by the I-LECS, or with new "fixed wireless" solutions, with all of this nationally connected with product bundling especially targeted at high-value customers. The effectiveness of such steps is uncertain, but we suspect these steps to be inadequate in the short-term to compensate for the profitability problems arising out of the basic overcapacity in the industry.

MANIPULATION

Historically, computer hardware and software have been tightly integrated in closed systems. With the advent of open systems, a real distinction has arisen between processing and storage hardware (i.e., equipment that physically transforms data), and the software which governs the manipulation of data (i.e., controls how user requests are handled and digital data are transformed). In the multimedia industry, two kinds of software will be needed. The first, which we might call "information superhighway software," enables the information superhighway to function as more than a simple data transmitter. This hybrid software combines elements of both manipulation and transmission. The second type, which we might call "traditional manipulation software," includes operating systems and stand-alone applications.

Information Superhighway Software The telecommunications and computer software industries are engaged in a fundamental conflict over the evolution of the information superhighway. The issue is whether, and to what degree, software for transmission and manipulation should reside on servers on the network or offline. We believe this is the single most important and difficult issue surrounding the future structure of the manipulation and transmission segments of the industry.

The telecommunications industry is trying to shift the balance toward intelligent networks, such as AIN, SS/7, and the Integrated Services Digital Network (ISDN). In this model, telephone networks would operate with a particular focus on "agency," with telco computers (next generation switches) serving as smart servers on behalf of network users. For example, the simple network might be able to locate any person anywhere by capturing and managing that person's signal as it travels from place to place. Further, a more intelligent network could proactively manage the verification, security, access limitation, and credit checks that allow messages to flow and transactions to be executed. Terminals would be "freed" of these connectivity tasks and/or would exploit or amplify those services. MCI and AT&T are quite advanced in moving in these directions embedded in their Internet offerings.

Naturally, the computer software industry ascribes a higher value to intelligent terminals. In this model, as in the conventional view of the Internet, the transmission infrastructure is not much more than a big dumb pipeline blindly switching messages from one location to another, manipulating them only minimally. All intelligence resides in users' computer terminals or in servers that are independent of the network.

Microsoft and Netscape are betting that, for the vast majority of applications, decentralized solutions using smart, off-network servers will prove to be faster, better, and cheaper for end users. If they can deliver standardized Internet service with the capacity to handle all the switched traffic transparently using the LEC network at a lower cost— albeit a lower quality service level—LECs would be positioned as "dumb" players in a low-return commodity transport business.[25]

Each of these approaches might deliver similar services to the customer. For example, one would deliver a smart picture phone linked to telephone company networks, whereas the other would deliver videoconferencing on the Internet. Each approach has technical advantages and disadvantages, and embodies quite different consumer behavior models, but neither is a priori superior. As a consequence, predicting which model will prevail is difficult. Success will depend on consumer preferences and the speed and skill the camps apply to innovative, creative solutions.

Today, the telecommunications industry, which offers applications such as call waiting, voice mail, and caller ID, is rapidly building deeper and broader bases of experience. The cost of such technical investments can be amortized among huge numbers of network subscribers. Moreover, to the extent that other industry segments require supervisory, security, and communications functions that are invisible to end users, the telecommunications industry's experience with real-time response software and connectivity problems in general will be an advantage. For its part, the computer industry, with its history of rapid technical innovation could pull together some complete solutions for the medium term, thus establishing a position that would be difficult to overcome. To the extent that the multimedia industry evolves in ways that require users, rather than networks, to manipulate data, the computer industry will have an advantage with its deep experience in man/computer interfaces.

The results of this competition will be products that can be sold to content packagers. Some products will be complete applications, such as software that enables video servers to dispense movies to set-top boxes in the home. AT&T, Oracle, and Microsoft, among others, are working on components for this application. Other products will be "middleware"—tools for constructing enduser applications or embedding code in resold applications. These will include tools that facilitate network use (e.g., search agents, such as those of General Magic) or make the network more accessible (e.g., the Graphical User Interfaces being offered by Microsoft and Bell Atlantic).[26]

The precise nature of these products is still uncertain; their design depends in part on the continuing debate about where network intelligence will reside, and on the speed with which workable solutions are offered to the marketplace. But a new tier of software tasks and functionality is emerging that will define the information elements of the superhighway. Like all prior software developments, this new tier will build on established software standards and approaches; progress will be uneven, as befits an intrinsically evolutionary and experimental process. Eventually, standards will emerge. As they do, the competitive structure of this new segment will shake out. However, as the network-level intelligence is finally partitioned, it will be marked by the emergence of standard network offerings, with at most three offerings surviving in any "wholesale" middleware or enduse application area.

Traditional Manipulation Software Operating systems for individual components of the information superhighway will remain the province of a few large competitors. Microsoft dominates operating systems for stand-alone personal computers and Novell dominates LAN operating systems. In each case, economies of scale and network externalities allow one firm to effectively set the standard, even if its technology is inferior. The only basis for competitive disequilibrium to be introduced is at the architectural level: for example, IBM, Sun, and others are attacking Microsoft and Intel with their Java applets network-computer prod-

product strategies. They will not displace Microsoft in stand-alone applications, but they are trying to restructure the bottleneck toward their strengths and give themselves a shot at growth as the "network" becomes intelligent. The same is likely to be true for makers of specific retail applications, from simple spreadsheets and databases to more complicated applications like CAD/CAM. Though markets for these products have unique requirements, they are still subject to typical economies of scale. Therefore, they will likely become relatively concentrated businesses—although the potential for superior applications to drive out inferior ones will be higher than it is in markets for tools, operating systems, and network standards.

Processing/Storage Hardware Because digitization allows all content to be processed and stored in the same way, the same hardware will be used to manipulate all content. As the cost of distributed computing becomes increasingly competitive, the mainframe will pass into history for most uses, except real-time processing of huge amounts of data (as in airline reservations or bank transactions processing).[27] The issue then becomes whether data and applications are held and processed centrally, or stored and manipulated locally, as personal computing and video games are today. We suspect the answer will be a combination of central and local processing, with the choice dependent primarily on frequency and volume of usage. For example, in the predicted move from videocassette rental to video on-demand, best sellers will probably be held on local file servers that can meet high demand without incurring long-distance transmission charges. Art house movies that are viewed less frequently would be held at more central locations, to optimize the mix of storage and transmission costs. Similarly, computer databases will be stored locally if they are used regularly and updated infrequently, or held centrally if they are searched infrequently and updated regularly.

Wherever processing power is held, the industry is heading toward the commodity supply of hardware. Intelligence will reside either in the manipulation of software or in specialized components (e.g., microprocessors). The production of processing and storage equipment will therefore be an unattractive industry.

Terminals

Market fragmentation is likely in the terminal segment of the industry. In the consumer market, the need to meet differentiated customer requirements will probably lead to a profusion of terminal types. Portable

Industry Segment	Structure
Content	• Fragmented and specialized • Broad distribution through multiple markets
Packaging	Distribution Packager • 3–4 Superpackagers with economies of scale • Remainder fragmented and specialized • Simple links to integrated systems, including selection and promotion
Transmission	Local Loop (4–9 players) • Wireless • Cable • Wireline Long-distance • More players than today • Overcapacity • Commodity pricing
Manipulation	Information Superhighway Software • Specialized • Based on telephone or Internet standards Traditional Manipulation Software • Fragmented Processing/Storage Hardware • Central and local processing
Terminals	• Fragmented and specialized • "Client" and small stand-alone devices

FIGURE 2-5   **Emerging Structure of the Multimedia Industry**

vs. fixed, small vs. large screen displays, high- vs. low-quality, and cheap single-function vs. expensive multifunction are some potential market segments. The most important functional difference will probably be wireless (portable) vs. wireline (fixed location) terminals.

Figure 2-5 summarizes our predictions for the structure of various segments of the emerging multimedia industry.

Key Success Factors and Capabilities

We have described the playing fields in each segment of the multimedia industry. The next task is to define key success factors in each segment. A brief review of the starting positions of players in each of today's three vertical industries indicates that some industry segments will be more competitive than others.

- *Content* is now provided by myriad players in many distinct businesses. In video/interactive offerings, the media/entertainment industry has a clear advantage.

- *Packaging* is divided among the three existing industries, with no dominant player. As a result, computer companies, cable and television programmers, current providers of information to telephone and online networks, as well as myriad new entrants, including probably the telephone companies themselves, will end up competing for control of the packaging function. Indeed, these players are already encroaching on each other (e.g., Sega is moving into cable and computer games).[28]

- *Transmission* is the domain of wireline and wireless telephone companies. The only threat to them is the possible use of cable as second local loop.

- *Manipulation* will have two very different competitive spheres. The information superhighway subsegment will be a battleground for the computer and telecommunications industries. Although traditional manipulation software and processing are likely to remain computer functions, the exact form of processing (file server versus workstation, for example), and its location (on or off the network) are debatable.

- The *terminal* market is almost equally divided among the telephone, television and personal computing industries suggesting that the "set-top box" market is up for grabs.[29]

In the following sections we will enlarge on each of these industry segments.

CONTENT

Content is the easiest segment to address because it will remain closest to its current form ("form" refers to production rather than distribution). While the multimedia revolution will overthrow existing distribution arrangements (such as retail outlets or mail order expertise), the key success factor in each of the discrete content businesses will be the production of the highest quality content at reasonable prices. In entertainment, the most uniquely creative content producers will be as successful as they are today—although because content will have to be created for more than one medium (i.e., film or television), new modes of creativity will be required. In news gathering, winners will be those entities that provide the desired coverage most cost effectively. That is, the firms that today excel at providing their particular content will continue to earn high returns, although with wide variance.

Content providers will not, in our view, have much of a struggle with packagers who are tempted to produce lower-quality content and force it on the consumers they control. We believe consumers will enable high-quality, independent content providers to survive and prosper; no superpackager will monopolize distribution. Although this implies that content suppliers need not integrate forward, there are strategic reasons why packagers and transmission firms will want preferential access to high-quality, recognizable content. Thus content providers will be approached by other industry players to form alliances. They will be in the driver's seat and should agree to participate only if they are offered substantial rewards over and above continuing independent operation.

PACKAGING

Key success factors for packagers will be customer ownership and appropriate vertical scope. Owning customers is difficult for packagers, who are intermediaries between content providers and customers. Moreover, packagers must also work through transmission companies, which have direct customer contacts. Thus, to be profitable, packagers must develop unique packages that override the reputations of content providers and direct customer contacts of transmission companies. Doing so will be difficult but not impossible. For example, MTV successfully plays this role today, notwithstanding attempts by record companies to create their own music network.[30]

The MTV example demonstrates two other critical determinants of customer ownership—first mover advantage and brand name. If Sony is considering switching from MTV to a new music network, it must recognize the distribution breadth and cost advantage MTV possesses. In particular, in businesses that exhibit huge economies of scale, the first mover is able to secure wide market access quickly, building a cost structure that is difficult for others to replicate. Typically, the first mover establishes an attractive brand name that strengthens its customer ownership. When consumers are deciding whether to source their multimedia needs from AT&T, the local LEC, the local cable company, or an entrepreneurial startup, the fact that their brand preference hierarchy probably matches that order will have a major impact on their decisions.

Another determinant of customer ownership will be a packager's technological capability. This might seem an unusual requirement for success in what is essentially a creative role, but given the enormous technological uncertainty surrounding the evolution of the multimedia industry, understanding and exploiting the limits of technological feasibility will be critical in the short term. In the early years of interactive television, for example, technology will determine the number of choices available to viewers for interactive responses. Designing interactive game shows will quickly become a redundant skill as interactivity extends to a much broader range of data. Thus, staying at the forefront of creativity will require a deep understanding not only of customers' needs, but more important, of the technical capabilities and limitations of the information superhighway.

Vertical scope—that is, the degree of integration with other segments (backward into content and forward into transmission)—will also be a key determinant of packagers' success. Early in the industry life cycle, broad scope in both directions will be important. Packagers will need access to the best content to assure customers that a new service offers the most desirable product. Access does not require ownership of content, but it does suggest that contracts or alliances with content providers will be critical.

At first, packagers will also have to extend themselves forward into transmission because network hardware and software will be inextricably linked to the development of effective packages. Here contracts will not be enough, at least in the beginning. Packagers will need to work closely with network providers to understand the technological limitations of a network, and if possible to establish network parameters. Due to the uncertainty inherent in the task, such working relationships cannot be arranged contractually.[31]

In the early years, of course, many packagers will be companies specializing in content or transmission, so at least one link will be internalized. Later, when standards have been established and uncertainty reduced, traditional contractual arrangements can be negotiated to capture the value of any remaining linkages between packaging and content or transmission. At that point these businesses will start to unbundle.

These principles apply particularly to firms that are striving to become broad-scope superpackagers. Clearly, these players will require enormous resources, as well as first mover advantages, to win. On the other hand, entering the fragmented, specialized packaging areas will be much easier. Any entrepreneur has the potential to become a viable niche packager.

TRANSMISSION

Two sets of success factors will exist in the transmission segment, one for local loops, and the other for long-distance transmission.

Local Loop Provided that one set of competitors does not achieve an overwhelming investment cost advantage, success in local loops will be based on the fact that this is primarily a customer service business. Although strategic pricing may produce differentially higher utilization, strength in packaging, provisioning, repair, billing, and brand name will determine success. The relative strengths and weaknesses of the four types of transmission players—local, long-distance, cable, and wireless—may be summarized as follows.

Due to regulatory pressures over the past decade, LECs are not only strong in most aspects of customer service; they are increasingly efficient in operations. These strengths position them very well for success in multimedia transmission. However, LECs lack the entertainment capability necessary for entry into the broader multimedia market. Unlike telephone service, in which price can be an important entry tactic, cable entry will probably require differentiated content to encourage customer switching. To acquire content, LECs will most likely form alliances with content providers or packagers (e.g., the Disney deal with three LECs,[32] or the aborted Bell Atlantic/TCI merger[33]). The strategic need for such an alliance will diminish as LECs establish a market presence, and market contracts for content replace more formally structured alliances.

Today, long-distance companies have strengths in sophisticated network management, brand name, and strategic pricing. They suffer from the lack of local loop infrastructure (and therefore from weak customer links). Their most logical mode of entry could be to resell LEC or cable facilities, an approach that puts them at somewhat of a disadvantage. In addition, the long-distance companies lack entertainment experience. Finally, AT&T in particular suffers from a lack of direct customer contact, because it has historically outsourced its billing, which is vital for success in local markets.

Cable companies are very poorly positioned. They have the worst customer service and brand reputation of any likely competitor; lack switching or sophisticated network management capabilities; and have not experienced the regulatory pressure to reduce costs and enhance service that has strengthened the LECs over the past decade. Cable companies have access to entertainment content now, but are likely to consolidate in the future in order to offer broad distribution to content providers and to counter the telephone companies' anticipated content alliances.[34] To generate telephone business they will probably have to form partnerships or merge with telephone companies, most likely out-of-territory LECs (e.g., US West and Continental Cable), or if permitted, a long-distance carrier. Clearly, such alliances would bring cable companies valuable capabilities in switching and network service management.

Wireless service will be seen as a complement to, rather than a substitute for, wireline communications for only five to eight years. Price differentials, limitations on data transmission, and the current lack of national coverage will slow wireless penetration into broad-based domestic markets, temporarily limiting it to high-volume telephone users. To offer national coverage that is the key to penetrating business markets, wireless players will need to form alliances. As the market broadens, the ability to market nationwide will create superior brand awareness and reduce marketing costs, attracting domestic customers and strengthening the advantage of nationwide coverage. This is the logic behind the current alliance activity in the wireless industry (such as Nextel's acquisition binge[35] and the alliance and now merger of Bell Atlantic and NYNEX).

Long-distance Long-distance transmission networks face the problem of retaining customer control. In principle, the transmission function is a wholesale commodity, which with recent advances in network quality, is essentially transparent to customers. Therefore, we might reasonably expect to see long-distance companies disintermediated by players that control customers, whether local loop or content packager. In this scenario, LECs would become resellers of long-distance minutes and would use simple low-cost routing algorithms and their enormous bargaining power to make long-distance transmission a very unprofitable, cost-driven business.

Long-distance companies could prevent this outcome by trying to maintain regulatory barriers to the resale of their product, or as AT&T is doing, by leveraging current brand name strengths in businesses that do provide customer contact. But even if AT&T becomes a packager or a local access provider, the long-distance transmission component of its business would best be treated as a stand-alone entity, for which the key to success will be low cost.

Thus, however the long-distance market evolves, the key to success in long-distance transmission will be low-cost service. Existing long-distance companies must retain customers while cutting the cost of basic network operations, and moving simultaneously into local loops and packaging businesses.

MANIPULATION

As the manipulation segment splits into three very different sub-segments—traditional manipulation software, information superhighway software, and processing/storage hardware—different success factors will emerge in each.

Traditional Manipulation Software Success in traditional manipulation software will probably continue to depend on the same factors that counted in the past. Therefore, we expect the same kinds of players, for instance, Microsoft, to win. The only change will be the decreasing frequency with which startups establish new standards within applications. The value of an installed customer base will provide incumbents with a major advantage, allowing them to gradually extend their scope to related markets.

Information Superhighway Software The experience of the software industry suggests that success in information superhighway software (including telecommunication and computer wholesale applications, as well as middleware) will derive from standard-setting prowess, which in turn, comes from technological capability, alliance building skills, and first mover advantage. Retail applications like the consumer Graphical User Interface are the traditional domain of Microsoft, which understands the consumer/computer interface and consumer needs extremely well. The proof of this is found in Microsoft's amazing repositioning of its entire company and product line. Specifically, having missed the full significance of the Internet as a new package, it developed Internet Explorer, redeveloped Office 97, and gained leadership back from Netscape—all in the span of eighteen months.

Wholesale, or computer/computer interface applications are a very different environment, in which Microsoft has traditionally had no presence. Though Microsoft should continue to perform well in the retail domain, its success in the wholesale market is more questionable.

The technological requirements of this new kind of software are so various—involving interactivity, connectivity, real time, and digital switching—that neither the computer nor the telecommunications industry has an overwhelming advantage. Today, the computer industry is focused on man/machine interactivity and complex manipulation and is only beginning to offer real-time products, most of which are relatively simple. The telecommunications industry, notably long-distance carriers, is producing a stream of real-time applications involving computer/computer interfaces (e.g., data filtering and amplification, call following, and caller signaling). They have the capability to develop nationwide real-time standards that will garner the lion's share of complex wholesale applications. Competition among telephone companies will then take place in terms of price, system reliability, and the fundamental design and ease of use of wholesale applications services offered to packagers. Competitive differentiation will come not from simply switching original information around the superhighway, but from improved processing of information. These intelligent networks will become "platforms" for network applications, much as DOS became for stand-alone applications.

Such applications hold the best hope for long-distance companies to build profitable market positions. To do so, however, they will have to acquire some of the skills of a manipulation company. We expect to see numerous alliances between transmission companies and computer and software companies with their database manipulation skills.

Such alliances will also benefit computer companies. The computer industry is working to develop smart servers that act as centralized data manipulators—an outcome Oracle and IBM would prefer. But industry participants must move closer to the transmission and software businesses if they are to escape the commoditization of basic processing and storage. Only in a scenario in which a relatively dumb network/server is complemented by smart terminals does Microsoft have a clear advantage. Microsoft wants to keep intelligence at the lowest, most componentized level, with minimal network interactions, so that it can capitalize on its power in standard setting in the business environment.

Given technological uncertainty, multiple proprietary and differentiated wholesale application packages will be developed for product offerings such as video on demand, global positioning satellite systems, and home shopping. However, in the long run, one may expect standardized offerings to emerge and one type of player to predominate.

Because these applications involve terminals, transmission, manipulation, and packagers, and because of their inherent profit potential, they are currently the focus of much alliance activity.[36] Some of the activity involves mergers and acquisitions, some joint ventures, and some prime contractor relationships. Although we cannot hope to predict which companies will win, or even the standards that will eventually emerge, we can suggest that there will be important advantages to being a first-mover in setting standards.[37] If a LEC, for example, establishes a successful standard in its interactive test market, that standard will be hard to dislodge, because of the huge complementary investments in switching, network infrastructure, set-top boxes, and so forth.

Processing/Storage Hardware In the processing subsegment, success will increasingly relate to the low-cost provision of commodity products. Differentiation may come from unique components, such as microprocessors, but computer storage and processing hardware boxes will continue to be commoditized. Even currently differentiated products (such as video servers) will rapidly become commodities. Thus, if computer companies are to survive, at least at the consumer end of the multimedia business, they will have to continue to lower costs and to improve their service and software products. Suppliers of differentiated components (e.g., displays) will capture the value from the hardware business, reducing computer companies to assemblers.

TERMINALS

Competitors with the resources and capabilities to succeed in the terminal segment are likely to have recognized two important features of that market. The first is that it will be a high-volume consumer market. The ubiquitous nature of the terminal and its potential combination with the telephone, television, video game player, personal computer, and video cassette player suggest a likely household penetration rate of over one hundred percent, and a U.S. domestic market of at least ten million units per annum. Worldwide sales of over fifty million units per annum are forecast.[38]

The second important aspect of the terminal market is that it is unlikely to be homogeneous, because horizontal and vertical differentiation in a market of that size is inevitable. Consumers will be differentiated from commercial and industrial users; their demands for portable and fixed bases, "smart" or "dumb" terminals, large- and small-screen displays, combination and single-use units, will also be highly differentiated. A single terminal is, in fact, highly unlikely to become the ubiquitous household unit, because individual preferences, needs, and incomes differ too widely.

The keys to success in such markets will be similar to those in the current consumer electronics market. High-volume manufacturing (primarily assembly) and product design and innovation capabilities, established brand names, and distribution channels will therefore become the most crucial to success. These factors favor the emergence of companies that serve mass markets, surrounded by specialists that focus on niche markets (e.g., Bang and Olufsen's unique Scandinavian design in the consumer electronics market) or supply unique components (e.g., Sharp's dominance in LCD screens). Indeed, consumer electronics companies will probably dominate the terminal market. Hardened to intense competition in successive waves of new product innovation, they have developed the capabilities needed to succeed in the terminals market.

The phenomenon of terminal companies acquiring content providers (e.g., Sony's purchase of Columbia) will be short-lived. After Sony failed to win over content providers to its VCR standard,[39] Sony decided to become a content provider in order to influence future terminal standards. However, the importance of content in terminal standards will disappear when content is distributed via digital networks. Thus, the link between content and terminal companies will be abolished. The content ventures of Sony, Philips (Polygram Records), and Matsushita will be spun off as independent businesses or sold to transmission or packager companies that value them more highly. The lesson of this experience is that attempts to fight the horizontal reconfiguration of the industry will fail. Trying to connect software content and terminal hardware in a unique vertical format will not succeed. For similar reasons, if Sega and Nintendo try to sustain video games as stand-alone vertical industries, they are likely to be overwhelmed.

Figure 2-6 summarizes the key success factors by industry segment.

Implications and Conclusions

Recognizing that three discrete vertical industries will be reconfiguring into five horizontal segments, we have a powerful framework for analyzing the future structure of the multimedia industry, the strategies and competitive advantages of individual players, and the wisdom of various kinds of alliances. In general, this framework suggests the following broad conclusions for players operating in each segment.

- *Content companies,* such as Disney, face excellent prospects. Providers of high-quality content now have the opportunity to enter into some very attractive alliances on favorable terms. Disney is doing just that, in its deals with three LECs.

- *Packagers* face perhaps the greatest challenges and opportunities, because this segment is the most novel, and companies are approaching it from different directions. These players need to

Industry Segment	Success Factors
Content	Cost/quality, independent of distribution
Packaging	Customer control • Creativity • High-quality content • Brand name • Early mover Technological acumen Vertical scope — content and transmission alliances
Transmission	Cost/quality of customer service and provisioning National coverage, interoperability, and branding Broadbanding service capabilities
Manipulation • Traditional Software • Information Highway Software • Processing Hardware	Incumbents Standard-setting, technological prowess Alliance skills Manipulation and transmission skills Low cost assembly Specialized components
Terminals	High volume assembly Product design and innovation Consumer marketing and distribution

FIGURE 2-6   **Key Multimedia Success Factors by Industry Segment**

make many alliances, and be prepared for big wins and big failures as the industry evolves.

- *LECs* will need to work simultaneously on upgrading their broadband network capabilities and building volume to fill that capacity while entering the long-distance business. Given the prospective overcapacity in local loops, LECs need to make very targeted facility investments. They are in a good position to build volume by developing roles as packagers through careful alliances.

- *Long-distance companies* face a similar challenge as they cope with entry by the LECs and must be careful about maintaining utilization of their capacity. They have bright prospects in other horizontal segments (specifically information superhighway software), but they must be prepared to confront and/or co-opt software companies, particularly Microsoft, Oracle, and the like.

- *Computer companies* need to recognize the limited future of their processing hardware and decide whether to move upstream into transmission or to remain in stand-alone applications.

- *Terminal producers* have the opportunity to shape consumer preferences for a multiplicity of new products.

As packagers and transmission companies try to lock up quality content to differentiate their consumer offerings, content providers are likely to become the focus of considerable alliance activity. Packagers should be interested in alliances with content providers in order to differentiate their product offerings, and with transmission companies in order to incorporate technological knowledge of network capabilities into their creative function. Transmission companies should be involved in alliances with one another. Wireless companies need to build nationwide networks; cable companies need to develop national distribution.

Clearly, there is enormous uncertainty about the future of the three industries that are converging into the multimedia superindustry. Though industry convergence has inspired a great deal of radical reorganization in many corporations, many of those moves cannot be explained by our framework. Rather, they seem driven by mimetic diversification ("It's all right for me to do this because my competitor just did it."), or naive heuristics ("This business must be worth investing in, because it will be the Microsoft of the future."). But that should not hinder our attempts to think in structured ways about the future. At this stage, the payoff of even a little knowledge is large enough to justify the investment. We believe the framework laid out in this paper will enable companies to better formulate strategies that will allow them to emerge as winners in the twenty-first century.

Endnotes

1. Anthony G. Oettinger, "Telling Ripe from Hype in Multimedia," (incidental paper, Boston, MA: Harvard University Center for Information Policy Research, July 1994).
2. Gary Hamel and C. K. Prahalad, *Competing for the Future* (Boston, MA: Harvard Business School Press, 1994).
3. Richard P. Simon and Barry A. Kaplan, "Communacopia: A Digital Communication Bounty," Goldman Sachs Investment Research, July 1992. John Hagel, III, and Thomas R. Eisenmann, "Navigating the Multimedia Landscape," *The McKinsey Quarterly* 3 (1994) 39–55.
4. Michael E. Porter, *Competitive Strategy* (New York: Free Press, 1980).

5. Birger Wernerfelt, "A Resource-based View of the Firm" *Strategic Management Journal* 5 (1984) 171–180. J. B. Barney, "Firm Resources and Sustained Competitive Advantage," *Journal of Management* 17 (1991) 99–120. M. A. Peteraf, "The Cornerstones of Competitive Advantage: A Resource-based View," *Strategic Management Journal* 14 (1993) 179–191.

6. Stephen P. Bradley and Jerry A. Hausman (eds.), *Future Competition in Telecommunications* (Boston, MA: Harvard Business School Press, 1989). Joseph Baylock, Stephen P. Bradley, and Eric K. Clemons, "Enhanced Communications Services: An Analysis of AT&T's Competitive Position," *Ibid.* Stephen P. Bradley, Jerry A. Hausman, and Richard L. Nolan, *Globalization, Technology, and Competition: The Fusion of Computers and Telecommunications in the 1990s* (Boston, MA: Harvard Business School Press, 1993). Stephen P. Bradley, "The Role of IT Networking in Sustaining Competitive Advantage," *Ibid.* David J. Collis, "The Evolution of Firm Boundaries: The Case of the Baby Bells," (working paper 93–064, Boston, MA: Harvard Business School, Division of Research, January 1993). "Rating the RHCs," *Telephony* 221 (1991) 26–29. P. William Bane, Ronald M. Serrano, and Debra McMahon, "LECs Must Learn the Marketing Game," *Telephony* 223 (1992) 22–24. "Telco Reduces OSP Trouble Reports: No News is Good News," *Telephone Engineer and Management* (April 1, 1993). Joao Baptista and Jerome Moitry, "PCS: An Exercise in Marketing Skills," (paper presented to IIRC PCS 1995 Conference, Paris, January 1995). Joao Baptista, Mitch Goldstein, and Peter Clark, "Can the European Operators Compete," *International Telecommunications Update*, 1995/96 (New York: Kensington Publications, 1995). P. William Bane, J. P. A. Baptista, J. Estin, and M. P. Goldstein, "International Carriers: Benchmarking Performance," *Telecommunications* (Americas Edition) 29 (1995).

7. Michael Fahey, "From Local to Global: Surveying the Fiber Landscape," *Telecommunications* (Americas Edition), 27 (1993) 33–38.

8. Charles F. Mason, "Iridium Forges Ahead With Its Grand PCN Plan," *Telephony* 225 (1993) 28–34.

9. Nielsen Media Research, "1992–1993 Report on Television," (Northbrook, IL: A.C. Nielsen Co., 1993) 8.

10. John Hagel, III, and William J. Lansing, "Who Owns the Customer," *The McKinsey Quarterly* (1994) 63–76.

11. Martin Dessaulies, Mercer Management Consulting, "Future Policy for Telecommunications Infrastructure and CATV Networks: A Path Toward Infrastructure Liberalization," (December 1994).

12. Catherine Arnst, "Phone Frenzy: Is There Anyone Who Doesn't Want to Be a Telecom Player?," *Business Week* (February 20, 1995) 92–97.

13. Joanie Wexler, "AT&T/McCaw Merger Could Lower Prices, Spur Innovation," *Network World* (September 26, 1994) 10–11.

14. Bruce DeMaeyer, "PCS Auctions: Ready or Not, Here They Come," *America's Network* (November 1, 1994) 34–35.

15. P. William Bane, Dekkers L. Davidson, and Ronald E. Grant, "The Making of Wireless Competition," *PCIA Journal* (June 1994) 16.

16. Naoyuki Koike, "Cable Television and Telephone Companies: Towards Residential Broadband Communications Services in the United States and Japan," (Boston, MA: Harvard University, Program on Information Resources Policy, 1990).

17. "Multimedia in Britain: Down the Line," *The Economist* (November 26, 1994) 76.

18. Mercer Management Consulting, "Future Policy for Telecommunications," 96–98.

19. Mercer, *Bloody Stalemate.*

20. Company confidential information.
21. David Rohde, "CAPs Invade the Suburbs," *Network World* (October 4, 1993) 33.
22. Mark Landler, "Baby Bells Advance in Long Distance," *New York Times*, Section 1 (April 29, 1995) 35.
23. Peter W. Huber, Michael K. Kellogg, and John Thorne, *The Geodesic Network II: 1993 Report on Competition in the Telephone Industry*, (Washington, DC: The Geodesic Company, 1992).
24. "International Prices Tumble at ICA Meeting," *Communications News* (July 1993) 32.
25. P. William Bane and Debra B. McMahon, "Break Up to Break Out," *Telephony* (September 16, 1996).
26. As a horizontal tool that can potentially be used in all applications interfaces, the Graphical User Interface can clearly be an enormous source of revenue.
27. Richard Ross, "Managing Distributed Computing," *Information Systems Management* (Summer 1994) 41–50.
28. Mark Berniker, "Sega Channel Readies for Debut," *Broadcasting & Cable* (June 20, 1994) 40.
29. Andrew Kupfer, "Set-top Box Wars," *Fortune* (August 22, 1994) 110–118.
30. Mark Landler, "Will MTV Have To Share the Stage?" *Business Week* (Industrial/Technology Edition) (February 21, 1994) 38.
31. Joseph Farrell and Garth Saloner, "Standardization, Compatibility, and Innovation," *Rand Journal of Economics* 16 (Spring 1985) 70–83.
32. Larry Armstrong, "The Baby Bells Go Hollywood," *Business Week* (August 29, 1994) 34–35.
33. Ian Scales, "Irreconcilable Differences?," *Communications International* (December 1994) 4–7.
34. Larry J. Yokell, "Cable TV Moves Into Telecom Markets," *Business Communications Review* (November 1994) 43–48.
35. Patrick Flanagan, "National Wireless Picture Getting Murkier," *Telecommunications* (Americas Edition) (November 1994) 15–16.
36. Jennifer Edstrom, "Hardware's Stake In Convergence," *Computer Reseller News* (November 14, 1994) SS27–SS30.
37. Michael Katz and Carl Shapiro, "Network Externalities, Competition, and Compatibility," *American Economic Review* 75 (1987) 424–440.
38. *Computer Industry Forecasts* (Second Quarter 1995).
39. Michael A. Cusumano, "Strategic Maneuvering and Mass-Market Dynamics: The Triumph of VHS Over Beta," *Business History Review* (Spring 1992) 51–94.

3 | Telecommunications: Building the Infrastructure for Value Creation

Jerry A. Hausman

OVER THE LAST DECADE, information service demand has grown by about twenty percent per year. In the last five years, connections to the Internet have grown about ten percent to twenty percent per month. We are in the midst of an "Internet mania" in which companies scramble to offer new services on the Internet. The stocks of companies that offer Internet products and services increased by two hundred to five hundred percent per year during 1995 and 1996. Online service providers such as Prodigy and America Online (AOL) are being joined by AT&T, MCI, and Microsoft. Software companies are offering products that permit easier use of the World Wide Web. This rapid increase in both consumer demand and competition is expected to continue.

However, the vast majority of service offerings have been limited by the copper wire pair that limits the bandwidth of service offerings to residential customers. This technology, in use in U.S. telephone networks since at least the 1920s, makes content more complicated than text extremely slow to transmit and receive. An existing technology, ISDN, over copper, increases bandwidth but still imposes a significant bandwidth limitation on multimedia content. Thus, multimedia offerings typically are supplied on CD ROMs. Use of CD ROMs has grown exponentially; CD ROM drives are now included as standard equipment on the majority of desktop PCs.

What would be the value of creating a new infrastructure for online multimedia offerings? The investment in the infrastructure for multimedia is likely to cost hundreds of billions of dollars. Is the value to consumers and the economy large enough to justify this expenditure? Economic analysis can be used to estimate the overall value to consumers and the economy. In this chapter, I will show that a single new successful service, voice messaging, has led to increased value to the economy of about $1.5 billion per year, and that the value of online services is estimated to be in the range of $10 to $25 billion per year.

Who is likely to build the infrastructure to provide the broadband capacity for online multimedia content? Local telephone companies and cable companies are the likely providers. However, government regulation is creating significant delays in building the needed infrastructure. This outmoded regulation must be eliminated or multimedia services are likely to be delayed in the United States for many years.

Then there is the Microsoft Network (MSN) debate. Many online service competitors, in particular AOL, have called for government regulation to decrease Microsoft's ability to compete in providing online services. While this action is expected from a competitor, it is surprising that the Department of Justice has taken these claims seriously. The MSN debate can be analyzed from a competitive perspective in terms of how the introduction of MSN is likely to affect consumers. The analysis shows that MSN will increase competition and benefit consumers. The Justice Department should not intervene because some competitors do not like competition.

Finally, who is likely to capture the value from the emerging online industry? By far the largest amount of value will be captured by consumers and business users of these new services. This result is not surprising to an economist, but it seems to be missed in much of the public policy debate. Among service providers, software providers and content providers are likely to be the most successful in capturing the (quasi) rents from online services. Equipment providers and transmission providers will face increased competition, which will not allow them to amass large rents. However, the outcome that consumers will benefit the most should not be lost among the charges of "unfair competition" from competitors who are trying to gain competitive advantage through government regulation, rather than by producing a superior product or service. The market has been successful to date in providing these consumer benefits. The dead hand of government regulation is certain to slow down progress and lead to competition among lobbyists and in the hearing room, rather than increased competition in the marketplace, which benefits consumers.

Estimating the Benefits and Efficiency of New Services

How should we estimate both the consumer value (benefits) and the overall value of new telecommunications services? This question can be approached in terms of economic efficiency. If the value of the new services is low in relation to their cost, then firms are unlikely to provide either services or the necessary infrastructure to carry them. In that case, the government should not become involved in attempts to accelerate infrastructure development. The development of voice messaging services provides a good illustration of this type of analysis. The consumer benefit from this new service turned out to be quite high. This example can be used to demonstrate how the value of a proposed new service can be estimated.

Consumer Value

To place a value on new telecommunications services, we will apply the method first introduced by the Nobel prize winning economist Sir J. R. Hicks (1940). I recently used this approach to value new varieties of consumer goods and telecommunications services (Hausman 1994, 1995a, 1995b). The basic idea of the economic approach to valuing new goods or services is to recognize that in their absence, consumers are unable to purchase them, no matter how much they might like to. Thus, in some sense, the price of the new good or service might as well be infinite, since it cannot be purchased at any price.

A more refined approach rests on a "virtual" or "reservation" price, at which demand for the new good or service is zero. At this virtual price, a "virtual equilibrium" exists between demand and supply, which is also zero. Estimation of the virtual price along with the expenditure function (demand curve) for the new good or service yields the economic value. The actual price of the new service will usually be well below the virtual price. The average difference between the virtual price and the actual market price is the *fundamental gain in value,* also called consumer surplus, from the new service. Thus, this economic approach uses market demand to value new goods and services; the market establishes what consumers are willing to pay.

Using this approach, I find that the introduction of new telecommunications services can produce very large gains in consumer value. Consider the introduction of voice messaging services by local telephone companies in 1990. Local voice messaging offered advanced voice mail features, including the ability to receive messages while the line is in use; partitioned mail boxes for various family members; and a broadcast feature for disseminating messages to a group of numbers, a feature useful for organizations or schools. Voice messaging, along with online information services, has been the great success story of enhanced service offerings in the past 15 years. By 1994, local telephone company voice messaging demand in the United States exceeded seven million subscribers. The average monthly price of voice messaging in that year was approximately $8. The gain in consumer welfare from these new services is estimated to be about $1.5 billion per year.[1]

The economic theory behind the estimation of the consumer value produced by new services was developed by Sir John Hicks. Hicks stated that for new products the "virtual" price in periods in which the goods did not exist would "just make the demands for these commodities equal to zero" (1940, 144).[2] Modern economists recognize this price as the shadow, or reservation, price, which when used in the demand function sets demand equal to zero. Given the demand function we can solve for the virtual price and the expenditure function (the indirect utility function) in order to evaluate a new product's contribution to the social welfare.

Let me use this approach to demonstrate the effect on the price index, or real income, of the introduction of a new good. Consider the demand for the new good, x_n, in period 1 to be a function of all prices and income, y:

$$x_n = g(p_1, \ldots, p_{n-1}, p_n, y). \qquad (3.1)$$

Now what if the good were *not* available in period 1? In that case, we can solve for the virtual price, p^*_n, which causes the demand for the new good to be equal to zero:

$$0 = x_n = g(p_1, \ldots, p_{n-1}, p^*_n, y). \qquad (3.2)$$

The approach Hicks used (1940) was to consider the change in real income (consumer value) to be the ratio $(p^*_n)(x_n)/(p_n)(x_n)$. While that approach is approximately correct, it does not account for the need to change income (y) as the price is increased in order to stay on the same indifference curve, so that the marginal value of income does not change. Thus, instead of using the Marshallian demand curve in equations (3.1) and (3.2), we should use the income-compensated and utility-constant Hicksian demand curve, which yields a more exact estimate of social welfare.[3] In terms of the expenditure function, we can solve the differential equation from Roy's identity, which corresponds to the demand function in equation (3.1), to find the (partial) expenditure function:

$$y = e(p_1, \ldots, p_{n-1}, p_n, u^1). \qquad (3.3)$$

The expenditure function gives the minimum amount of income, y, needed to achieve the utility level, utility u^1, which corresponds to the demand function of equation (3.1) and the expenditure function of equation (3.3).

To solve for the amount of income needed to achieve utility level u^1 in the absence of the new good, we can use the expenditure function from equation (3.3):

$$y^* = e(p_1, \ldots, p_{n-1}, p^*_n, u^1). \qquad (3.4)$$

The change in consumer welfare when the price decreases from the virtual price level, p^*_n, to the actual price level, p_n, keeping utility at the level u^1, is $y^* - y$. Note that to use this approach, we must estimate a demand curve, as in equation (3.1), which in turn implies the expenditure function and the ability to do the exact welfare calculation of equations (3.3) and (3.4). Thus, the only assumption required is to specify a parametric (or nonparametric) form of the demand function. Once the demand function has been specified and estimated, the expenditure function can be estimated, using the techniques of Hausman (1981) or

Vartia (1984) in the parametric case, or the method of Hausman-Newey (1995) in the nonparametric case.

The required formula to measure the consumer surplus, or consumer value, from the introduction of a new good is given in equation (3.4). Using this equation, we can estimate the value of voice messaging to be about $1.5 billion per year. Obviously, large amounts of value are created by new services that prove popular with consumers. Using equation (3.4) typically requires sufficient data to estimate a demand curve. However, to estimate the approximate size of consumer benefits without sufficient data, we can use the linear (lower bound) and log linear (upper bound) demand curves, assuming small income effects. Thus, the consumer surplus, CS, from a new service is:

$$(0.5\, p_n q_n)/\delta < CS < (p_n q_n)/(\delta - 1) \tag{3.5}$$

where $p_n q_n$ is the revenue from the service and δ is the price elasticity at current demand levels.

Equation (3.5) can be used to value online information services. The latest estimate of total subscribers is about 17 million. Using an average revenue figure of $18 per month yields a yearly revenue estimate of $3.02 billion. Assuming that the market price elasticity of online services is the same as that for voice messaging, we could estimate consumer surplus to be in the range of $1.4 to $12.2 billion. The midpoint of that range is about $6.8 billion per year, which is a large gain in consumer welfare.

An important implication of equation (3.5) is that consumer welfare grows quickly as the number of subscribers increases. Both bounds grow at the same rate as the number of subscribers (holding price constant). The number of households using the Internet has nearly doubled since July 1995 so consumer welfare continues to grow very fast from Internet usage. Thus, if subscribers (demand) increase by 10%, both bounds increase by the same percentage. The conclusion is that *if a new provider can increase demand beyond what it would otherwise be through greater ease of use, advertising, marketing, brand name user, improved content, or other features, consumer value will increase by the same percentage (approximately) as demand.* Thus, the entry of new service providers like Microsoft and AT&T is likely to increase consumer value from online services significantly. In addition, the entry of local phone companies or cable TV, both of whom can market directly to a large customer base, would likely produce large gains in consumer value.[4] Companies like Microsoft, AT&T, local phone companies, and others should be permitted to use advantages they possess to increase demand. Consumer value will increase as a result.

TOTAL ECONOMIC VALUE

To estimate the total economic value derived from a new service, we must turn to the other half of the value equation, the value to firms that produce the new services. Total value equals consumer surplus plus producer surplus (PS), which is approximated by total "gross margin." The formula is:

$$\text{Total Value} = CS + PS = (p_n q_n)/(\delta - 1) + [(p_n - mc) * q_n] \qquad (3.6)$$

where mc is the marginal cost of producing the service.[5] For most telecommunications services, the marginal cost is quite low compared with the price, because of the large fixed (sunk) costs of the service. Thus, an online service can usually provide service to additional customers at little extra cost.

Estimates of producer surplus are often difficult to make unless cost information is available. But based on experience in telecommunications, producer surplus is often between ten and twenty percent of the size of consumer surplus. Thus, significant additional value arises from producer surplus. As equation (3.6) demonstrates, producer surplus also increases at the same rate as demand, so that the expansion of demand by new service providers has a positive effect. Note that *the gain to consumers is typically considerably much larger than the gain to producers.* This finding is common to the introduction of new goods and services.

Increasing the Supply of Bandwidth for New Services

The vast majority of online customers receive services over copper wire provided by their local telephone companies. This technology has remained essentially the same for about the last seventy-five years. It is basically an analog system modified for use with digital transmission. The ubiquitous modem translates from digital to analog and back, so a PC can interact with the telephone network. Modem speeds have advanced from 300 bps to 28.8 kbps over the past decade, greatly accelerating their interaction with online networks. At the present time, 56 kbps modems are becoming available. However, this method of reception is still painstakingly slow. It places limits on online interaction and is much too slow for video transmission.

The existing copper-wire network can be upgraded using ISDN technology. Two 64-kbs channels (equivalent to the channels used for voice or data) plus a signaling channel (a 16-kbs packet channel) are transmitted over the copper wire, permitting video transmission of a somewhat "jagged" or "shaky" quality. Though ISDN is still limited, its quality may well improve with improved digital compression techniques. However, video will likely continue to be limited to CD ROM drives, as it is now.

Bandwidth is likely to expand in the near future, however. Much greater capacity is expected—at a minimum, DS1 bandwidth (1.544 Mbps), which is equivalent to 24 voice-grade lines in terms of capacity. DS3 bandwidth or higher would be required to provide full-motion video service. Such service would require much greater use of fiber optic transmission, either a pure fiber system or a combined fiber-coaxial system. Transmission would be entirely digital, and sufficient capacity would exist to offer multimedia services.

Two sets of likely providers exist for this transmission capacity. The first are local telephone companies. In most central business districts, sufficient fiber capacity already exists, since large companies and long distance carriers currently make extensive use of DS1s and DS3s. To deliver DS1 capacity to residential customers, phone companies would need to adopt a "fiber to the curb" or a hybrid fiber-coaxial system. Either approach will require them to lay significant amounts of new fiber. Pacific Bell is installing a hybrid fiber coaxial system, though it has slowed down the installation rate recently. However, a new technology, ADSL, could allow very high transmission over the copper wires that currently are used for residential lines. ADSL can be thought of as an extremely high speed modem that will allow transmission speed of 6 megabytes in one direction.[6] ADSL is still an unproven technology in the field, although recent tests are quite promising. If ADSL can be implemented at a low price, it will solve the "copper wire" problem without the necessity of the hundreds of millions of dollars being spent to construct fiber optic networks.

The other likely provider is a combination of competitive access providers (CAPs), for instance, Teleport and MFS, and local cable companies. CAPs currently provide DS1 level or above service in most central business districts in the United States—they serve over forty metropolitan statistical areas and are expanding rapidly. Cable companies operate coaxial networks throughout most of the United States; ninety-six percent of all houses are passed by cable. However, current cable networks are unsuitable for DS1 transmission; they are largely one-way ring-type systems rather than two-way fiber optic networks with switching capability. The existing coaxial drops to houses may or may not be useable, depending on quality and age of installation. The investment required to update them will be large. Cable companies have begun to offer cable modems over their updated networks. Cable modems allow a transmission speed of 10 megabytes in one direction. They are also in an experimental state, although more advanced than ADSL. Again, the question arises over the price of cable modems, and whether the demand for them will be sufficient to justify the required investment to upgrade cable networks.

What is the greatest obstacle to the expansion of high-capacity networks in the United States? The federal government. While the current administration extols the coming of the "information superhighway," obsolete government regulations provide the greatest obstacle to the highway's construction. For telephone companies, the Federal Communications Commission (FCC) requires Section 214 authorization before an LEC can build a fiber network. Section 214 authorization requires the LEC to describe its technology and to "prove" that the investment will be profitable. Over the past few years, the FCC has taken on average over two years to approve these applications, and a number of LECs have now withdrawn their applications because they have decided to change their technology. The FCC appears unable to keep pace with the pace of changing technology.[7] Section 214 authorization actually has no real economic role (beyond allowing competitors to use the regulatory process to delay competition). Section 214 authorizations are an obstacle that was set up under now obsolete cost-based (rate of return) regulation in which telephone rates were based on regulatory cost estimates. The FCC now uses price cap regulation where service specific regulatory costs are not used to set regulated telephone rates. Thus, the potential problem of cross subsidy, which justified Section 214 applications, has been eliminated by modern regulation. The FCC also regulates and limits the financial interest in content that a LEC can deliver over its network. In recent years, several Federal courts have ruled this limitation unconstitutional.[8]

From the cable companies' viewpoint, the current FCC regulation limits the prices and earning of cable companies. Cable companies, which typically have very high debt levels, have slowed down their ambitious network modification plans. The FCC regulation arises from a lack of competition since Congress decided in 1991 not to allow LEC competition with cable, but instead to have the FCC regulate cable.

The obvious solution to these political obstacles to improved networks is Congressional legislation. Congress did pass legislation in January 1996. Despite the passage of the Telecommunications Act of 1996, which was supposed to eliminate much of the government regulation to permit increased competition, the FCC regulatory order of August 1996 is likely to lead to *decreased* investment in the public telephone network. The FCC order requires telephone companies to sell their technology to competitors at incremental (marginal) cost. This rule will not allow telephone companies to recover their investment in new technology. Decreased investment will lead to decreased new services and to harm to consumers. The FCC has failed to recognize the importance of innovation in dynamic industries such as telecommunications.

Encouraging Competition Among Online Service Providers

Online subscription growth ha s been increasing at a rate of nearly seventy-five percent per year. As of July 1997, total online subscribers to network service offerings exceeded seventeen million. America Online (AOL) and Prodigy are growing rapidly, pursued by new entrants Microsoft Network (MSN) and AT&T. None of the companies in the field has experienced problems raising capital. AOL's stock price increased 480% since January 1995; companies that offer "browsers" and other software for use on the Internet experienced even greater increases. So long as a business plan mentions the Internet or the World Wide Web, almost any idea can find a venture capitalist.

GOVERNMENT REGULATION OF INFORMATION SERVICES

Before passage of the Telecommunications Act of 1996, government regulation was slow to change and did not keep pace with technological changes. Let us return to the voice messaging services discussed earlier, which created consumer value worth about $1.5 billion per year in 1994 alone. The delay in implementing this new technology, caused by government regulation, is estimated to have cost consumers and the U.S. economy tens of billions of dollars in lost value.

Voice messaging using central office telephone technology was sufficiently well developed to begin operation in the early 1980s.[9] In 1981, AT&T applied for permission from the FCC to provide "Custom Calling II" services, which included voice messaging, along with basic local service. The FCC rejected AT&T's request, mainly because AT&T had claimed it would need to redesign its network equipment at substantial delay and cost.[10] The FCC decided that since it was "technically possible" to provide separate voice messaging, AT&T would not be allowed to provide it on an integrated basis (¶53). The extra economic cost of separate service played only a minor role in the FCC's decision.

Shortly after the FCC's decision, in August 1982, the Modification of Final Judgment on the breakup of AT&T went into effect. The judgment prohibited the Bell Operating Companies (BOCs) from providing "information services" (similar in definition to the FCC's definition of "enhanced service"):

Information service means the offering of a capability for generating, acquiring, storing, transforming, processing, retrieving, utilizing, or making available information which may be conveyed via telecommunications. . . .

Under this restriction the BOCs were not allowed to offer voice messaging services that required the storage and retrieval of information, nor to generate content associated with information services.

The combined effect of the judgment and the FCC's decision was to prevent the BOCs from offering voice messaging to residential and small business customers.[11] Nor did competing service providers offer voice messaging, despite their claims that the equipment already existed, and despite the FCC's belief that competing service providers would offer such services (ibid., ¶85, ¶103). Thus, residential and small business customers were denied the opportunity to purchase voice messaging services.

In March 1988, Judge Greene modified his judgment and authorized the "Baby Bells" to provide transmission-based (but not content-based) information services.[12] Also in 1988, the FCC began approving comparably efficient interconnection (CEI) plans, which allowed the Baby Bells to provide enhanced services like voice messaging on an integrated basis. These regulatory changes permitted the Baby Bells to begin to offer voice messaging. In practice, they began to offer the service in 1990.

Growth in demand for voice messaging has been extremely rapid; in 1996 about seven million Baby Bell customers subscribed to the service. Clearly, demand for voice messaging existed in the United States in the 1980s, as did the technology to offer it on an economical basis. The effect on consumer welfare of the delay in permitting voice messaging service cost the U.S. consumer $5.4 billion in lost welfare (in 1994 dollars).

Now suppose the FCC had not delayed, but had instead allowed the Baby Bells to provide voice messaging on an integrated basis from 1984. For illustrative purposes, suppose the technology had not been as advanced, or the competition from other forms of voice messaging as stiff.[13] In this scenario, we will assume that the price would have

TABLE 3-1   Estimated Loss in Consumer Welfare Because of Delay in Offering Voice Messaging, 1988 (in 1994 dollars)

Scenario	Market Penetration	Assumed Price	Lost Welfare
1. Similar to 1994	1994 level	1994 price	$1.5 billion
2. Higher price	1994 level	50% higher	$1.2 billion

been fifty percent higher. Consumer surplus would have decreased by about $270 million—a small amount compared with the $1.5 billion loss caused by regulatory and judicial delay. These calculations are summarized in Table 3-1.

The calculations in Table 3-1 demonstrate an important result of economic analysis. Gains in consumer welfare from the introduction of a successful new product are usually quite large. Not to allow the introduction of such a product has an economic effect similar to that of a quota or nontradable ration tickets. In fact, the effect is even greater because the quota or the number of ration tickets is essentially zero when regulation holds up the introduction of a good or service. As the estimates in Table 3-1 demonstrate, regulatory delay in or prohibitions of the introduction of new goods and services can have an especially negative effect. The U.S. economy can sustain billions of dollars of losses for each year of delay in the introduction of a new service consumers value and will purchase. Overall, the lost consumer value from regulatory delay in approving voice messaging is estimated to have exceeded $5 billion (in 1994 dollars).

THE DEBATE OVER MICROSOFT NETWORK

In the summer of 1995, shortly before the introduction of Windows 95, the Department of Justice launched an investigation that threatened to delay the launch. Competitors claimed that the program's inclusion of an icon, or access button, for the Microsoft Network would give Microsoft an "unfair" competitive advantage. For instance, the president of AOL complained that one-button access was anticompetitive, since no other online service was allowed a launch button in Windows 95. To an economist, such reasoning is incorrect, because to the extent that easy access to the Internet increases the convenience of using online services and expands demand, consumers benefit—as equation (3.5) demonstrates. Thus, one-button access is procompetitive, because it increases demand and consumer value.

Why would an industry invite examination by government regulators, especially given the history of regulatory delays just discussed? The answer lies in anticompetitive claims that Microsoft would use its market advantage in Windows 95 to gain a competitive advantage in providing online services. Only at the last moment did the Department of Justice back off from its threat to sue Microsoft.

The correct method of evaluating competitors' claims is to examine the effect of Microsoft's service on consumer value and economic efficiency. Thus, an "unfair" outcome would arise if prices were higher, or quality lower, because of Microsoft's misusing its control of Windows to impede competition. The following pages will deal with and dispose of that possibility.

Bundling of Microsoft Network in Windows 95 The first claim to evaluate is whether consumers would be harmed by the "bundling" of Microsoft's Network with Windows 95. *Bundling* refers to the sale of two goods together. It is common practice in the U.S. economy: software is bundled with PCs and Macs, film is bundled with processing, new cellular telephones are bundled with service contracts. Economists consider bundling to be generally procompetitive, unless it retards entry or causes firms to exit an industry, in which case its effect can be either procompetitive or anticompetitive. So long as bundling increases consumer demand, however, it will almost always be procompetitive. Using the formula in equations (3.5) and (3.6) demonstrates this proposition.[14]

Opponents of bundling often incorrectly complain about monopoly leveraging. The idea of monopoly leveraging is that a firm with market power extends that power to an adjacent market in an anticompetitive manner. But just because a firm has market power, its competition in an adjacent market is *not* necessarily anticompetitive. Indeed, its entry will typically be procompetitive, because the firm can use economies of scope to lower costs and charge lower prices in the new market. Lower prices, of course, benefit consumers, although competitors may be harmed.

Bundling, or "leveraging," is anticompetitive only when a firm with market power is able to exercise its power by restricting output or raising prices. This fundamental reasoning is now well accepted by the Federal courts.[15] To possess a competitive advantage is not monopoly leveraging.

Windows As an Essential Facility   Another argument used against Microsoft was that Windows is an essential facility because of its ubiquitousness.[16] An essential facility has a precise legal definition. Typically, an essential facility is subject to government regulation, which forces its owner to allow competitors to use it. The primary example is the local telephone network, to which competitors of the local phone companies are guaranteed access. In the heat of debate over MSN, Steven Case, president of AOL, claimed that Windows was an essential facility, and that AOL should be allowed to insert its own icon in the program.

The legal definition of an essential facility has the following elements.

1. A competitor requires its use to provide a given service.

2. The service cannot be purchased from another supplier at a reasonable cost.

3. The functions of the service cannot be supplied in an alternative manner at a reasonable economic cost.

Windows provides a distribution service for Microsoft Network. Is Windows an essential facility for other online service providers? The answer, using these criteria, is no. Competitors have been able to distribute their products without using Windows. They are bundled into computers and distributed through 800 numbers, magazine ads, online ads, and sometimes even in cereal boxes. Thus, Microsoft cannot use Windows to eliminate competition in online services; Windows is not an essential facility. Windows may well provide MSN a competitive advantage, but a competitive advantage is not an essential facility. IBM could have bundled Prodigy into its PCs, and AT&T can bundle its online service disk into the bills it sends its long distance customers. These marketing strategies are the essence of competition. The mythical "level playing field" sought by Microsoft's competitors does not—and should not—exist. Each company should use its advantages to the utmost to gain a competitive advantage over its rivals. Consumers typically benefit from these actions.

Finally, economists and legal scholars recognize that government regulation is potentially dangerous, because it deters investment in new innovation. If a company invents a new product that is very successful, and competitors convince the government to force their access to its use, the economic incentive to invest in new products will diminish. Since new products create large amounts of new consumer value, as was just demonstrated, such government action is likely to harm consumers. Furthermore, competitors do not share the risk of investment in potentially unsuccessful products. They only demand access to successful new products. So government action to force access to a new product will deter investment in new products.[17]

Microsoft's Economic Incentives   Economic analysis demonstrates that consumers will benefit from Microsoft's method of introducing Microsoft Network. If Microsoft had no online service product of its own, most economists would favor Microsoft's auctioning off exclusive one-button launch rights to another online service provider. Prodigy, AOL, or any other company could bid for the rights. Consumers would benefit from wide distribution of the successful bidder's service in Windows, through more convenient network access. If they liked the service, they would make greater use of it. Economic analysis demonstrates that when consumers patronize an improved product or service and demand for the product or service rises significantly, consumer welfare increases.[18]

Now consider the question of whether Microsoft should be allowed to enter the bidding for single-button access to an online network. Microsoft will provide the service itself only if it can make more money by providing it than by auctioning off the button rights. But Microsoft can make more money only if it can increase demand by providing a better online service, one consumers will buy.[19] Other providers of such services—AOL and Prodigy, each of which has over a million subscribers—will continue to provide strong competition. Indeed, AOL recently announced it had enrolled more than six hundred thousand new subscribers in the fourth quarter of its 1997 fiscal year. Thus, Microsoft's decision to create MSN and include it in Windows 95 will likely increase consumer welfare and should not be stopped by the government.

Competitors' complaints about Microsoft's distribution advantage are not surprising. But their proposed "regulatory solution" would be a serious mistake in an unregulated industry, such as computer software. It would force Microsoft to share its economic return from Windows with competitors. If that were to happen, not only Microsoft, but other companies, would draw back from investing in R&D and innovative products. Ultimately, permitting free riding by competitors would result in a less innovative economy.

Recently, Microsoft's strategy has shifted away from providing a proprietary service. It now offers a basic Internet access service. The MSN has about two million subscribers whereas AOL has grown over eight million subscribers in the past year. Competition in online services has *increased* since the entry of Microsoft and other firms, such as AT&T. Microsoft's chief competitor is now Netscape, which offers browser software competition with Microsoft's. Netscape has recently claimed that its product is the largest selling applications program in history. Netscape has sold or given away between eighty and ninety percent of the browsers in use. Nevertheless, Netscape has approached the Department of Justice, which began another investigation of Microsoft in September 1996. The outcome of the investigation will once again raise the question of whether consumers or competitors are protected by Department of Justice actions.

Who Will Capture the Value in the Growth of Information Services?

Today, online and other information services are growing rapidly. The Internet has the potential to cause major changes in social and business activities. As a result, Internet-related companies have experienced huge stock price increases over the past few years. Who will capture the value in this explosion in the use of online services? Six groups will benefit.

1. *Infrastructure providers.* Companies like the AT&T equipment spinoff, Lucent, will see a significant outward shift in their demand curves, because of the need for high-capacity bandwidth. The "rewiring of America" should benefit construction companies as well. Since this technology is well established, radical changes are not likely in this sector.

2. *Hardware manufacturers.* The changeover to digital switches is now largely complete in the United States. However, demand for broadband services could create demand for broadband switches, which would benefit switch manufacturers. The changeover could also radically alter the industry's structure, because of the massive sunk cost investments required.[20] Another radical change will be in the demand for set-top boxes, cable modems, and ADSL chip sets. This technology is presently in flux. There has also been some discussion of the replacement of PCs by "dumb terminals" for navigating the Internet. Thus, hardware manufacturers could either benefit or become much less important because of Internet-based technology.

3. *Software producers.* Software producers could see boom times if software plays a major role in controlling the network at the consumer end. On the other hand, the Internet could reduce the

importance of software. In either situation, applications-based software and software that enables consumers to better use the Internet are likely to be a major source of value creation.

4. *Network service providers.* The ability to provide transmission capacity is unlikely to lead to major value creation. Transmission capacity will decrease in price, and competition will increase dramatically. Ultimately, transmission capacity will become a commodity, with little opportunity to profit from value-added services. This outcome should become clear relatively soon, when the government permits competition.

5. *Content providers.* Much value, perhaps most, will be created by content. However, content providers—firms that develop content—are unlikely to capture all the value. Increasingly, much of the value (rents) from content will be captured by the individuals who create it. This outcome arises from a lack of talent, not from a scarcity of companies to package and sell it. Thus, as the supply of transmission capacity grows, content providers will find economical outlets for their products. But the individuals who create the content will be the most valuable resource.

6. *Business users and consumers.* By far the largest beneficiaries of the online revolution will be business users and consumers. I have demonstrated that consumers typically capture very large proportions of the value from new services. That should hold true in the future, as numerous new services, most of which are not now available, come online. Many new services will be failures, but some will be wildly successful. These successful new services will benefit users, both business and consumers.

The next step is to develop networks that will permit these new services. They are likely to be broadband or ADSL-based networks and will probably be delivered competitively by cable companies and telephone companies. However, the government must remove the legal and regulatory obstacles that are currently delaying their introduction costing consumers billions of dollars a year in lost value. Congress must quit playing favorites, and regulators must "let go," so competition can take over. Even an imperfectly competitive outcome will produce hundreds of billions of dollars worth of increased value by ushering in the technological and economic era that is within our grasp.

Endnotes

1. Similarly, the introduction of cellular telephone services is estimated to have produced gains in consumer welfare in excess of $25 billion per year (Hausman 1995a).
2. Hicks's theory was extended by E. Rothbarth (1941). See Hausman (1994) for a further discussion.
3. In equation (3.2) income, y, is solved out in terms of the utility level, u^1, to find the Hicksian demand curve given the Marshallian demand curve specification. Hausman (1981) demonstrates this solution procedure.
4. This increased competition is likely to lower prices as well, which creates an added benefit to consumers.
5. This total value equation also represents the gain to economy efficiency. The difference between price and marginal cost is the quasi rent which goes to the firm that supplies the service.
6. The transmission speed is about 350 kbs in the other direction.
7. Of course, the LECs' competitors, the cable companies have attempted to use the regulatory process to impede the LECs' Section 214 applications.
8. The Telecommunications Act of 1996 has caused this issue to become moot.
9. See R. F. Rey (ed.), *Engineering and Operations in the Bell System* (1983) for a description of the early development of AT&T's custom calling services.
10. AT&T Petition for Waiver of Section 64.702 of the Commission's Rules and Regulations ¶18, 88 F.C.C. 2d 1 (1981). The FCC recognized the presence of economies of scope in voice messaging (¶17), but feared a "slippery slope" that would create regulatory uncertainty.
11. Medium- and large-sized businesses were able to use voice messaging services through their PBXs, many of which were similar in design to the Central Office Switches (COS) used by the Baby Bells.
12. Opinion on the First Triennial Review, September 10, 1987, Section V.
13. Indeed, in the early 1980s the technology would have been based on a mainframe system; current technology is based on the PC. Thus, the price could well have been fifty percent higher in the earlier period.
14. For further discussion, see J. Hausman, "When Does Improved Quality Lead to Increased Consumer Welfare?," 1995 draft mimeo.
15. See, e.g., *US v. Western Electric Co.*, 900 F. 2d 283 (D.C. Cir., 1990): "New entry or increased competition in any market typically hurts and sometimes even destroys existing competitors. A court's solicitude for those firms—ostensibly in an effort to foster competition—may well come at the expense of competition. . . . Accordingly, unless the entering [firm] will have the ability to raise prices or restrict output in the market it seeks to enter, there can be no substantial possibilities that it could use its monopoly power to 'impede competition.'" Both the DC Circuit, the 9th Circuit (in *Alaska Airlines v. United Airlines*, 1991) and numerous lower courts have recognized that the earlier decision on leveraging merely confers a competitive advantage but not market power, in *Berkey Photo v. Eastman Kodak Co.*, 603 F. 2d 263 (2d Cir., 1979), is incorrect.
16. This claim has recently been made in a particularly ill-informed article by a Microsoft competitor, J. Gleick, "Making Microsoft Safe for Capitalism," *The New York Times*, November 5, 1995, Section 6, p. 50.
17. This effect would arise from the FCC order of August 1996, as discussed above.
18. For a more thorough analysis of this point see J. Hausman, "When Does Improved Quality Lead to Increased Consumer Welfare?," 1995 draft mimeo.

See also my invited testimony to the Federal Trade Commission, "Merger Policy in Declining Demand Industries," November 14, 1995.

19. The only other method by which Microsoft could make additional money by keeping the launch rights for itself would be to raise the price of Microsoft Network above the current competitive level. But Microsoft could not do so, because it lacks market power in online services. Competition from others would keep the price at competitive levels.

20. See J. Hausman and E. Kohlberg (1989) for an analysis of the central office switch industry.

References

J. Hausman, "Exact Consumer's Surplus and Deadweight Loss," *American Economic Review* 71 (1981).

——, "Valuation of New Goods Under Perfect and Imperfect Competition," (working paper, Boston, MA: MIT, June 1994), forthcoming in R. Gordon and T. Bresnahan (eds.), *The Economics of New Goods* (Chicago: University of Chicago Press, 1997) 209–237.

——, "The Cost of Cellular Telephone Regulation," mimeo, 1995.

——, "When Does Quality Improvement Lead to Increased Consumer Welfare?," mimeo, 1995.

—— and E. Kohlberg, "The Evolution of the Central Office Switch Industry," in S. Bradley and J. Hausman (eds.), *Future Competition in Telecommunications* (Boston, MA: Harvard Business School Press, 1989).

—— and W. Newey, "Non-parametric Estimation of Exact Consumer Surplus and Deadweight Loss," *Econometrica* 62 (1995).

—— and T. Tardiff, "Valuation and Regulation of New Services in Telecommunications," mimeo, 1995.

J. R. Hicks, "The Valuation of the Social Income," *Economic Journal* (1940).

R. F. Rey (ed.), Engineering and Operations in the Bell System (1983).

E. Rothbarth, "The Measurement of Changes in Real Income Under Conditions of Rationing," *Review of Economic Studies* (1941) 100–107.

Y. Vartia, "Efficient Methods of Measuring Welfare Change and Compensated Income in Terms of Ordinary Demand Functions," *Econometrica* 51 (1984).

PART TWO

Sensing the Customer

4 | *Strategic Uncertainty and the Future of Online Consumer Interaction*

Eric K. Clemons and Stephen P. Bradley

GIVEN THE CHANGES driven or enabled by the increasing popularity of the Internet and the World Wide Web, predicting the future of retailing is extremely difficult. Inevitably, we will be surprised by the changing balance between online consumer interaction (home shopping) and more traditional forms of retailing, such as in-store shopping and catalog sales. The rate of consumer adoption of online retailing is likely to be much faster than many traditional retailers expect, though certainly far slower than many futurists, consultants, and electronic service providers claim. Moreover, online retailing has implications for the profitability of retailers and the relative profitability and balance of power among manufacturers and primary service providers, distributors, retailers, and electronic service bundlers.

As one of our colleagues notes, "The problem with surprise is that it is so often unexpected." That is, not only are we surprised by unforeseen changes, we are surprised by

Acknowledgments: The assistance of Lawrence Wilkinson of Global Business Network and of the participants of several scenario workshops on the future of retailing is gratefully acknowledged.

the speed with which those changes occur, and even by the areas in which they occur. Thus, although many of us believe we will be prepared for the changes created by widespread adoption of online consumer interaction, most will in fact be unable to predict its implications. More importantly, many companies will be surprised even by the ways in which they are unable to predict, and by the means through which their operations, their profitability, and their competitive positioning will be altered.

The "unanticipated nature of surprise" affects not only amateurs, the technologically unsophisticated, and those individuals foolish enough to venture predictions outside their domains of expertise; increasingly, it affects experts as well. For example, scholars who study globalization are in danger of being eclipsed by a combination of air travel and the Internet. One of the authors has a seven-year-old daughter who helps to plan family vacations by looking at a globe: "Paris would be nice for Christmas Eve, for the food. It would be nice to see Hong Kong this year, before it's returned to the mainland, while it's still an island! I'm not sure what I'll eat in Tokyo . . . Oh, right, there's a Wendy's on the Ginza." Indeed, many of our children and most denizens of the Net already live in borderless global world. The last people to understand this reality may well be those scholars who study globalization as a separate discipline.

In an earlier book in this series, published in 1993 (Bradley et al.), we speculated on the long-term prospects of "zero-cost bandwidth" (that is, free and unlimited telecommunications capability) and its implications for commerce and the structure of the firm. Zero-cost bandwidth implies nearly cost-free interactions with customers and suppliers, which is becoming a reality far faster than we anticipated in 1993. At that time we considered the implications for interfirm transactions, and the changing nature of the interfirm market for intermediate goods and services—that is, the changing balance between making components or providing services internally and procuring those components and services from other firms. We now realize that the costs of such interactions have fallen so low that they will fundamentally alter not only the relationships between firms and their major customers and suppliers, but between firms and end consumers, even the most infrequent consumers of the least expensive packaged goods.

Zero-cost interactions will have a wide range of applications which have not previously been examined, and a wide range of effects that are certain not to be anticipated. Applications include the following:

- Initial applications affected business-to-business interactions, the cost, and altering risks associated with close interfirm cooperation and the economics of the make-or-buy decision (Clemons, Reddi, and Row, 1993).

- Current applications include interactions that allow custom design for major corporate accounts—for example, shared virtual reality for interactive tractor design.

- Emerging applications include custom-designed products for individual consumers, such as custom-cut jeans and shoes.

In this chapter we introduce the concept of strategic uncertainty and describe the sources of uncertainty introduced by online consumer interaction. We then describe scenario analysis, a powerful tool for dealing with strategic uncertainty. Using scenario analysis, we explore the strategic alternatives that may confront retailers. Finally, we examine the strategic responses available to firms and the barriers that will likely inhibit their ability to implement necessary changes.

Six Strategic Uncertainties in Online Consumer Interaction

Emerging alternatives to traditional shopping will affect all aspects of retailing, including marketing, merchandising, consumer choice, physical distribution, and the relative power and profitability of retailers, manufacturers, and intermediaries. Changes this dramatic are almost always misunderstood. Do consumers know what the change to online retailing implies? Do retailers, manufacturers, distributors, or service bundlers know? Do those in the academic community know?

Six sources of uncertainty compound the difficulty in understanding and planning for coming changes in retailing:

- How will online consumer interaction evolve, and which market segments will be affected first?
- What will be the role of the brand name in an online market?
- What role will consumer confidence play in cybermarketing?
- What use will be made of detailed information on individual consumers and their transactions with specific manufacturers and service providers?
- Who will own and control and benefit from information on consumers?
- Who will the channel members be in online consumer interaction?

These sources of uncertainty are addressed in the section that follows.

MARKET SEGMENTATION

How will online consumer interaction evolve, and which market segments will be affected first? Though ATM adoption now appears to have been inevitable, in most U.S. cities it was a surprisingly slow process. For a long time, a twenty-five percent consumer adoption rate was considered to be the maximum achievable, and marketers spoke of "hitting the [consumer adoption] wall." Even today, consumers' use of ATMs is restricted largely to their own banks' machines, almost exclusively to obtain cash; use of other banks' machines, and use of ATMs for making deposits is extremely limited.

Likewise, online shopping is likely to grow slowly. Thus, it is useful for us to consider which consumer segments will prove the most willing adopters, and which products and services will prove to be best suited to online retailing.

BRANDING

What will be the role of the brand name in an online market? Will online distribution eliminate barriers to entry, opening the retailing channel to all providers? Will it offer consumers such profound new sources of product information that branding and advertising will become irrelevant? Or will branding increase in importance, as consumers rely on brand reputation to support their confidence in online distribution? If so, whose brand will predominate, the primary supplier's, the bundler/re-packaging service's, or the final retailer's?

The importance of this last question is already evident in some services. For example, in first-class air travel, the brand is clearly the airline's. Consumers are confident that their tickets will be honored, so they choose an airline based on its service offering and schedule, and perhaps its loyalty programs. However, in discount air travel, the travel packager's is probably the relevant brand, because consumers must choose carefully to ensure quality of service and financial stability. Similarly, in buying a camcorder or other consumer durable, the consumer may want to deal with a manufacturer with a strong brand, to ensure that problems will be unlikely; or with a retailer with a strong reputation for customer service, to ensure that if problems do arise, they will be resolved quickly and satisfactorily.

CONSUMER CONFIDENCE

What role will consumer confidence play in cybermarketing? Will it matter? Consumer confidence in online shopping and virtual stores is determined to some extent by consumers' willingness to accept risk and by their assessment of the degree of risk involved. Purchasing canned tuna online is no more risky than purchasing detergent; one need not inspect its appearance to assess its freshness nor ensure its timely delivery. However, purchasing fresh shellfish is a different matter. Likewise, purchasing jeans by mail or through an electronic catalog is not risky, since a poorly fitted pair of jeans is a limited inconvenience, and consumers often have considerable legal recourse on mail-order and credit-card purchases. But a poor selection of an insurance carrier can have catastrophic implications, if one must make a claim.

USE OF CONSUMER PROFILES

What use will be made of detailed information on individual consumers and their transactions with specific manufacturers and service providers? In an online environment, are consumers likely to "surf" from one shopping venue or virtual store to another, or are they likely to develop stable, ongoing relationships with a limited number of virtual stores? Will consumers object to the compilation of information on their purchases by retailers and service providers as an invasion of their privacy, or will they encourage it because of the improved service it enables? Use of detailed consumer profiles could make electronic shopping easier and less time consuming than traditional shopping, for consumers would no longer need to search the aisles for their usual purchases, but could instead simply specify their usual order. How will such convenience affect the patronage of physical versus virtual stores?

CONTROL OF CONSUMER DATABANKS

Who will own, control, and benefit from information on consumers? That is, who will determine how information will be shared and with whom it will be shared? A new corporation, Abacus, seeks to provide a central database for such information. Abacus makes its data available to all retailers, thus reducing the value of ongoing relationships with consumers. Other service providers hope to create insurmountable switching costs for owners of ongoing relationship data, locking in their accounts indefinitely.[1] Consumer advocates believe that consumers will ultimately own and control their own profiles, bringing them to all their online activities. In the process, they will create an environment in which first-time visits to virtual stores are as satisfying as repeat visits.

Since control over consumer information is likely to confer significant influence over consumer activities, the answer to the question of who captures, controls, owns, and uses consumer information implies an answer to the question of who controls consumer activities. Thus, the profitability of manufacturers, service bundlers, distributors, and both physical and virtual retailers, and the distribution of benefits among them and among consumers, is at stake.

CHANNEL MEMBERSHIP

Who will be the channel members in online retailing? Will consumers interact with traditional retailers or their online counterparts with service bundlers like America Online (AOL), with credit-card issuers, or directly with manufacturers, thereby bypassing retailers, wholesalers, and distributors? Clearly, the answer to this question will dramatically affect the role of all channel members, their economic power, and the share of retailing profit they retain.

INTERDEPENDENCY AMONG STRATEGIC UNCERTAINTIES

Each of the strategic uncertainties just addressed is likely to be interdependent with some or all of the others. That is, some consumers will soon be very comfortable purchasing shelf-stable packaged goods electronically. Yet, they will be extremely reluctant to purchase durable goods like automobiles without first developing a personal relationship with a dealer. Likewise, though some consumers may soon be willing to shop for hotel accommodations for a business trip through an Internet-based service, the same individuals may still require intensive coaching from travel agents when planning a major vacation. Thus, retailers need to determine which products and services are appropriate for online distribution, under which conditions, and to which consumers.

IMPLICATIONS OF STRATEGIC UNCERTAINTY

The slow adoption of ATMs by consumers suggests that online shopping is likely to grow slowly, at least initially. However, many technologies exhibit slow adoption at first, then suddenly achieve nearly universal adoption when some "tipping point" is reached. Fax use grew so slowly from its introduction before World War II that in 1982, Federal Express could seriously consider offering Zap Mail.[2] Two years later, the use of fax machines by consumers and corporations had become so widespread that Federal Express canceled Zap Mail and wrote off its investment. The possibility that adoption of a new technology may suddenly accelerate suggests that corporations will need to make some investment in online services, even when consumers appear indifferent to it. The most critical decision may be which partners to keep and which to support or abandon; that is, firms will need to make strategic commitments under considerable strategic uncertainty.

The expected risks and returns of early strategic alliances are very high. Firms that make the correct decisions may in the long run find that they have merely recognized strategic necessities, thus retaining parity with other firms that have correctly interpreted the trends and implemented the appropriate measures. Firms that make the wrong decisions may find themselves at a significant disadvantage. Indeed, if they have offended the wrong business partners, or waited too long before creating strategic alliances, their corporations may fail in the new competitive marketplace.

Exploring Strategic Uncertainty Through Scenario Analysis

Scenario analysis is useful in strategic planning during times of rapid change when discontinuities in the business environment make extrapolation from available historical data misleading or meaningless. Scenario analysis attempts to identify the environment in which a firm may have to operate, expressed as a set of scenarios that covers virtu-ally any eventuality the firm may encounter. These scenarios are not intended to represent good, bad, or average cases. Rather, they are based on those fundamental driving forces that will determine the busi-ness environment. In general, the relative importance of those driving forces will not be known in advance. Unknown and perhaps unknow-able, they are so important to planning for the future that if they *were* known firms would know everything they need to know to develop an effective strategy.

Scenario analysis does not rely on data. It relies instead on the identi-fication of uncertainties on which data would be useful, and on an explo-ration of the implications of assuming the most extreme values for such data. Although scenario analysis doesn't require data, it is still highly structured. Different practitioners follow slightly different procedures, but generally the following steps are performed in the following order:[3]

1. *Surface the key uncertainties.* Identify questions that cannot be an-swered, but which appear to matter greatly.

2. *Rank the key uncertainties to determine the key drivers.* Identify the two or three most important unanswerable questions—the things that cannot be known, that if known, would tell strategic planners precisely what they need to know.

3. *Combine the key uncertainties to yield concrete scenarios.* That is, de-fine alternative futures in which each uncertainty is assumed to take an extreme value.

4. *Provide details.* Turn each scenario into a plausible story, explaining how it might come about and how consumers, executives in the firm, and executives in competing firms would feel about it.

A simplifying assumption of scenario analysis is to assume initially that one and only one of the alternative scenarios will emerge. This assump-tion allows planners to develop alternative views of the future and to prepare a strategy for each alternative. These strategies are contingent strategies, in that their appropriateness cannot be determined until more information is available. Still, the development of such strategies enables more thorough planning, and the beginning of strategic nego-tiations with potential alliance partners. That, in turn, enables a more rapid response when the shape of things to come has become clearer. The assumption that only one scenario will be realized is, of course, unrealistic and is always dropped at some point in the planning process.

Five Strategic Scenarios for Online Consumer Interaction

The scenarios presented in this section reflect a preliminary analysis of the future of online consumer interaction. They are based on workshops conducted with retailers and manufacturers over the course of several years.

Scenario analysis may be diagrammed graphically (see Figure 4-1). Each of the key drivers is represented on the horizontal or vertical axis of a four-quadrant matrix. The horizontal axis represents the most critical uncertainty in online consumer interaction, the nature of the interaction. The ends of this axis represent the following alternatives:

- the degree to which consumers will interact with retailers online (on the left), and

- the degree to which consumers will interact with retailers in traditional ways, face-to-face (on the right).

This question is critical because it will determine the intermediaries with which the consumer interacts, as well as the degree to which retailers' physical resources (e.g., their investment in physical plant and real

FIGURE 4-1   Five Strategic Scenarios for Online Consumer Interaction

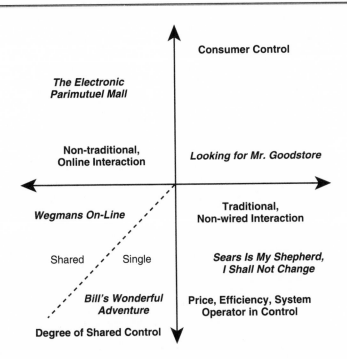

estate) and skills (e.g., merchandising, display, and selection of store locations) will retain their value. Note that whether consumers engage in
face-to-face interaction in traditional retail stores or move to online
shopping, intermediaries will be involved. The need for efficient logistics
to support the distribution of all but the most expensive products and the
need to reduce risk in the distribution of the most expensive, suggest that
intermediaries will remain involved for the foreseeable future.

The vertical axis represents a second critical uncertainty, the consumer's intention in the shopping experience. The extremes of this axis
represent the following alternatives:

- the degree to which the consumer seeks a rewarding shopping
  experience, and thus seeks control of the interaction (the top of
  the axis), and

- the degree to which the consumer desires efficiency, speed, simplicity, and low price, and thus is willing to allow others to control the shopping experience in order to achieve those objectives
  (the bottom of the axis).

The quadrant that represents a high degree of online activity and a low
degree of consumer control can be subdivided based on the degree of
shared control over the shopping experience—that is, the degree to
which control of the shopping experience is shared among service providers or retained by a single provider. This third subsidiary axis represents the following extremes:

- *Open, shared control.* The extent to which the telecommunica
  tions environment offers universal access and interoperability.

- *Limited control.* The extent to which one or a few major players (a
  major telecommunications and cable consortium, or an alliance
  between Microsoft and Visa) controls access to online commerce.

Five scenarios result from the analysis of the key drivers represented in
Figure 4-1: Looking for Mr. Goodstore; Sears is My Shepherd, I Shall
Not Change; The Electronic Parimutuel Mall; Wegmans On-Line; and
Bill's Wonderful Adventure.[4]

LOOKING FOR MR. GOODSTORE

The Looking for Mr. Goodstore scenario (upper right quadrant) is characterized by a high degree of consumer control over the shopping experience, and by continued reliance on traditional in-store shopping. In this
scenario, consumers enjoy and actively seek out shopping experiences,

displaying a traditional need to own the right merchandise and wear the right labels, and exhibiting a traditional willingness to visit retail stores. For this scenario to be realized, consumers must have sufficient disposable income and sufficient time to shop. They may even consider shopping to be a social activity and a form of recreation, and they must consider shopping to be safe. But these conditions may not exist in the future, suggesting that this form of retailing may decrease in importance. The potential for dramatic change in the importance of this scenario has strategic implications for retailers. Yet this scenario is embraced by many retailers, who have based much of their short-term strategic positioning on it.

SEARS IS MY SHEPHERD, I SHALL NOT CHANGE

In the Sears Is My Shepherd scenario, consumers are more concerned with price and efficiency than with the experiential aspects of shopping. However, they continue to shop in the traditional way, visiting retailers' store locations rather than their web sites, even though doing so may be more expensive and less efficient than online shopping. Consumers in this quadrant are not shopping for enjoyment or companionship; rather, they are down-market, low-income rejecters of advanced technology, and aging traditionalists who are loyal to the stores where they have always shopped. These consumers respond favorably to long-standing relationships with merchants they have come to trust.

There is considerable uncertainty concerning how rapidly this scenario will be replaced by online consumer interaction. However, it is likely to remain important for some time. The example of ATMs, which achieved no more than thirty percent adoption the first decade after their introduction, is illustrative, as are the demographics of early ATM adoption. The largest number of ATM adopters came from up-market segments; aging and technophobic lower-income consumers tended to remain with traditional teller service. Barring changes in related factors—significant increases in educational level and technological acceptance among low-income consumers, dramatic improvements in the ease of use of home shopping systems, or further rapid deterioration of traditional shopping locations—this scenario should endure for some time.

THE ELECTRONIC PARIMUTUEL MALL

In The Electronic Parimutuel Mall scenario, consumers shop in an online marketplace, exercising considerable control over their shopping experience in the process. As the cost of searching for merchandise and ascertaining its quality drops, consumers will increasingly be able to determine which goods and services best meet their needs, and who is offering them at the most attractive prices. Additionally, as the cost of communicating with manufacturers and potential suppliers drops, consumers will participate actively in the design of their goods and services. Thus, they need not settle for selecting the best available alternative at the best price. Consumers are likely to be well served in this scenario. However, competition is likely to be quite high, placing considerable strain on all the participants in this market environment.

WEGMANS ON-LINE

The Wegmans On-Line scenario is characterized by full consumer acceptance of online shopping, considerable consumer sensitivity to pricing, and only limited consumer control of the shopping experience (i.e., consumers will select from a narrow set of options determined for them). Ownership of consumer profiles and control over the shopping experience will be shared by traditional retailers, online retailers, and service providers. This scenario entails only limited mastery of the Net and its navigation by consumers. For that reason, we assume consumers will not be able to locate all items at the best available price, or even to locate items on their own, without assistance.

BILL'S WONDERFUL ADVENTURE

Like Wegmans On-Line, the Bill's Wonderful Adventure scenario is characterized by full consumer acceptance of online shopping and by limited consumer control over the shopping experience. This limited control may be due not to consumer preference but to the structure of the online environment, which allows a small set of powerful consortia to maintain a closed system, limit consumer choice, and restrict or eliminate the use of interfaces or search agents. This is the scenario with the greatest potential for economic exploitation. Like the other scenarios which involve nontraditional distribution, it is radically different from the current retailing environment. Unlike the nearly utopian Electronic Parimutuel Mall, however, this is a bleak scenario in which the operators of cyberspace have almost unlimited power to determine who can occupy retail locations in cyberspace and which "agents" will determine what individual consumers will be shown. They will also have unparalleled power over manufacturers—well beyond that enjoyed by Wal*Mart or Kmart today.

The Five Scenarios Explored

Because the strategic implications of each of the five scenarios are different, the strategies manufacturers, retailers, and system operators should consider will differ dramatically as well. In reality, of course, the future retailing environment will not resemble any one of the five scenarios exclusively, but rather some combination of them. Different consumers will employ different ways of interacting with retailers. Even individual consumers are likely to employ different shopping modes to obtain different products and services.

LOOKING FOR MR. GOODSTORE

The Looking for Mr. Goodstore scenario, characterized by a high degree of service, high margins, and traditional stores that offer traditional shopping experience, is well understood by most retailers. The reliance on physical stores means that retailers can continue to benefit from their skills in product display, merchandising, and customer service. The current roles of retailers, wholesalers, distributors, and manufacturers will remain much the same, implying a more or less stable distribution of power and profitability. Because this scenario is well understood, and because it offers high margins, it is the one for which many retailers are doing most of their planning, and to which they are committing most of their resources.

SEARS IS MY SHEPHERD, I SHALL NOT CHANGE

The Sears Is My Shepherd scenario is in many ways the most conservative of the five, suggesting that for most consumers, the future of retailing will be a down-market, low-margin, simple, and efficient shopping experience. This is the world of Wal*Mart, Kmart, and Sam's Club stores. Although margins are low, efficient operators can be as successful as Wal*Mart has been.

THE ELECTRONIC PARIMUTUEL MALL

The Electronic Parimutuel Mall scenario is perhaps the most attractive for consumers, who can find or design products to precisely meet their needs, their budgets, and their personal taste. But because of the high degree of competition implied by efficient access to market information, this scenario may be a very difficult one for retailers and manufacturers. That is, competition will keep margins much lower in this scenario than the Looking for Mr. Goodstore scenario. Retailers may attempt to keep margins high by bundling products, to obscure the price of individual products or services. But consumers can readily design alternative bundles, determine the price of individual offerings, and obtain each at the lowest available price. In this scenario, most value will be captured by consumers.

This scenario is profoundly different from that of the current retailing environment and will require major and perhaps painful changes by retailers, distributors, and manufacturers. Specifically:

- For both retailers and manufacturers, traditional advertising will be less effective, less valuable, and in extreme cases perhaps even unnecessary. Consumers will know what they want, where to find it, and what to pay for it.

- Mass merchandising and physical display of products will be unnecessary.

- Throughout the retailing system margins will quickly be eroded by competition, suggesting that high margins will be earned only by the earliest entrants into any market niche. Thus rapid interpretation of trends and fast response product design and production will become increasingly important.

- Many manufacturers will need to respond to individual requests for custom-designed products and services and in a timely and cost effective manner. This trend toward "mass customization" will bring important changes in the economics of production.

WEGMANS ON-LINE

The Wegmans On-Line scenario is characterized by a high degree of consumer acceptance of online interaction and shopping as well as of outside control over their shopping experience. In this scenario, consumers expect shopping to be fast, easy, and relatively cost effective. They do not wish to "surf the net," or control their profile data and are not likely to drive prices and margins down as low as in The Electronic Parimutuel Mall. Since a large number of competing virtual stores and virtual malls will exist in this scenario, however, competition will be sufficient to ensure against monopoly prices.

This scenario is almost certainly the most attractive for the majority of retailers and manufacturers. It is very different from the current re-

tailing environment, and will require substantial changes by all participants. Specifically:

- Retailers will capture information on consumers in the process of
  capturing their orders. The information will enable retailers to
  make the shopping experience extremely efficient for consumers,
  by selecting merchandise based on their individual preferences
  and income.

- Access to information on consumer preferences will create considerable shifts in economic power. Since virtual stores can be recon-
  figured at will, store operators can drop a brand or brands from the
  product list seen by consumers who are indifferent to choice in
  some categories. (For instance, they can drop one brand of paper
  towels from the list seen by consumers who are indifferent to
  brands in that category.) Such reconfigurations damage the manufacturer without inconveniencing the consumer or causing the retailer to lose sales. The power to reconfigure for each consumer thus
  will enable operators of virtual stores to display the highest margin
  items to most consumers, and thus to squeeze payments from
  manufacturers. In essence, operators will be able to charge manufacturers considerable economic rents for virtual shelf space.

- Consumers are unlikely to want to learn several different interfaces—one for dairy products, another for vegetables, a third for
  detergents and a fourth for frozen foods. Thus, manufacturers who
  want to break into online retailing to avoid losing economic power
  to retailers will be forced to create strategic alliances with many
  different manufacturers, and perhaps even direct competitors.

- Since in this scenario consumers will have not yet learned to surf
  the Net, affiliation with the right network service providers may
  be vitally important. Consumers may be unable to find merchants
  who do not participate in one or more of the prime "virtual malls"
  in cyberspace: being a cybershop on a cyberspace backwater will
  be like being bypassed by an interstate or supplanted by a major
  shopping mall. Thus, virtual mall operators will have an opportunity to charge considerable "economic rents."

In this scenario, economic value will be shared by manufacturers, electronic retailers, and consumers, as is true today. However, as retailers
begin to accumulate and use more detailed information on consumers
than is available to manufacturers, they will be able to capture more of
this value.

Finally, physical assets like prime locations may be worth considerably less in this scenario, along with traditional skills like merchandising and space allocation. Considerable resistance to change may develop among the currently dominant players, which may contribute to a significant decline in their economic power and market share. However, the potential for disruption associated with this scenario may prevent established participants from perceiving its plausibility, from perceiving the threat it represents, and thus from responding in a timely manner.

BILL'S WONDERFUL ADVENTURE

The Bill's Wonderful Adventure scenario is characterized by a high degree of acceptance of online consumer interaction and reliance upon online shopping. Like the Wegmans On-Line scenario, it also implies that some participants will retain considerable control over the consumers' shopping experience. Unlike that scenario, however, in the Bill's Wonderful Adventure scenario control over consumer profiles and online activity in general is retained by a small group of systems operators, virtual mall owners, and software developers. While this scenario offers shopping that is fast, easy, and relatively cost effective, prices and margins will not be driven down by stiff competition, as in The Electronic Parimutuel Mall scenario. Since only a few virtual stores and virtual malls will be available, however, much of the profit that would have been earned by retailers and manufacturers will instead be retained by systems operators and software developers.[5]

As in the Wegmans On-Line scenario, Bill's Wonderful Adventure will significantly change the value of traditional retailing resources and expertise:

- The resources and skills of traditional merchants—prime center-city locations, efficient space management—will become far less valuable, to the significant disadvantage of the owners and operators of retail properties.

- Interface skills—the strength of Microsoft and other software vendors—will become increasingly important.

- First-mover effects may sustain and reinforce advantages gained early, since more consumers will go to cybermalls with more merchants, and more merchants will go to cybermalls with more consumers.

In this scenario, as in the Wegmans On-Line scenario, value will be shared among manufacturers, electronic retailers, and consumers.

However, the shift in power toward online retailers, and the resulting increase in the share of the value they capture, will be even greater than in the Wegmans On-Line scenario.

Once again, making the necessary changes will be painful and difficult for retailing firms that are currently successful, since these firms may experience a significant decrease in power and profitability. This scenario will probably produce the worst economic outcomes for current participants in the retail channel, suggesting that early cooperative action to avoid it is well advised. Again, the potential for disruption associated with this scenario may prevent established participants from perceiving its plausibility, the threat that it represents, and the necessity of responding in a timely manner.

Fortunately, even if the Bill's Wonderful Adventure scenario were to emerge, it would be unlikely to last. With a minimum of regulatory encouragement, the development of intelligent agents would allow consumers to surge the Net and control their shopping experiences, prompting a transition to The Electronic Parimutuel Mall scenario.

Figure 4-2 summarizes the strategic implications of the five scenarios.

FIGURE 4-2   Strategic Implications of the Five Scenarios

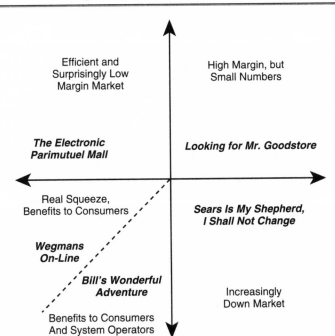

Strategic Responses to Uncertainty

Companies that are contemplating the uncertainties associated with the advent of online retailing face an apparent paradox. They must respond immediately, at least with initial preparations, despite the high degree of strategic uncertainty. Yet they cannot know how to respond. There is too much uncertainty, and the differences between alternative scenarios are too great to permit preparation for all eventualities.

For example, if an airline expects the transition to online ticket distribution to occur rapidly, it might begin the process of disintermediation that would allow it to retain the commissions travel agents now receive for ticket distribution. Similarly, if a packaged goods manufacturer anticipates a rapid transition to online distribution of its products, it might try to gain control of the consumer interface, to avoid losing power to online retailers. Both these actions would be likely to involve strategic alliances with new partners. Moreover, both would be certain to offend owners of travel agencies and retail stores, which are essential to success in the current retailing environment. Therefore, they are certain to provoke retribution from agencies and retailers that retain the power to punish suppliers who attempt to bypass them. Thus, strategic actions that may be essential to success in one scenario may be costly, even catastrophic, in others.

Basically, companies that are contemplating the transition to online commerce and online consumer interaction can choose from the following responses to strategic uncertainty:

- They can attempt to hide and to avoid confronting strategic challenges for as long as possible.

- They can attempt to exercise some control over which scenario emerges. For example, early formation of strategic industry alliances can avert the scenario Bill's Wonderful Adventure, and the associated loss of control, power, and profitability.

- They can place their bets now. But how large should their bets be, and how many should they place? And how public can those bets be?

- They can invest in options for strategic positioning, learn more, and wait until the environment becomes more clear. That is, they can develop contingent strategies, make the investments and begin the negotiations to form the alliances to implement those strategies, wait, and learn. As the passage of time reduces strategic uncertainty, they can invoke or cancel contingent strategies as appropriate. Some—perhaps many—strategic investments may be wasted, but they are likely to have been small, since they were investments in the preparation for rapid implementation of a strategy rather than in full implementation of a strategy. Should quick action become necessary when a tipping point is reached, firms will be prepared.

Clearly, hiding is not a good strategy. The choice among the other options must be made on a case-by-case basis. Some established companies will have a great deal to lose under certain scenarios. The loss to Lever Brothers and Procter & Gamble, to Wal*Mart and Krogers, if the Bill's Wonderful Adventure scenario were to arise, would be unacceptable. Thus, those companies should attempt to influence the future within which they will operate. Only for the largest corporations will this option be a viable one, however.

Other companies will have nothing to lose. Some may be close to bankruptcy and will be able to place only one bet. Others will be startups; if they guess correctly and place the right bets, their return on investment will be enormous. If they guess incorrectly, their principals will write off several months of intense effort and get back to work. Clearly, for these firms, the preferred strategy is to bet what one can and hope for the best.

Most of the time, established firms will lack the power and influence needed to ensure their preferred scenario, and will have too much to lose to place only one bet. Those firms will need to rely on the strategy of investing in strategic options, waiting, and learning more. Properly done, this strategy is not a passive one. First, firms will be actively evaluating their strategic options, making contingent investments based on their evaluations and constantly updating their assessments of the business environment. Consequently, their portfolio of strategic options will be changing constantly. Second, one need not always wait to learn more; often the firm can undertake active experiments to test consumer behavior, competitors' actions, regulatory responses, and other essential aspects of their environment.

Barriers to Change

Experience suggests that scenario analysis can be useful in several ways. It can serve as the basis for a discussion of alternative views of the future, providing a common basis for understanding and a common vocabulary for exploring implications for the future. Properly extended and tailored to the needs of individual companies or industries, it can also provide the basis for strategic planning, including contingency planning both for threatening scenarios and for promising scenarios that offer real business opportunities. Finally, by making a company more sensitive to early warning signs and indicators of emerging scenarios, scenario analysis can facilitate environmental scanning and accelerate a company's strategic responses. Early environmental cues may be so indistinct, and run so counter to prevailing expertise and intuition in the firm, that they would be discounted without the heightened awareness created by scenario analysis.

That said, we must warn that a successful organizational response is not ensured, even after completion of a scenario analysis. The changes organizations may be required to make must of course be initiated by a firm's senior executives. Paradoxically, changes that may reduce risks to the firm may greatly increase risks to those officers. For instance, changes that reduce the importance of store location, in-store product merchandising, or mass production and distribution may be resisted by those who are skilled at those activities, since such changes will be seen as a devaluation of their competence and their personal competitive advantage (Tushman and Anderson 1986; Argyris 1990). Similarly, changes that diminish the importance of shelf space allocation and elevate the importance of software design are likely to be resisted as well.

Experience has shown how difficult it is for organizations to divest themselves of once-productive physical assets that have outlived their usefulness. Individuals find it even harder to divest themselves of once-valued skills. Executives of retailers, manufacturers, and other participants in today's retailing environment who attempt to change their firms will be required not only to divest assets that they own, but also assets that they are.

In sum, preparing for the new retailing environment will require painful decisions regarding changes that cannot be avoided. The safest and least painful way to prepare for an uncertain future is to invest to enable a rapid response to multiple contingencies and to monitor the environment for clues to emerging scenarios. For most firms, controlling the future is not possible, and betting the future of the firm on a single strategic scenario would violate fiduciary responsibility. Thus, hedging one's bets, waiting for more information, and learning, and then responding as quickly as possible when it is appropriate to act is probably the best strategy.

Endnotes

1. Indeed, one insurance company's chief executive has compared the strategic use of detailed information on customers' transactions to "pouring concrete over the customers' ankles," so that they cannot change service providers. We consider the analogy inappropriate at best; moreover, we think it unlikely that an electronic marketplace will eliminate consumers' opportunity to choose.
2. Zap Mail was a proprietary system in which Federal Express used its trucks to pick up documents and take them to fax centers, where they were transmitted to fax centers in the recipients' cities and then delivered by truck. This door-to-door process required two to four hours—far faster than overnight delivery of hard copy documents. Although it now is hard to imagine, the offering initially appeared to be enormously successful.
3. See Schwartz (1991) or Schoemaker (1995) for a more detailed treatment of the scenario process. Pierre Wack (1985a, 1985b) provides two of the earliest references. Arie de Geus (1988) uses scenario planning as an exercise much as we do in this chapter. Peter Schwartz (1992) provides useful insight in how to turn each scenario into a detailed basis for the planning exercise. See Clemons (1995) for a more detailed treatment of the use of scenario analysis in determining competitive strategies in an environment of technologically driven strategic uncertainty.
4. The chatty and familiar sounding names selected are typical of many scenario workshops. Participants frequently pick names that provide vivid images, trigger a strong emotional response, and are easily remembered.
5. This is not unlike the current situation in IBM-compatible personal computers, in which Microsoft's earnings on each machine manufactured appear to be greater than the manufacturer's earnings.

References

C. Argyris, *Overcoming Organizational Defenses* (Boston: Allyn and Bacon, 1990).

S. P. Bradley, J. A. Hausman, and R. L. Nolan (eds.), *Globalization, Technology, and Competition: The Fusion of Computers and Telecommunications in the 1990s* (Boston: Harvard Business School Press, 1993).

E. K. Clemons, "Using Scenario Analysis to Manage the Strategic Risks of Reengineering," *Sloan Management Review* (Summer 1995) 61–71.

—— S. P. Reddi, and M. C. Row, "The Impact of Information Technology on the Organization of Economic Activity: The 'Move to the Middle' Hypothesis," *Journal of Management Information Systems* (Fall 1993) 9–35.

A. de Geus, "Planning as Learning," *Harvard Business Review* 66 (1988) 70–74.

P. J. H. Schoemaker, "Scenario Planning: A Tool for Strategic Thinking," *Sloan Management Review* (Spring 1995).

P. Schwartz, *The Art of the Long View* (New York: Doubleday, 1991).

—— "Composing a Plot for Your Scenario," *Planning Review* 20,46 (1992) 4–8.

M. Tushman and P. Anderson, "Technological Discontinuities and Organizational Environments,"*Administrative Sciences Quarterly* 31(1986) 439–465.

Pierre Wack, "Scenarios: Uncharted Waters Ahead," *Harvard Business Review* 63 (1985) 72–79.

—— "Scenarios: Shooting the Rapids," *Harvard Business Review* 63 (1985) 139–150.

5 | Delivering Customer Value Through the World Wide Web

Kathy Biro

WITH THE ADVENT OF THE Information Superhighway, companies are racing to establish a presence on the World Wide Web (WWW), the latest in a long line of New Media. But the business landscape is littered with New Media failures. History suggests that these investments present enormous risks: they require consumers to change fundamentally their behavior, which consumers are notoriously reluctant to do. Companies focusing on the promise of the technology rather than on delivering true consumer benefit tend to overstate the business case and understate true costs, both human and financial. All too often the result is escalating costs, low revenues, and mounting losses.

But investing in the New Media can be profitable, provided that companies focus on consumers rather than on enabling technologies. This chapter provides a framework for managing investments in New Media, using L.L. Bean's WWW site as an example of effective use of New Media to serve customers. The context for this example is the partnership between L.L. Bean and Strategic Interactive Group (SIG), an interactive media and marketing agency that provides strategic consulting services, as well as creative and technical implementation on the WWW. SIG has been responsible for the creative and technical development of L.L. Bean's site since it launched in September 1995.

New Media Failures: Of Cake Mixes and Picturephones

The marketing challenges inherent in New Media are considerable. Historically, consumer acceptance of new technologies has been slow and cumbersome, delaying anticipated profits by decades. Indeed, consumer acceptance of any innovation is typically slow, despite extraordinary benefits and convenience.

When cake mixes were first created, they required consumers to only add water—a major behavioral shift. Consumers felt a cake made with such a mix could not possibly be as good as a homemade cake. So cake mix formulas were revised to require the addition of an egg and milk. The new mixes met with great success, because the behavior shift required of consumers was minor. Eventually some consumers became comfortable adding only water (some never will).

The issue of behavioral change is compounded by technological innovations, the benefits of which consumers have great difficulty imagining. Consider recent advances in telephone technology. Why did the cellular phone experience such rapid success, while Picturephone technology has languished for decades? The answer has to do with the degree of behavioral shift required by each. The cellular phone asks for little in the way of true behavioral change—it is used the same way as a traditional phone, with the terrific advantage of portability. But the Picturephone changes the consumers' living room and requires the caller to be seen rather than unseen—altering the nature of the telephone experience. Moreover, the Picturephone must be marketed in consumer clusters. Others in the consumer's circle must buy it, or it will be useless. Clearly these hurdles are the reason consumers are not clamoring for this technology.

Likewise, while much has been written about Intuit's Quicken and its home-banking capabilities, home banking has been in painful, expensive development for more than a decade. In 1984, Chase Manhattan Bank launched its home banking system. A key part of this launch was a partnership with a division of AT&T to develop a device that could link consumers to the bank through their television sets. This was a crucial aspect of the plan, given the slowness of personal computer adoption rates at the time. (Sales of personal computers for the home took more than a decade to reach the level industry pundits had first predicted.)

The device AT&T came up with was a marvel. A keyboard with a built in card-reader, it could connect consumers to the home-banking service instantly, with the swipe of a card. Management was ecstatic. They could sell these boxes (or even give them away) and create a ready market for a service they had spent millions developing. Moreover, lab-based research was encouraging: consumers found the device easy to use, especially the card-reader.

But the device failed the living room test. To hook it up, users had to plug it into an outlet, a phone jack, and a TV—not hard to do. The problem was that phone jacks, televisions, and electrical outlets typically were not located in the same vicinity. Thus, connecting the device required consumers to create an asterisk of wires in the center of their living rooms—a condition that turned the nifty card-reader into a bristling techno-nightmare. For the privilege of checking their bank balances, consumers had to wreck their living rooms, when a simple phone call would have served just as well.

Thus, the effort was doomed from the start. From the beginning, Chase was asking consumers to conduct their banking in a materially different way—which far from being convenient, took much more time and patience than the traditional paper-and-pencil method. Asking consumers to rearrange their furniture compounded the problem.

The Myth of Proprietary Advantage

Like home banking, many promising technologies never achieve significant market penetration, despite expenditures in the millions. Unfortunately, few organizations have the horsepower (or stomach lining) to tolerate years of investment with limited returns. Yet the returns are frequently overestimated by companies seeking new markets and distribution channels. In pursuit of the technological imperative (translation: We *can* build it so someone must want it), companies may even ignore evidence of consumer rejection. Once a great deal of money has been spent chasing a promising new technology, companies tend to blind themselves to consumers' responses, convinced these consumers will eventually come around.

Today, many companies are striving to be the first to exploit technologies, and in so doing to create a proprietary competitive advantage. This approach assumes they can build sufficient barriers to entry in a cost-effective manner. However, history suggests that beyond the benefit of organizational learning, most pioneers reap limited advantages, especially if they do not end up owning the distribution channel, but merely using it to market their goods and services. This is the flip side of the early adopter phenomenon: like early adopters, corporate first movers also get burned. As they learn from their mistakes, they pave the way for others to follow in a more cost-effective way, creating only a limited proprietary advantage in the process. The contrast between the quick popularity of America Online (AOL) and the slow, expensive growth of the first mover Prodigy is a perfect illustration. Similarly, the new wave of personal digital assistants, such as U.S. Robotics's Pilot, are faring far better than Apple's Newton, as developers have learned from Apple's mistakes.

A primary impetus in technological change is clearly corporate ego—a desire to be first, to be innovative, to change the competitive landscape. Such risk-taking requires missionary zeal, the kind that can develop a vision of the future before others can make out the current landscape. But a balance must be struck between missionary zeal and misguided fanaticism; otherwise a cycle of failure will unfold. It begins with enormous excitement for a technology—an enthusiasm that far exceeds its capabilities, either because of inherent technological limitations or because of an organizational inability to fully exploit the technology's potential. Fueled by a desire for proprietary advantage, companies overstate the technology's market potential and understate its true cost—especially that of the infrastructure it requires, whose cost typically exceeds all estimates. Few resources are left for creative content development. Ultimately, poor-quality content hampers the technology's adoption potential, slowing market penetration. When the true costs of delivering ongoing service become apparent, usually in a year or two, the balloon of enthusiasm bursts and funding halts.

Many such experiments miss the mark by wide, not narrow, margins. Clearly, if companies were to subject their New Media efforts to the acid test of consumer interest, much of what is now failing in the marketplace would never have been developed in the first place. Companies need to focus less on technology and more on consumer behavior; less on organizational benefit and more on consumer benefit. True consumer behavior change comes slowly.

Because the success of an innovation lies in the hands of consumers rather than technologists, companies must refocus on delivering a quality consumer experience.

New Media Success: L.L. Bean on the World Wide Web

L.L. Bean, one of the most admired companies in the world, exemplifies true customer focus and the highest quality service. At the core of its brand identity are its roots as an outdoor company. In a world of countless wannabe outdoor catalog companies, Bean can claim years of experience as a provider of high-quality outdoor equipment.

Yet when Bean's executives contacted me, Bean was at a crossroads in its marketing approach. Its traditional communications vehicles did not convey Bean's heritage with the richness and historical sense it deserved. To differentiate itself from the pack of Madison Avenue-created catalogs that masquerade as outdoor outfitters, Bean had decided to turn to the WWW. Beyond communicating its story and uniqueness, Bean saw the WWW as a way to build deeper and more enduring customer relationships by enriching customers' experiences of the company. Most of all, Bean sought to deliver an experience fully consistent with its reputation as a premiere company.

Bean is now using the WWW to add value and richness to its customers' experience of the great outdoors. Moving beyond the product information in its catalog, Bean is sharing its outdoor expertise, creating true customer value in the process. Providing customers with deep, rich content to enhance their participation in outdoor activities extends the context within which they evaluate L.L. Bean products. Bean can then promote its product lines within the context of their intended use. As customers learn more about specific activities and explore the great outdoors, they develop a deeper understanding of the features and benefits of Bean products.

To achieve these objectives, Bean first had to answer some difficult questions. How could its roots in the outdoors be reconciled with the high technology web interface? Absent the catalog environment, what would Bean look like, even sound like on the WWW? Bean's exploration of the WWW was fundamentally an exploration in doing business without walls, freeing customers from the inherent limitations of the catalog and storefront. The world of the WWW transcends the limitations of bricks and mortar, paper and postage, sales force productivity, and return per square foot of retail store selling space or square inch of catalog copy. Instead, transactions occur in a kind of market space, where the customer experiences a closer, far more intimate view of the company's identity and expertise. Once this concept became clear to managers, the exercise became one of helping the customer to discover the company behind the catalog. Bean set about building a web site that would deliver enduring customer value, starting with the first contact.

EASY SETUP

The importance of a positive first experience with a new technology cannot be overestimated. Unlike the experts who design computer systems, most consumers lack the patience or ability to handle complex setups. They often reject products and services before they are even up and running because of technical complexities. Barriers to trial can include special equipment requirements, complicated application processes, new accounts to open, and unfamiliar payment mechanisms. Long or painful setup processes discourage consumers, ultimately dooming a new product or service to failure.

First, Bean wisely chose not to assume the burden of educating consumers in web technology. The choice of the WWW rather than a CD-ROM meant that Bean could rely on the fair amount of technical expertise among web-savvy consumers. In contrast to some other web sites, on Bean's home page there are no accounts to open, no passwords to enter, no clues to hunt for or transactions to search through—no unnecessary hurdles to the experience. (Of course, most web hurdles relate to the system's vastness and anarchy, against which the best defense is a coherent search vehicle.)

TRAILBLAZING INTERFACE

Adding interactivity to the consumer experience is a highly complex exercise that takes time to master. Since consumers will no longer be consuming the content on a linear basis, each content component must be treated as a self-contained module. Development of an easy-to-follow navigation scheme and simple user interface is essential. Consumers must be able to get the lay of the land quickly, without wading through layers and layers of screens. An intuitive and easy-to-use navigational metaphor that is consistent with the sponsoring organization's brand identity is desirable, but difficult to execute. For example, the first WWW site of a competitor of L.L. Bean effectively communicated its brand identity, but fell short in providing navigational assistance. The first screen provided little explanation of how the site was organized, and consumers had to wade through nine subcategories before they could reach the retailer's products.

From a creative standpoint, print issues such as tone, manner, and voice get translated into "look and feel" in multimedia. The experience is more emotional and intuitive, less logical, more visual and experiential than a text-based experience. Companies with highly defined ways of communicating with consumers through traditional media may find this new environment somewhat daunting. Practitioners must effectively translate brand equity into a very different consumer experience—one that is less controllable but has the potential to be far richer.

Bean had developed a highly sophisticated voice through traditional print media. On the WWW, the challenge was to devise a new metaphor through the use of video, stills, animation, and text. Managers were tempted to reproduce the catalog metaphor; customers were familiar with it and extending it to the WWW would simplify the development process. However, on-screen catalogs are simply not as convenient and entertaining as print catalogs. Moreover, mere online reproduction of the print catalog would not help Bean achieve its objective of communicating its outdoor heritage and expertise more richly. To realize its goal of doing business without walls, Bean had to free itself from the constraints of its print catalog.

And so they settled on the idea of a trail system—that is, a network of trails and signs—to help users navigate through the content, as if finding their way through a national park. From the opening screen, with Bean's signature watercolor painting of the outdoors, to the use of organic trail signs as navigation buttons, Bean's web site is a unique environment through which the customer navigates intuitively, with a keen sense of adventure. Exploring this site is like exploring the great outdoors: though you may never have been there, you feel you know where you are going.

To ensure that the trail interface truly embodied the look, feel, and voice of Bean, strict guidelines were developed and enforced. Everything from the use of watercolors to typefaces, logo treatments, and color schemes was discussed and codified so consumers would experience the Bean they have grown to know and love. New elements, such as icons and tool bars, had to reflect Bean-like graphic design while at the same time conforming to "netiquette." Like the catalog, the web site was planned to be seasonal, its images and content changing every few months with the weather.

DELIVERING TRUE CUSTOMER VALUE: THE FOUR C'S

Central to a successful New Media introduction is whether an innovation delivers true customer value and benefit. True value is created when an innovation meets at least one of four primary criteria—ideally, it will meet all four: content, commerce, community, and customization. These criteria provide a blueprint for New Media concept development, serving as an acid test of whether a company has succeeded in delivering true customer benefit. Bean succeeded in meeting all four.

Content: Outdoor Lore To exploit the creative potential of New Media cost effectively, companies must take stock of their existing content. These assets, such as text, stock photographs, video clips, and even employee expertise, should be identified, catalogued, and reorchestrated in the new context. To add dimension to the consumer experience, such content should be enhanced with new graphics, video, animation, and text. Considerable expertise is required to turn existing content into worthwhile media content. The disappointing nature of some early CD-ROMs like *En Passant*, a CD-ROM that was little more than a catalog translated to disk, or the early electronic books, illustrates the difficulties. Multimedia applications demand increased entertainment value and breakthrough metaphors rather than a literal translation from one medium to the next. Content developers must experiment widely, taking their cues from the entertainment and education industries, which possess considerable expertise in compelling and user-friendly content creation.

Care must be taken to strike the appropriate balance between content and cost. A content analysis must include "make versus buy" decisions that weigh the cost of developing original content against the cost of purchasing or licensing content. Similarly, the cost of increased depth and breadth needs to be analyzed, as well as degree of interactivity and the overall complexity or elegance of the user interface. Consumer requirements, rather than the appeal of technical wizardry, should dominate in these decisions.

Regardless of how it is sourced, content needs to be truly value-added to actively engage the consumer. Informative, entertaining, compelling, hard-to-find, innovatively conveyed, or conveniently compiled, it must save consumers time or enhance their experience in an area of keen interest. It cannot be gratuitous or found elsewhere in a more convenient form.

Bean conducted a comprehensive internal content review: from archived catalogs to outdoor activity guides and equipment checklists, from tips on cross-country ski techniques to guidelines on selecting a canoe by paddling style, Bean had a wealth of content about its unique heritage and expertise. Like many companies, however, much of this content was intellectual capital—information that existed inside the heads of outdoor guides and fly-fishing enthusiasts—not necessarily written down, but part of the company's lore. To get at this treasure trove of outdoor expertise, managers held internal focus groups, reviewed files, and unearthed old catalogs and flyers. They interviewed retail store employees, customers, and product managers, carefully recording their insights.

Once collected, this content was mapped, catalogued, and stored in a digital-asset warehouse, from which web site developers could choose appropriate content for various applications. Creation of the warehouse uncovered information gaps that needed to be filled; Bean's site visitors are currently being polled for their thoughts on how to fill them. The end result is a deep and rich multimedia content experience, ranging from historical artifacts to tips on fly-casting, tailored to the outdoor enthusiast. This digital asset warehouse is an enduring multimedia asset, leverageable across the full range of New Media opportunities, from CD-ROM to online services and diskettes. Having invested in digital content once, Bean can deploy it as needed across multiple multimedia channels.

Commerce: Closer to the Customer Much of the extraordinary interest in the WWW is fueled by the promise of electronic commerce. In its broadest sense, electronic commerce involves enabling a customer to buy, seek, refer to, transact with, sample, and exchange information. For most companies, however, the real promise lies in the vision of doing business without walls in a market space rather than a physical location. This is a vision being pursued by virtually every major company in the United States.

Robust electronic commerce, however, is only beginning to take hold. Not only do consumers have justifiable security concerns; they need to be weaned from traditional ways of doing business. From a consumer-behavior standpoint, web users progress through a hierarchy of activities, beginning with browsing and followed by active search, eventually evolving to basic transactions. Marketers would do well to follow this natural progression in their web activities, gently educating consumers to eventually overcome their wariness of online purchases.

Clearly, commerce is at the core of L.L. Bean's business as a catalog merchant. However, Bean recognized consumer concerns—indeed had its own concerns with respect to delivering world-class customer service and bulletproof security. Consequently, Bean began with the limited intent of developing a closer relationship with customers through personalized information exchange. Phase one included collecting information on customer demographics and activity interests; initiating simple transactions, such as catalog requests; and integrating easy-to-use templates for e-mail and market research surveys. The results of these initiatives have been used to forecast the potential impact of true electronic commerce. In subsequent phases, Bean registered customers for outdoor skills courses and offered online inventory-checking. Most important, during the fall of 1996, Bean began to offer online product ordering, and in doing so, legitimized the WWW as a direct-order vehicle.

Community: Outdoor Enthusiasts While industry pundits once assumed that content would fuel the information revolution and feed the growth of online services, experience indicates otherwise. To date, the online revolution has been fueled not by a voracious appetite for knowledge and data, but rather by the need to communicate and stay in touch, to meet like-minded others in the comfort of one's home, protected by the cloak of anonymity. Indeed, the experience of AOL with the popularity of members' chat rooms indicates that boredom and loneliness are important drivers of the online revolution.

While the prospect of millions bathed in the blue light of their computer screens, communicating anonymously with strangers, would appear to be a depressing one, the phenomenon is real. It is a migration from the passive experience of television to a far more compelling, active experience. Fundamentally, the interactive age is about connectedness—the deep-seated need to be part of something in a controlled, ultimately safe way. This need is both basic and powerful. Those who succeed in creating community on the WWW will dominate the interactive age.

Community is clearly part of L.L. Bean's heritage. Many customers can recount stories of trips to the Bean store in Freeport, Maine, to find out where the fish were biting, to drink coffee and eat donuts late into a Sunday night, or just to belong to "the Bean mystique." Customers can call Bean for advice on outdoor activities and be connected with an outdoor enthusiast—the genuine article. Only a few in-the-know customers enjoy these aspects of the Bean relationship, however. Clearly, the WWW offers Bean a way to foster community among a far broader range of consumers, and in doing so to add value to the customer experience.

Bean plans a community-building functionality in which product and activity experts can communicate with consumers on their topics of interest, moderated by Bean's Outdoor Discovery guides. For example, consumers will be able to register for outdoor schools, such as the Bean Fly Fishing School. The result of these community initiatives is the creation of a series of tightly knit communities organized by activity dedicated to sharing tips and techniques, planning outings, and comparing sporting gear. For the outdoor enthusiast from beginner to expert, Bean has become a source of shared information, much of it coming from consumers themselves. Communities will grow from common interest and evolve as needed based on consumer interest and inclination.

Customization: Personalized Outfitting The notion of delivering customized goods and services is a fundamental tenet of the interactive revolution. Hitherto, customization has meant the offering of packaged variations of mass-produced goods and services. With fully developed interactive tools, however, companies can begin to individualize their offerings. Carefully constructed, an interactive interface can ensure that each consumer's experiences are unique and reflective of individual needs.

On the WWW, customization is related to the way content is stored and accessed. It is fundamentally a database concept, in which search tools and survey questions are used to help consumers filter content. In its ultimate expression, customization will derive from "intelligent agents," which can adjust to an individual's unique taste and preferences. Over time, technology can be expected to evolve in increasingly sophisticated ways, allowing companies to transcend physical boundaries in their interaction with consumers.

For Bean, phase one of customization began with the development of a database on national parks and the activities permitted in them. Customers planning trips can input their specific needs and interests, such as canoeing in the midwest, and receive a list of appropriate locations, along with directions on how to get there and a list of other activities permitted in the area. In subsequent phases, Bean will use its technology and customers' measurements to facilitate custom outfitting, recommending specific items in stock to meet customers' activity style and personal proportions. Ultimately, the vision is to provide personalized, customized catalogs for customers, based on their measurements, activity style, and other relevant considerations.

PROMISES KEPT

It is tempting to conceive of the delivery of a high-quality consumer experience in terms of the content of the product or service alone, rather than the total package of delivery and usage. Experience shows, however, that care must be taken to ensure high quality at every contact with the customer, from sign-up to fulfillment and reliability during usage. Having defined consumer benefit across the four C's, companies need to ensure consumers of a consistently reliable experience.

A recent experience with a retailer on a major online service comes to mind. The offer was for brownies, gift-wrapped and delivered in time for Christmas. A colleague of mine happily placed an order, aglow with the arrival of the information age. Seven days later he received a post-card through the mail, indicating that the item was out of stock. Or consider the much-touted home pages on the WWW, many of which ask visitors to send questions or comments to the host companies. Many of the resulting questions appear to be falling into an electronic black hole. Some companies are rushing so quickly to the WWW, their home pages are perpetually under construction—empty stores, not open for business.

Consider for a moment the impression created by these kinds of experiences. First, they make it painfully clear that many of these innovations are merely dazzling front ends, supported by a primitive back-office with cranky clerks and piles of unanswered customer complaints. But more critically, they erode brand equity. Companies who would find it appalling to have customer service issues go unaddressed in their core business omit entire aspects of the business process as they experiment with New Media.

Because much of Bean's marketplace reputation is derived from its world-class service, avoiding such gaffes was of great concern to Bean's managers. A cross-functional team was established to provide input into the planning process, thus ensuring that total quality process and procedures were put in place throughout. For example, Bean did not wish customers to order without also being able to check inventory status online. Similarly, Bean would not solicit customers' feedback via e-mail without ensuring that their comments would be handled expeditiously. Bean's thoughtful, measured implementation, including the decision not to provide online ordering initially, was in keeping with its desire to deliver flawless service across all dimensions, from initial contact to fulfillment to ongoing usage.

Ongoing Improvement

The true power of interactive media lies in the availability of real-time data to support continuous improvement of customer relationships. This ability to sense and respond to consumers through real-time marketing based on data capture, analysis, and adjustment is a fundamental premise of New Media. On the WWW, this takes the form of continuous monitoring of consumer use of content in order to enhance its utility, emphasize or de-emphasize certain topics, and create new ones. It also involves a clear commitment to respond proactively to consumer input—a commitment that does not come naturally to companies that are used to thinking in terms of months or even years rather than days. However, such a commitment is essential in order to capture the real benefits of New Media.

At Bean, ongoing improvement was deemed a necessity. Was the company indeed meeting consumer expectations, sensing and responding to their needs? What needed to be fixed? Enhanced? Deleted? To answer these questions, ongoing tracking of site activities and business performance was given top priority. Specific marketing efficiency measures, including catalog inquiries, cost per inquiry, and revenue per product page, are taken on an ongoing basis. As one would expect from a company as quantitatively oriented as Bean, this type of performance tracking is a standard practice there. At companies accustomed to "softer" performance measures or a mass-marketing view, this disciplined analytic approach yields results that are revealing, exerting a tremendous impact on their overall performance.

For Bean, the WWW is already proving its value. It enables Bean to target desirable customers more effectively with lower acquisition costs, compared with traditional communications vehicles. These customers are more likely to purchase from Bean, with higher average order values, and higher lifetime value. Clearly, the WWW's potential contribution for Bean is no longer a matter of speculation: Bean has proven the WWW's strategic and business contribution and is now poised to fully exploit it.

Managing New Media Investments: Conclusions

Over the near term companies should not expect a substantial return on their investment in New Media. Most New Media have a limited base of current users; market extension is hampered by the general lack of technical literacy among a significant portion of consumers. Consequently, any pioneer in New Media will pay dearly in the form of higher costs. Over the long term, however, New Media marketing initiatives may have a substantial payback. As the new technology becomes more pervasive, prices will fall and the user base grow. Continued development of these services will drive their adoption and foster new markets for products and services.

In the near term, then, New Media opportunities must be viewed in terms of organizational learning. Invaluable knowledge can be gained in creative development, implementation, transaction management, and consumer acceptance. Organizations can search for the most cost-effective means of deploying digital assets across multiple vehicles without reinventing content in the process. Finally, they can gain consumer input well before products and services are introduced to the marketplace—an advantage critical to success in New Media.

Maximizing Organizational Learning

A critical challenge for organizations is the strategic integration of New Media experimentation. Frequently, New Media departments are consigned to the fringes of an organization, where they have little or no contact with core businesses. It is not unusual to find a communications department focusing on media placement on the Internet, while in another part of the company, unknown to them, the technology department is busily setting up a web page. Confusion is rampant concerning the role of New Media in the broader scheme of things. Is this a new marketing channel? Or is it a new business?

If New Media are viewed as new communications channels, then clearly they must be developed in a way that is complementary to core marketing activities. However, some companies see New Media such as the WWW or CD-ROM disks as a new business opportunity rather than as a new marketing channel. Either way, because New Media are most often viewed as highly technical and ill-understood mechanisms for reaching customers, they tend to be approached through task forces or splinter groups rather than through the organizational mainstream. As a result, they may bear little relationship to an institution's core strategies.

Approaching New Media in a way that is divorced from core strategies is a highly expensive and risky proposition. Fringe experiments tend to take on a life of their own, reinventing the wheel in terms of processes and market intelligence; duplicating resources; and jockeying for dollars without being compared with mature, more cost-effective marketing channels. Thus, one finds companies experimenting on the WWW without attempting to value its exposure there compared with traditional channels; without forecasting its costs, including ongoing maintenance; and without attending to the total customer experience, with its associated impact on brand equity. Such companies need to concentrate less on how the WWW operates, and more on how WWW exposure relates to their overall marketing activities; less on how to market on the WWW, and more on how to communicate synergistically across all marketing vehicles. Strategic and tactical integration at the conceptual, if not the structural, level is fundamental to maximizing overall organizational learning while controlling financial risk.

This is not to say that New Media exercises always need to compare favorably with traditional marketing methods before they are worth exploiting. An economic value can and should be assigned to organizational learning, much as it is to R&D. But valuing organizational learning should not be used as an excuse to pursue a series of disconnected New Media experiments. Rather, organizational learning should be a deliberate, planned process of learning how to deliver a quality consumer experience, how to manage the development process, and how to recycle digital content. Mastering these processes is essential to competing in the integrated communication format of the future—possibly interactive television. Even if the interactive appliance of the future turns out to be the personal computer, the skills required to succeed in the new marketing environment will be the same.

Armed with an understanding of the learning required for successful content development, companies should select a combination of short-term tactical exercises and strategic experiments to build organizational know-how. Starting with relatively simple exercises, like providing content to an online service or initiating an interactive fax capability, companies can begin to design content with consumer appeal. Later, they can explore interactive kiosks, games, and CD-ROMs as a kind of dress rehearsal for interactive television.

Structured as a portfolio of projects rather than as a series of one-shot experiments bearing little relationship, these exercises can provide content to be used across all media. An example is L.L. Bean's centralized digital-content database, in which reside everything from digitized catalog copies and photos to full-motion videos and editorials about the out-of-doors. This approach allows Bean to spread its development expense across multiple projects, thereby controlling costs while building organizational learning. Its flexibility also helps to control risk in a rapidly changing technological environment.

CONTROLLING RISK

The pursuit of a portfolio of experiments, rather than "betting the store" on one particular technology, helps to control the risk inherent in new technologies. Uncertainty with respect to consumer acceptance also suggests minimization of investment and risk. Risk can be controlled through prototyping rather than full-scale development; alliances rather than individual efforts; and the use of proven technologies rather than the pioneering of new ones.

Proceeding with caution—moving quickly and carefully to build critical organizational learning, though not so quickly as to forge ahead alone—also helps to control risk. Clearly, companies need to beware of the temptation to be a first mover. For some, there are advantages to be gained, and indeed someone has to be first, or innovation would never occur. But companies must strike an appropriate balance between fact and fancy, corporate ego and consumer benefit—and most important, between the capabilities of a technology and consumer needs.

Finally, risk is controlled by setting realistic expectations. If a company is reconciled to limited near-term profit, it can more appropriately (and more cost effectively) brace for the long haul without the continued pressure of short-term results. By taking the long view, a company has a better chance of having its technology in place when the consumer at last arrives.

Imagining the Future

Over the next decade, New Media will profoundly change the way many companies interact with their customers. Companies will use the power of multimedia to deliver far more robust communications than are possible through traditional media, markedly improving their ability to differentiate themselves and express their core identity, heritage, and unique intellectual capital. They will also improve their ability to sense and respond to consumer needs through continuous data collection and analysis and truly responsive real-time marketing. The result will be radically improved marketing efficiency. And companies will use the new technologies to empower customers to help themselves. World-class companies will develop world-class electronic service strategies, delivering a higher level of service at a lower cost.

For their part, customers will delight in the immediacy and simplicity of e-mail communication of service problems; online product comparisons, account and order status inquiries, and inventory checking; and of course electronic ordering of goods and services. They will feel a new sense of connectedness and access, and a renewed sense of individual attention. New electronic communities will form in "clean, well-lit spaces," where a company's customers will congregate, meet like-minded others, and share ideas of mutual interest.

Finally, businesses will emerge, unencumbered by the limitations of a physical presence. The results of all these changes will be profound. New technologies will define the business agenda over the next decade. As companies learn how to do business without walls, they will use their new technology to deliver true customer value—leveraging their investments in the process.

6 | Using Geographic Information Systems to Sense and Respond to Customers

Brian E. Mennecke, Jack Dangermond,
PJ Santoro, and Mark W. Darling

A LOCATION IS MORE THAN just an address. Consider
that statement for a moment—what is it that makes an
address meaningful? Numbers and place names are in
themselves insignificant. A location's surroundings and
its position in relation to them are what define a particular site. For example, as lunch approaches you may
begin to think about that new bagel shop and deli down
the street. In doing so, you probably will not think too
much about its address. Rather, you will think about
the shop in relation to your current location, as well as

Note: The authors would like to acknowledge and thank the
many people who assisted with the completion of this chapter.
Several of the more prominent supporters include Rick
Baumgartner (the IBM Corporation, Falls Church, VA), Daniel
Cory (The Microsoft Corporation, Redmond, WA), Martin
Crossland (SW Missouri State University, Springfield, MO),
Michael Johnson (the InfoNow Corporation, Denver, CO), Sara
Mayo (East Carolina University, Greenville, NC), Martin Schardt
(Union Pacific Resources, Houston, TX), Karen Steede (Creative
Consulting, Marketing, and Mapping Services, Austin, TX),
Steve Trammel (ESRI, Redlands, CA), and Arun Vaidya (the
Conrail Corporation, Philadelphia, PA).

all the other places—the copy center, bakery, sub shop (the other option for lunch)—you may want to visit on your trip to the deli.

Unfortunately, the average desktop computer is not likely to process and store information related to an address in the same way you do. In fact, address data in most databases are used more often to generate mailings than to visualize a location—the position of a site in relation to surrounding points of interest. That is a shame, because an address holds information that lends itself to an abundance of uses by managers and decision makers.

This chapter describes a promising new technology for storing and manipulating information related to geographic location. It begins by defining the origins and capabilities of the Geographic Information System and a related technology, the Global Positioning System. Two cases illustrate how, when linked with a firm's proprietary information system, this new technology can provide businesses with a significant strategic advantage. American Isuzu Motors has used the Geographic Information System to locate new dealerships, launch new products, and improve dealer relations. Levi Strauss & Co. has employed the system to customize its products and adjust its product mix, as well as to place its advertising and promotion. A description of current applications of the technology, including charting and mapping tools, desktop applications, and enterprise-wide tools, follows. The chapter concludes with a discussion of future directions in this groundbreaking new technology.

Capabilities and Strategic Implications of GIS

A geographic information system[1] (GIS) is a technology that can be used to unlock the wealth of information inherent in an address field, as well as in other data that describe location (zip codes, county codes, latitude, and longitude). A GIS supports data management, analysis, and decision making by creating a platform on which attribute data—billing records, customer demographics, sales force statistics—can be integrated with spatial data (maps)[2] to give meaning to a location. In this platform, maps can be used to query a database, or a database can be used to create maps and other visual displays. Thus, a GIS forms the heart of a powerful system for monitoring resources, tracking operations, and reaching out to customers based on location, a variable critical to almost every business activity.

Although the GIS industry is quite large, exceeding $1 billion dollars, the business market for GIS has begun to expand only recently. Growth in GIS use has been fueled by the evolution of desktop computing, which has provided end users with the computing power needed to run GIS, and by the availability of inexpensive yet detailed demographic, consumer, and map data. In fact, much of the growth in GIS use in the United States can be attributed directly to the Census Bureau's release in 1990 of detailed map data for the entire United States. These map data, called TIGER (Topologically Integrated Geographic Encoding and Referencing) files, provide coverage down to the scale of a city block and are accurate to within several hundred feet. TIGER data, when combined with the detailed demographic and customer data that is now available, bring powerful geographic analysis capabilities to the desktop PC.

However, what could you do if there were no way to acquire digital data? For example, most countries do not generate data that is comparable with TIGER files in scope or coverage. How would you acquire data in one of these countries? The answer is that you could collect it using a GPS, or Global Positioning System. GPSs consist of twenty-five U.S. Department of Defense (DOD) satellites orbiting the earth at an altitude of greater than eleven thousand miles. These satellites broadcast radio waves that can be picked up by a GPS receiver on the Earth's surface.[3] A GPS receiver trilaterates from at least three satellites to receive a two-dimensional position (without elevation) and four or more satellites to yield a three-dimensional position (with elevation). Locational information captured using the GPS can be entered directly into a storage unit or notebook computer. Originally, GPSs were used exclusively by the DOD for military applications. Recently, however, several of civilian applications have been developed including vehicle tracking; shipboard, airplane, and in-vehicle navigation; location marking or for criminal trials; tragedies like the TWA crash; wilderness exploration and survival; and updating and maintenance of GIS databases.

Yet, desktop GIS and GPS applications represent but the tip of the proverbial iceberg. The true potential of geographic technologies is unleashed when their map and customer data are integrated with the proprietary data located in a firm's corporate information system. Such integrated, enterprise-wide GIS can provide firms with a significant competitive advantage in a business climate that is fluid and quickly changing. GIS technology has the potential to provide this competitive advantage by enabling a firm to implement tactics that help it to achieve core strategic objectives:[4] to learn, innovate, and adapt; to manage risks and identify opportunities; and to achieve operational efficiency (Table 6-1). The ability to sense and respond to customers, competitors, suppliers, and other organizational and environmental factors is fundamental to achieving these strategic objectives.

For these and other applications, geographic technologies are critical. Yet, they will likely become even more essential as communication and information technologies continue to evolve, redefining how and where people work and conduct business. We can expect that the physical boundaries that once defined and restricted organizations will be replaced by less constraining virtual boundaries. For example, as cellular technology and mobile computing have enabled salespeople to move their offices into their vehicles, the nature of, and in some cases the need for, a regional sales office has changed.

Those who are called on to manage organizations operating in these dynamic and unstructured environments will increasingly face myriad new, unforeseen challenges. For example, to increase market share and carve out and control new markets, many firms have replaced broadcast and mass-marketing techniques with more focused marketing strategies. These strategies require firms to capture, maintain, and use detailed information about a variety of market variables in order to build and nurture customer relationships. To do so successfully, firms must often develop new alliances with suppliers, retailers, and other segments of the value chain. Yet, the ultimate goal of all of these efforts is usually to bring a product or service to someone, somewhere; thus geography is a pivotal factor in these undertakings. In fact, geography is often the one factor that is common to the many diverse tasks firms engage in as they serve their customers. Because a GIS can be used to monitor an organization's resources, clients, and competitors based on their location, it is a powerful tool for sensing and responding to changing competitive environments, and to the needs of the boundaryless organization.

Sensing and Responding Through GIS: Two Cases

The goal of the sense and respond strategy is to attract and retain the most profitable customers. To do so, a firm must be able to sense the needs of its customers and respond by delivering the goods or services required to build and maintain long-term customer relationships. How-

TABLE 6-1   **Applications for Geographic Technologies in Achieving an Organization's Strategic Objectives**

Learn, Innovate, and Adapt

- Define market segments using precise demographic data
- Analyze demand and customer base
- Estimate consumer expenditures by product category
- Manage and respond to customer feedback

- Forecast sales
- Test market new products
- Evaluate advertising
- Examine customer satisfaction
- Track rapidly growing markets
- Precision lead generation
- Relationship marketing

Manage Risks and Identify Opportunities

- Analyze markets
- Analyze customer geodemographics
- Data mining
- Monitor competitors
- Monitor product launches
- Manage pricing

- Customer segmentation
- Targeting markets and customers
- Advertising support and promotion decisions
- Model the performance of markets
- Environmental and regulatory compliance

Achieve Efficiency in Operations

- Site location analysis
- Facilities management
- Sales sorce allocation
- Manufacturing management
- Quality control
- Vehicle tracking
- Product development
- Transportation management
- Sales territory alignment

- Product delivery
- Product management
- Merchandise mixing
- Store formatting
- Inventory management
- Space management
- Retail management
- In-store promotion planning
- Media allocation

ever, for a firm to sense and respond to customers, it must be able to identify, monitor, and manage its own operations, external threats and opportunities, and the boundaries that lie both within and outside of the organization. Regis McKenna made this point quite clearly in discussing the potential of technology to develop and manage customer relationships when he noted that "once companies open themselves up to customers, they must have the systems, processes, and people in place to support the interaction fully."[5]

To realize the full profit-potential from each customer relationship, firms must attend to specific and often mundane business functions including data collection and market intelligence; data management, analysis, and decision making; and process and logistics management.[6] While various tools and techniques are needed to perform these functions, GIS takes advantage of the logical link that geography provides for tying these and other business functions together. Because location is critical to so much of what businesses do, more and more firms are relying on GIS to address some or all of their market management activities. In fact, many cutting-edge firms have made GIS a primary tool for managing customer relationships. We document the experiences of two companies—American Isuzu Motors and Levi Strauss & Co.—that are using geographic technologies to manage their relationships with customers.

SENSING CUSTOMER NEEDS: AMERICAN ISUZU MOTORS

Businesses can listen to their customers in many different ways, through many different media. Some use both the Internet and toll-free phone lines to capture information about customer preferences, complaints, and problems. But these media, although critical to the task of listening, form only one link in the feedback chain. To truly listen to customers, a firm must be able to filter out the noise, integrate information, and build meaningful customer profiles. Moreover, while the ability to learn from customers is powerful, and will increasingly be required to maintain a competitive advantage,[7] other links in the technological feedback chain are no less important. Those additional links include information technologies that allow managers to collect and manage data, make decisions based on that information, and manage operational processes that facilitate the building of relationships. For an increasing number of firms, GIS is the information technology that binds this feedback chain together.

Consider, for example, a customer who travels thirty miles to visit a retailer who carries essentially the same line of products as a retailer located five miles from the customer's home. That the customer would travel an extra twenty five miles says something important about the customer's attitudes and perhaps even the loyalty to both retailers. Information such as this is essential to understanding consumer behavior, and it can only be analyzed and understood by considering the geodemographic characteristics of a firm's customer base.

The American Isuzu Motors Company[8] has built a strategic advantage by using GIS to capture and manage information about its customers. Isuzu has been operating in the U.S. market since 1980 and is probably best known for its Isuzu Trooper® sports-utility vehicle. Other product lines include the Rodeo®, a mid-scale compact sports-utility vehicle; utility pick-up trucks; commercial vehicles; and the Oasis® minivan. The markets in which Isuzu operates are quite competitive and plagued by continuously shrinking margins. Because most Isuzu dealers also market other manufacturers' products, Isuzu must treat its dealers like customers. Its goal is to maintain a high satisfaction rate so dealers will favorably represent Isuzu products to the car-buying public.

New Dealerships Isuzu's GIS project was initiated in 1988 and implemented in 1989. Its first application was the identification of optimal locations for new dealerships—a significant change in the company's site selection process. Isuzu was accustomed to following the lead of other automobile manufacturers—management would select a new site in an existing auto mall, primarily because other auto companies had already done so. GIS enabled Isuzu to be proactive, positioning its dealerships based on customer profiles rather than in reaction to the decisions made by its competitors.

New Product Launches The importance of GIS was quickly demonstrated in one of its earliest applications at Isuzu, which involved integrating the system into new product launches. When the Amigo® was first introduced in the late 1980s, Isuzu used GIS to identify specific regions in which the product was expected to succeed. Based on demographic information about its customer base, GIS predicted the Chicago area would be the Amigo®'s best market. Although several managers felt the *Windy City* had an unsuitable climate for a soft-top sports-utility vehicle, the company proceeded with the launch. As predicted, Chicago generated the highest sales of all the markets in which the Amigo® was introduced.

Isuzu used GIS again in planning the launch of its revised Trooper® in 1992. The new model was significantly different from the preceding one in terms of style, features, and price. Isuzu used GIS and demographic data to identify likely customers for the models based on income, lifestyle, and proximity to selected dealerships. The company then sent personalized letters to potential customers in their primary target market, offering to let them take the vehicle on an extended three-day test drive. This approach proved quite successful: approximately one out of every six people who received the offer took the test drive. Actual sales for the two dealers who participated in the promotion increased by four hundred fifty percent and two hundred seventy-five percent, respectively.

Dealer Relations Because Isuzu relies on its dealers to sell products, it also uses geographic technologies to optimize its dealer relationships. The company recently began to use GIS as the core tool in an initiative called the *Dealer Counselor program*. The goal of the program is to redefine the role of Isuzu sales representatives so as to increase their exposure to dealer sales managers. The goal is accomplished through GIS-based analysis systems that sales representatives can use while at a dealership. The systems allow representatives to assist sales managers in analyzing sales trends, exploring regional markets, identifying and learning about potential customers, and locating other market opportunities. (Figure 6-1 shows a typical map generated in such an analysis.) In effect, the sales representative acts as a consultant to the dealership. Because Isuzu representatives must compete with other manufacturers' representatives for the time and attention of dealer sales managers, Isuzu has effectively used GIS to gain a competitive advantage by adding value to its relationship with dealers. Its closer ties with dealers, in turn, allow its representatives to collect more information from dealers—in other words, to better sense their needs.

Future Directions Thus, GIS has become an essential tool in Isuzu's marketing intelligence system, growing more important as the company continues to fine tune its marketing strategy. The company has redefined its culture and marketing philosophy by refocusing its marketing efforts on understanding and targeting customers more precisely—a change enabled by GIS.[9] Isuzu recognizes four specific advantages of GIS. First, it allows databases to be managed geographically. Second, the declining cost of implementing a desktop GIS increases its value as a database management tool compared with mainframe environments. Third, GIS can be used to manage new approaches to relationship marketing and direct marketing made possible by new communication channels. Fi-

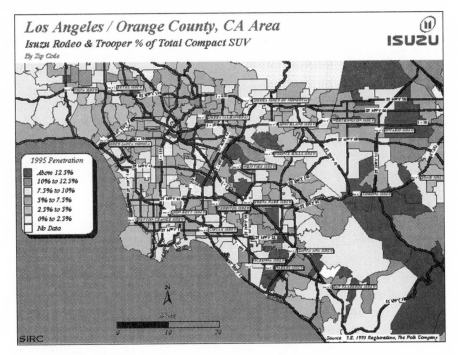

FIGURE 6-1   Thematic Map Showing the Market Penetration of Isuzu Products
Reprinted with permission from Isuzu.

nally, GIS has statistical modeling capabilities that enhance customer profiling techniques. Isuzu views GIS as a tool that can be used to build on its three core competencies: its product, its operational excellence, and its intimate knowledge of customers.

Isuzu has a variety of objectives in using GIS technology. First, it seeks to reduce distribution and marketing costs by segmenting markets and positioning its products more effectively. Second, the company strives to realign its internal functions and processes with those of its direct customer—the dealer—to help the dealer, in turn, to forge a long-term relationship with the customer. Third, Isuzu seeks to exploit real-time information at the retail level to create customer value. Finally, the company wants to redefine and expand the responsibilities of its field organization to enhance its relationship with dealers and diffuse the shift of power from manufacturer to retailer. The ultimate goal is to better listen to and understand customers in order to respond more effectively to both dealers and customers.

RESPONDING TO CUSTOMER NEEDS: LEVI STRAUSS & CO.

To be successful, firms must not only listen; they must follow through by bringing customers goods and services that satisfy their needs and preferences. In other words, "Companies . . . can do more than use information systems to sense the needs of their customers. They can also use technology to respond to customers by creating service experiences for them."[10] GIS has an important role to play in the process of providing *service experiences*, because a firm's task in responding involves bringing the product to the customer—in most cases a location-dependent problem. Somehow, somewhere, the product and the customer must be brought together.

Customized Jeans The company recently introduced Personal Pair™ jeans,[11] a concept that gives women the opportunity to order jeans to satisfy their personal preferences. Personal Pair™ jeans are available only from Original Levi's® Stores and Personal Pair™ stores. While the idea of providing clothing designed to match the personal preferences of individual women is simple conceptually, it is not simple in practice. To implement this strategy, the firm needed a way to manage customers individually from sales all the way through the manufacturing process.

Because Personal Pair™ jeans are available only through Original Levi's® Stores, when a customer contacts the company about the product through the World Wide Web or a toll-free number, GIS technology is used to direct her to the nearest location that carries it. In some cases, customers do not live or work within a reasonable distance of an Original Levi's® Store. Information about the inquiry is then placed in the customer database and eventually used to evaluate market potential during site selection. When a new Original Levi's® Store is opened, customers who live within the new trade area receive a personalized invitation to visit the store, complete with customized directions on how to reach it.

Product Mix Managers use GIS to define the product mix both for Original Levi's® Stores and for other retailers that carry Levi Strauss & Co. products. To do so, they examine regional market-demand characteristics revealed by geodemographic data and information stored in the customer database. By overlaying information about anticipated demand with information about product availability, they can quickly identify specific stores in which product supply is too low. In this way, managers can match supply and demand on a store-by-store basis.

Advertising and Promotions To customize their regional advertising and promotions, managers use GIS to select billboards[12] based on location, traffic patterns, and visibility; to select and customize the content of billboards and other local advertisements based on regional demographics; and to customize advertising associated with promotions for special events, such as concerts or jazz festivals, based on the demographics of local communities. Similarly, managers use GIS to support national promotional efforts, such as new product launches, target marketing, custom mailings, advertising, and media selection.

Merchandise coordinators work with individual retail stores to make certain that Levi Strauss & Co. products are displayed properly, that they are in adequate supply, and that in-store promotional materials are properly positioned and displayed. GIS is used to define the optimal territory for each coordinator and to manage the routing and sequencing of their visits to the stores, enabling coordinators to visit more stores, spend more time at each store, and, in general, use their time more effectively.

The Future of GIS

In the future, consumers will see the effects of GIS everywhere, though they will not always notice its presence. Geographic technologies will be embedded in everything from executive information systems to the family automobile. Because they are important for a multitude of business functions, and by extension, for a multitude of human activities, GIS and GPS will become part of most of the tools consumers use routinely (e.g., finding their way to a new restaurant, perhaps using an in-vehicle satellite navigation system in combination with a database of restaurants).

Current GIS Functions

GIS business applications can be divided into three broad functional categories:[13] charting and spreadsheet mapping tools; desktop GIS for specialized analyses; and enterprise GIS for strategic and corporate-wide analyses.

Charting and Mapping Tools In general, the tools in this category are designed to have a low start-up cost and to be easy to use, but they possess limited functionality compared with more advanced GIS. Typical of entry-level GIS packages are the spreadsheet mapping tools like Microsoft's Excel Microsoft Map™ and Lotus Maps.™ These applications are designed to provide simple, easy-to-use thematic mapping functions for end users. For example, Dan Cory of Microsoft says that their strategy for Microsoft Map™ is to make the application so easy to use that a manager or decision maker can churn out a map with no more than 10 minutes of training. Furthermore, because these tools are standard add-ons, they are available to anyone who uses one of these spreadsheets.

Another entry-level charting and mapping tool is BusinessMap,®[14] which was developed by Environmental Systems Research Institute, an organization with which one of the authors of this chapter is affiliated. BusinessMap® is an easy to use Windows-based application designed for users who possess limited experience with geographic technologies and who need to do more than thematic mapping. The program is designed to work with data from the most popular spreadsheet and database vendors, and, compared with the spreadsheet mapping tools, support a greater variety of business and managerial analyses (e.g., queries, map layer control, locating addresses).

An important factor that has limited the penetration of GIS into a wider variety of business settings is the difficulty of learning to use the software. Mapping and charting tools that are easy to use and readily accessible are designed to bridge this gap by bringing the power of geographic analysis to the average PC user.

Desktop Tools Through the first half of the 1990s, much of the growth in GIS industry was fueled by the increased use of the second category of GIS applications, desktop GIS. In general, state-of-the-art desktop GIS software offers users a full suite of analysis and data management capabilities. Desktop GIS—including products such as ArcView,®[15] Atlas GIS,®[16] and MapInfo,®[17]—provide data handling functionality comparable with that of leading PC-based database management systems, plus the ability to analyze, integrate, and display spatial and attribute data. A package such as ArcView® can also be used to capture new data (e.g., using a GPS); to import data from other sources (e.g., Bureau of the Census map data or customer information from the corporate database); or to perform complex statistical and modeling analyses (e.g., to examine and predict potential sales for consumer electronics products—Figure 6-2).

The role of desktop GIS has evolved considerably over the past decade. Traditionally, many desktop systems were used primarily on stand-alone personal computers or workstations by GIS Specialists. In this context, GIS was often merely a tool to support unique and specialized analyses, perhaps even one-time tasks like preparing reports or performing site-

FIGURE 6-2   ESRI's ArcView® GIS Used for an Analysis of the Consumer Electronics Market
Reprinted with permission from ESRI.

selection analyses. In other words, desktop GIS was often treated like other specialized computing tools (e.g., computer aided design [CAD] systems), in that it had to be operated by a specialist who understood both the software and the principles of geography (but unfortunately, in too many cases, little about business). End-users of the systems' output often never touched the keyboard, because these systems were not integrated into the corporate information system. Of course, that limited the potential of GIS as an organizational enabling force.

Within the last several years, this pattern of use has changed dramatically. Increasingly, business users have moved GIS out of its old role as a specialty tool and into a much broader set of routine business applications. This is due in part to the evolving functionality and usability of desktop tools, but also to the availability of new types of geographic software. For example, MapObjects®[18] is an object-oriented development tool that enables developers to integrate spatial functionality into Windows and Internet applications (Figure 6-3). Thus, spatial

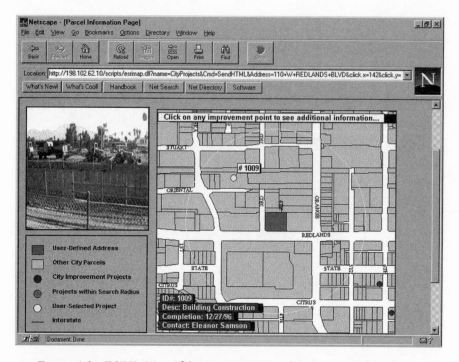

FIGURE 6-3   ESRI's MapObjects® Integrated into a World Wide Web Application
Reprinted with permission from ESRI.

analysis capabilities can be integrated into applications in multiple environments across an organization's information system.

Today, as with spreadsheets, organizations that rely on GIS have integrated it into a variety of core business functions and systems. A desktop GIS like ArcView® is now most often used by managers, business analysts, and others as a platform for addressing a variety of common decision making and managerial tasks.

Enterprise-Wide Tools The third category of GIS, enterprise GIS, takes geographic information technology beyond the desktop into the heart of the corporate information system. Enterprise GIS is characterized by wide diffusion through the organization so that a large number of organizational members have access to part or all of its functions. Because it is used for routine organizational tasks, it is tightly integrated into the corporate information system. Enterprise-wide GIS can be implemented using a spatial database system, such as the Spatial Database Engine (SDE®),[19] combined with client GIS software, such as a desktop

GIS application. Through advances in client-server computing and database management technologies, enterprise-wide GIS solutions like SDE® enable users to manage and integrate large quantities of geographic and attribute data (databases with one hundred million records are not unusual) and to deliver these data anywhere on a local or wide area network. Further, because they are usually implemented in a standard relational database, they are portable to most database environments. Tools like SDE® can therefore be used to build high-speed applications; to embed sophisticated geoprocessing capabilities into software applications; to deliver these applications on a variety of hardware and software platforms; to increase the availability of geographic data; and, perhaps most important, integrate geographic data into existing corporate database management systems.

Several organizations have GIS installations that are utilized enterprise wide. In general, these applications have been most important for industries in which the management of geography is a mission-critical activity—firms that must manage large infrastructures or facilities (e.g., utilities such as Pacific Gas and Electric, which uses GIS to manage power lines and other infrastructure); firms that manage or exploit natural resources (e.g., major petroleum companies, which use GPS to first locate their wells and pipelines, and then use this information in conjunction with GIS to manage exploration, production, and distribution activities); or firms in the trucking or transportation industries (e.g., railroads that use GIS to manage information about rail maintenance history down to the individual rails).

Conrail, which operates an eleven thousand mile rail freight network in twelve Northeastern and Midwestern states and the Province of Quebec, first prototyped an enterprise-wide GIS for multidepartmental applications to visualize data with geographic context and to create a framework for integrating, distributing, and analyzing disparate internal and external information. For example, the Operating Assets Department uses GIS to cost-effectively manage the corporate assets of about $7 billion while delivering service to Conrail's Service Groups. This integrated GIS is used both to manage a data warehouse and to apply this asset for managing operations and structuring costs. This GIS-supported data warehouse is being shared among multifunctional groups to deliver customer-focused service to each of the organization's Service Groups.

Conrail's GIS is also being developed to keep information about track configuration and geographic location current and accurate. For example, it ensures that "as-built" construction information updates the base physical plant data. Electronic monuments (in-track transponders) have been installed at all track intersections to provide synchronization points for automatic data collection and to maintain data integrity. Further, maintenance crews are being equipped with GPS data collection terminals to enable accurate on-site data collection and reporting. This permits Conrail to use dynamic segmentation tools to display detailed information about the maintenance history and costs for each route (e.g., down to individual rail segments).

Several of Conrail's key business management issues and their associated costs are being addressed using GIS. These include issues and tasks such as maintaining information about track ownership, trackage rights, tonnage hauled, and the configuration and classification of rail networks. Further, Conrail uses GIS to monitor its communication and dispatching sites, grade crossings, track clearance, track defects, the condition and location of in-transit cars and locomotives, crew worksites, and travel logistics. The scope of these undertakings is deemed pioneering in the rail industry.

FUTURE DIRECTIONS FOR GEOGRAPHIC TECHNOLOGIES

Although geographic information technology has been available and widely used for many years,[20] only recently has its use in business begun to accelerate. As with other technologies that have experienced dramatic growth, several factors are driving this phenomenon. First, global competition, decreasing profit margins, rapid and unforeseen changes in technology (e.g., the Internet and deregulation of telecommunications), as well as other changes in the competitive landscape have forced organizations to seek more effective ways of managing, monitoring, and understanding their operations, their markets, and their customers. Second, as with other software tools, the rapid increase in performance and simultaneous decrease in the cost of these computing resources have enabled both small and large users to adopt this technology. Third, the availability of digital map data, demographic data, and other data about individual customer buying behaviors has provided GIS users with low-cost data sources for a variety of business applications. Finally, GIS software has become easier to use, with the result that GIS is now accessible even to users with minimal training.

Nevertheless, this growth is likely to be inconsequential compared with future growth. Geographic technologies will undoubtedly be integrated into many, if not most, information technologies, and for that matter, many consumer products (e.g., automobiles—GIS-based navigation systems are already available in a number of luxury cars such as the Cadillac and BMW). For this type of growth to occur, changes will need to be made in the functionality and ease of use of geographic technologies. GIS must become seamlessly integrated into other technologies so that its presence is taken for granted by users. In this context, the paradigm for GIS use and application development must shift. Currently, many vendors and users regard GIS only as a specialty technology. GIS and other geographic technologies must come to be seen as a critical part of the process people use to solve business problems—a process in which geographic analysis is recognized as an important component of the problem-solving process. Yet, because GIS will not be the only information technology on which firms rely, to be successful GIS will need to be designed to function as a part of a firm's broader information processing paradigm. Rick Baumgartner, a Business Unit Executive at IBM, puts it this way: "To become really successful, GIS will have to assimilate itself into the existing corporate infrastructure."

The Spatial Database Engine (SDE®) is an example of a geographic technology that is designed around such a paradigm. SDE® enables users to build high-speed applications with integrated geoprocessing capabilities that can tap into the large data sets that reside in existing information systems and databases. These capabilities are important for firms that must efficiently access large, mission-critical data resources. For example, several firms in the petroleum industry have begun to use this technology to manage the vast amounts of data that are needed for petroleum exploration. Union Pacific Resources (UPR), a subsidiary of the Union Pacific Corporation, uses SDE®[21] to manage and query more than six gigabytes of data about one and one half million exploratory wells, three hundred thousand seismic profiles, and hundreds of thousands of other types of records about various land resources. Data that previously took minutes or hours to be queried are now accessible in seconds or minutes. SDE® has also enabled UPR to access and analyze data nationwide, to integrate data from multiple sources and formats, and to use the data proactively for decision support and analysis.

In the future, geographic applications like SDE® will be used by a growing number of firms in a variety of industries to exploit the power of spatial data. For example, Visa Plus® is using a World Wide Web product called FindNow[SM] to provide an innovative Internet service for locating ATM machines.[22] FindNow[SM], which was developed by the InfoNow Corporation using SDE® technology, enables users to find the location of the three ATM machines that are nearest to a user-specified address or street intersection. To do this, SDE® is used to query a data set with hundreds of thousands of records to identify and display

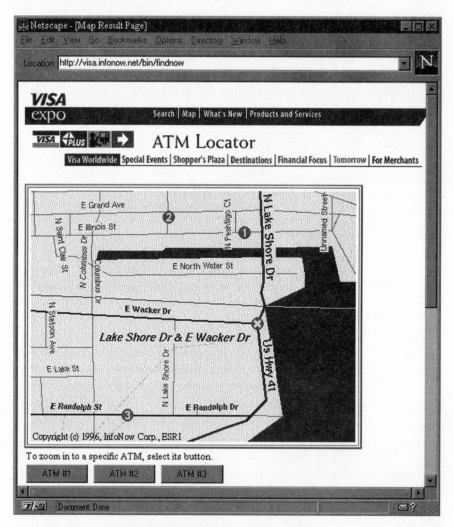

FIGURE 6-4   The Visa® Plus ATM Locator Service
Reprinted with permission from InfoNow.

within seconds a reference map showing the specified area and the location of the ATM machines. Figure 6-4 shows an example of a map generated using the Visa Plus® service; in this case, for the three closest ATMs to the intersection of Lake Shore Drive and Wacker Drive in Chicago, Illinois. In this way, Visa Plus® is using advanced spatial technology to add unique value to the service they provide to their customers.

These examples illustrate how advanced geographic technologies can be used to develop and manage very large databases. Geographic technologies can be used to spatially enable—and thereby enhance—an assortment of high-end, mission-critical applications, including data warehousing.[23]

It is estimated that more than eighty percent of all business data can be linked by some type of geographic component, but these spatial characteristics are too often not factored into the design of data warehouses. Although most organizations have an intense desire to *know* their customers, they often possess an incomplete paradigm of the actual data that describe these customers. In reality, the process of sensing customers should be considered a by-product, or extension of the organization's existing customer knowledge that is shared in the data warehouse. The process of defining and extending organizational knowledge about customers—which includes providing necessary process improvements and tools to actually sense, describe, and respond to customers—can be significantly enabled by geographic technologies. Data can be organized in a spatial order; the very same organizational order that is used by most managers when they *think* about their operations and markets.

In addition, the process of building or enhancing corporate data can also be improved by recognizing that a large and constantly growing list of GIS-based data resources is available that can be used to complement many organizational analysis requirements. For example, when a competitive retail survey that is required for the purchase of a shopping center is completed, locational data from a third-party data vendor can provide a wealth of additional information (i.e., ownership, complementary commercial uses, square footage) that would complement the acquisition process. Today, GIS-based data sources vary from satellite imagery used to validate the number of new houses in a retail market to the individual *people-point* data of the consumers living in those houses.

A logical next step would be to integrate GIS into collaborative technologies to create spatially-enabled groupware. IBM has taken an important step in this direction by using SDE® and MapObjects® to integrate spatial data-handling and analysis capabilities into Lotus Notes.™ Collaborative GIS applications such as these are important because they enable teams and other organizational units to integrate spatial data into group analysis and problem solving activities.

Summary and Conclusions

This chapter began with the statement "A *location* is more than just an *address*!," with the goal of highlighting the importance of geography in the tasks of defining, understanding, managing, and solving business problems. Most, if not all, decision makers and managers have at least a tacit understanding of this; however, too often they either lack the information system tools to manage geography or they have not become fully cognizant of how geography can effectively be integrated into solving their problems and understanding their customers. For example, consider a situation that is typical of the stories we hear repeatedly as we interact with managers and business leaders. On a recent shuttle flight, one of the authors of this chapter encountered a manager for a nationwide financial institution that specializes in consumer loans. In the discussion that ensued, he began to talk about the purpose of his travels, which in this case was to help one of his company's regional offices examine its market potential. One of the first comments out of his mouth was "I wish there was a tool to help me *see* where customers are located!" As he was subsequently shown a GIS working on a laptop computer, he expressed delight by noting that "This is *exactly* what I need!"

Geography can be used to provide value in business. Many firms are using geographic technologies to improve their abilities to sense the needs of customers and respond accordingly. The requirement to sense and respond accurately and quickly will increase because, as the theme of this book suggests, business and, for that matter, government organizations, must compete in a marketplace that is vastly different from that which existed just a few years ago. Because of telecommunications and other forms of technology, organizational boundaries are more fluid and less likely to be constrained or defined by existing geographic boundaries. In this context, GIS offers organizations the opportunity to respond to and manage these new organizational forms by integrating geography into the decision-making process.

Endnotes

1. The term *geographical information system* is the preferred term for this technology in Europe.
2. Two types of data are typically used in GIS applications: map (or locational) data and attribute data. *Map data* define the location of objects, and may include boundaries (e.g., county); lines (e.g., roads); or points (e.g., office buildings). *Attribute data* describe objects and may include a customer's name, address, or demographic information.
3. Unfortunately, the DOD purposely degrades positional accuracy with a process called Selective Availability (S/A). One way to counter this is to apply Differential GPS (DGPS), which uses base station data from a known location to offset the error. Use of the GPS signal is free; however, accuracy can be improved by using higher quality receivers. For example, by using DGPS, positional accuracy can be improved from a resolution of two to five meters to within one meter.

4. See Sumantra Ghoshal, "Global Strategy: An Organizing Framework," *Strategic Management Journal*, 8 (1987) 425–440.

5. Regis McKenna, "Real-Time Marketing," *Harvard Business Review*, July–August (1995) 92.

6. See W. H. Grant and L. Schlesinger, "Realize Your Customers' Full Profit Potential," *Harvard Business Review*, September–October, 1995, for a more detailed discussion of this topic.

7. See Joseph Pine, II, Don Peppers, and Martha Rogers, "Do You Want to Keep Your Customers Forever?" *Harvard Business Review*, March–April, 1995.

8. See http://www.isuzu.com

9. See Frederick E. Webster, "Executing the New Marketing Concept," *Marketing Management*, 3, No. 1, 1994.

10. Regis, McKenna, op cit.

11. Ibid.

12. GPS is increasingly being used to select the location of and content for marketing tools such as outdoor billboards. Outdoor Technologies, a company based in Austin, Texas, markets a database of billboard locations. Using GPS, the billboard locations and their attributes are recorded and downloaded into a GIS. The GIS can then be used to analyze street and highway traffic patterns and to perform demographic analysis of neighborhoods surrounding the billboards. Subscriptions to this database are sold to advertising companies so that their billboard advertising campaigns for existing clients can be targeted to specific demographic groups.

13. These are by no means the only geographically based applications currently available. Myriad consumer products are available for education (e.g., Broderbund's *Where in the World is Carmen Sandiego?*®), reference work (e.g., Microsoft's Encarta® 96 World Atlas), and travel planning (e.g., Delorme's *Map'n'Go*® trip-routing software and Microsoft's AutoMap" travel planner).

14. BusinessMap is a Registered Trademark of the Environmental Systems Research Institute, or ESRI, see http://www.esri.com/

15. ArcView is a Registered Trademark of ESRI, see http://www.esri.com/

16. Atlas GIS is a Registered Trademark of ESRI.

17. MapInfo is a Registered Trademark of the MapInfo Corporation, see http://www.mapinfo.com/

18. MapObjects® is a registered trademark of ESRI.

19. SDE® is a registered trademark of ESRI.

20. Jack Dangermond, one of the authors of this chapter, founded ESRI in 1969 and produced and marketed GIS software from that time until now (see http://www.esri.com). The primary users of GIS during the last three decades have been various agencies within the federal and state governments, as well as large private-sector firms such as utilities and petroleum companies.

21. This custom ArcView® and SDE® application, called LandGIS,® was developed for UPR jointly by Eagle Information Mapping and Innovation Business Solutions, Inc.

22. See http://www.visa.com for the Visa Plus® ATM locator and http://www.infonow.com for the FindNow[SM] service.

23. The father of data warehousing, W. H. Inmon, says that a data warehouse is a subject-oriented, integrated, time-variant, nonvolatile collection of data in support of management's decision-making process. In practice, most data warehouse applications are quite large, often containing millions of records. Conversely, a "data mart" is a scaled down, less expensive, and simpler version of the data warehouse application. See W. H. Inmon, *Building the Data Warehouse*, 2nd ed., (QED Publishing Group; New York: Wiley Computer Publishing, 1996).

7 | *Seeing Through the Customer's Eyes with Computer Imaging*

Gerald Zaltman and Linda J. Schuck

THIS ARTICLE DESCRIBES a research tool that helps customers express their thoughts and feelings more fully. It is unique in three ways. First, it is based on wide-ranging research on images and the mind. Second, it employs what is at once the oldest and most complex multimedia technology available to human kind—the link between perception and cognition. Thought is rooted in the senses. Third, it uses computer imaging techniques to help customers explore and express their ideas. The tool is called the Zaltman Metaphor Elicitation Technique (ZMET).

Impressive progress has been made in the study of the representation of the external world in the mind. That progress has provided considerable insight into ways of conveying information to customers. Much less progress has been made in the study of the representation of the mind to the external world. Our capacity to *tell* people exceeds our capacity to let others *tell us*. Put somewhat differently, *firms are much better at helping customers to understand product and service offerings than they are at helping customers to express their deep and latent thoughts and feelings.* Since a firm's response to those thoughts and feelings is the ultimate basis for its success in the marketplace, doing better at the task of helping customers to represent their thinking is essential.

Lack of progress in letting others tell us their deep thoughts underlies a familiar complaint about market research; that customers are unable to express important untapped needs and hence can offer little guidance in the development of new products or innovative strategies. In fact, *the primary obstacles customers encounter in articulating their needs are imposed on them by market research.* Although human expressive capabilities may have limits, conventional research techniques have a long way to go before encountering them.

The gulf between customers and researchers is affected by the boundaries between customers and managers, researchers and managers, and researchers and creative or product design staffs. Researchers, creative staffs, designers, managers, and customers are separate if co-dependent cultures, each with its own unique frame of reference (Barabba and Zaltman, 1991). These multiple mind-sets must be managed successfully if there is to be a meeting of the minds between customers and managers. (See especially Barabba, 1995.)

Boundaries exist within these communities as well. Problems arise not so much from the existence of different frames of reference—indeed, their presence can be very productive—but from the failure to acknowledge and understand them. Thus, an important challenge in "getting the inside out" for any group is to acknowledge the different frames of reference and work with them. For example, it is desirable to map not only how customers think about a topic, but how managers, creative staffs, and researchers think customers think about a topic. The ZMET has shown promise in helping with this task.

The following section describes ZMET, a research method that enables customers to probe and share knowledge that is hidden or difficult to express. Succeeding sections recount its application at the Pacific Gas and Electric Company (PG&E).

The Zaltman Metaphor Elicitation Technique

The ZMET is a patented research tool that enables subjects both to understand their own thinking more fully and to share it with researchers. ZMET surfaces basic constructs or ideas and the connections among them, and does so in a user-friendly way.

BASIC PREMISES

ZMET is based on current research and thinking in diverse fields such as cognitive neuroscience, neurobiology, artistic and literary criticism, visual anthropology, visual sociology, semiotics, the philosophy of the mind, art therapy, and psycholinguistics. Specifically, it is built on seven basic premises.

Most Social Communication Is Nonverbal It is estimated that eighty percent of all human communication is nonverbal (Weiser 1988). This estimate is consistent with the finding that two-thirds of all stimuli reaching the brain are visual, with the balance conveyed by sound, taste, smell, and touch. Nonverbal communication includes paralanguage, or the tone, pitch, and other qualities of speech that determine whether we literally mean what we say (cf. Gibbs 1994). Paradoxically, the majority of all market research techniques are verbocentric; they rely on literal verbal language. While verbal language is important, the task facing market researchers is how to use both verbal and nonverbal language more effectively.

Thoughts Occur as Images Thus, having thoughts and expressing them in words can be quite different. What do we have, then, when we have a thought? Two useful insights are provided by the neurobiologist Antonio R. Damasio and by Steven Pinker, director of the Center for Cognitive Neuroscience at MIT. According to Damasio (1994):

> [Brains] still have no mind, if they do not meet an essential condition: the ability to display images internally and to order those images in a process called thought. (The images are not solely visual; there are also "sound images," "olfactory images," and so on.) . . . My view then is that having a mind means that an organism forms neural representations which can become images, be manipulated in a process called thought, and eventually influence behavior. . . . (pp. 89, 90)

Images, then, are central to thought. But what about words? According to Pinker (1994):

Is thought dependent on words? . . . Or are our thoughts merely couched in words whenever we need to communicate them to a listener? (italics in original, p. 56) . . . The idea that thought is the same thing as language is an example of what can be called a conventional absurdity (p. 57) . . . there is no scientific evidence that languages dramatically shape their speakers' way of thinking. (p. 58)

Thoughts, then, are images; only infrequently are they verbal images. For this reason, it is important to help customers to represent their images in nonverbal terms, moving researchers closer to the state in which thoughts occur. Verbal language is an indispensable part of this process. Linked directly with specific visual images, language helps customers to convey their internal representations or meanings to researchers and managers.

Metaphors Are Central to Cognition   In the past two decades, a consensus has emerged among scholars in many disciplines that metaphor, the representation of one thing in terms of another, is fundamental to thinking and knowing.

Recent advances in cognitive linguistics, philosophy, anthropology, and psychology show that not only is much of our language metaphorically structured, but so is much of our cognition. People conceptualize their experiences in figurative terms via metaphor, metonymy, irony, oxymoron, and so on, and these principles underlie the way we think, reason, and imagine. (Gibbs 1994, p. 5)

Metaphors actively create and shape thought. Because we cannot know anything unless it is perceived as an instance of one thing and not of another (Lakoff 1987), thought is inherently figurative. Consequently, by paying more attention to the metaphors customers use to express their images, we can learn more about their thoughts and feelings.

Cognition is Grounded in Embodied Experience   This premise, although supported by research in many fields, is less widely known. It states that abstract thought is shaped by perceptual and motor experiences (cf. Johnson 1987, 1991; Gibbs 1994, Leyton 1991; Damasio 1994; McAdams and Bigard 1993; Varela et al. 1991). Perceptual experience includes all sensory systems, not just vision. Basically, metaphorical understanding and associated mental models are grounded in everyday bodily experience.

This premise suggests that various senses and the interaction among them (called *synesthesia*) are useful in probing deep thought structures. Again, consider the neurobiological perspective:

> . . . that the body, as represented in the brain, may constitute the indispensable frame of reference for the neural processes that we experience as the mind; that our very organism rather than some absolute external reality is used as the ground reference for the constructions we make of the world around us and for the construction of the ever-present sense of subjectivity that is part and parcel of our experiences; that our most refined thoughts and best actions, our greatest joys and deepest sorrows, use the body as a yardstick. (Damasio 1994, p. xvi)

Viewing the body as a multimedia system that shapes our thinking suggests that its various subsystems, such as the visual system, can be used to "get the inside out."

Deep Structures of Thought Can Be Accessed All customers have conscious thoughts about a business that they need help in articulating. Customers also have many hidden thoughts—ideas they are not aware of possessing, but are willing to share once discovered. A variety of techniques used in art therapy, especially phototherapy, can be very effective in bringing such thoughts to the surface (Ziller 1990). Judy Weiser (1993) has expressed their relevance this way:

> All art therapy is based on the idea that visual-symbolic representation is far less interruptive and distortive than verbal translations of sensory-based experiences, and that we not only often project unconscious meaning through such metaphoric communications from deep inside but also tap into those areas while simply reacting or responding to symbolic imagery produced by others. . . .Verbal translation [provides] good hiding places for rationalizations, defenses, excuses, and other protections. . . . Most of us think, feel, and recall memories not in words directly, but rather in iconic imagery. . . . All of these make up the mental maps that we use when later trying to cognitively communicate about things, whether using words or artistic symbolic representations of them. . . . What a person notices [in a picture] will always mirror the inner map that she or he is unconsciously using to organize and understand what the senses are perceiving.

Used appropriately, these and other techniques allow researchers to delve more deeply into customers' thoughts than has been customary.

The symbolic images Weiser refers to are often missing pieces of more fundamental thought structures. They are "deep" in the sense that they are generally not accessible using research techniques like focus groups, which surface knowledge customers can readily convey.[1]

The Meaning of a Thought Is Shaped by Its Association with Other Thoughts Any given thought or idea has meaning only in relation to other thoughts or ideas. It is important, then, to learn how particular thoughts are associated. For example, when a customer discusses a firm's responsiveness to their problems, it is necessary to understand what other thoughts give rise to the idea of responsiveness and what thoughts are activated by responsiveness. Knowing which ideas in a network of ideas are "buttons," which when pressed or activated, become co-active with other ideas, can be of great value in planning corporate strategy. For this reason, it is useful to present ideas or constructs that are connected in a reasoning chain in the form of a causal model.

Reason, Emotion, and Experience Co-mingle Human thought involves both reasoning and emotion, so does effective decision making, whether by customers or managers.[2] Therefore emotion, logical inference, and embodied experience must be considered mutually dependent and inseparable dynamics (de Sousa 1987; Varela et al. 1991; Edelman 1992; Damasio 1994).

THE ZMET INTERVIEW

These seven basic premises underlie the Zaltman techniques, which begin with an interview in which customers explore their thoughts and feelings about a business. A customer might collect pictures representing thoughts and feelings about the firm from sources such as family albums, catalogs, magazines, or photographs taken specifically for the interview. It is essential that customers seek or collect their own pictures rather than selecting from images provided by the researcher. Most participants report spending about six to seven hours over several days thinking about the assignment and locating pictures. Many comment on their high level of involvement. Customers, then, arrive for the interview at an advanced stage of thinking.

The one-on-one, face-to-face interview takes approximately two hours. It involves several steps carefully designed to engage different aspects of a customer's thought process and allow deep, often hidden ideas to emerge. At the same time, each step overlaps somewhat with at least one other step. When different steps surface the same idea, researchers can be more confident about its significance.

Thus, the interview procedure increases the likelihood of uncovering important ideas, provides convergent validation for ideas, and permits an assessment of the salience of an idea to participants.

During the typical interview, participants tell a story about each picture; describe any images they wanted to find but could not, and the ideas those images would have expressed; elaborate on the most representative picture; and describe an image that conveys the opposite of the topic. Customers are also asked what a company (or a specific group, such as product managers, designers, or sales personnel) thinks of them, and what picture(s) would express that. (Some ZMET projects have focused exclusively on this issue.)

Further into the interview, the Kelly Repertory Grid (a construct elicitation method used in clinical psychology) and a laddering technique (a probing procedure) are used to elicit and probe key ideas in a different way. Then, a variety of phototherapy techniques are employed to explore selected images from still other perspectives. Next, nonvisual images are explored—what is and is not the touch, taste, and smell of a company—and participants are asked to explain the link between these nonvisual images and the company.

The participant is also asked to create a thirty-second vignette or video expressing the more important ideas elicited in the interview. Finally, with the help of a specialist in computer graphics, the participant uses digital imaging techniques to create a collage that summarizes his or her thoughts and feelings. For most participants, this is one of the most engaging and self-revealing aspects of the interview.

Interviewers are trained in using ZMET and in the disciplinary underpinnings of the technique. The number of steps and their implementation varies from project to project, but each involves an R&D component to ensure continual improvement in the technique.

An Example: Pacific Gas & Electric

The Pacific Gas & Electric Company has used ZMET to position itself competitively in preparation for restructuring of the electric utility industry. In just a few years, increasing numbers of PG&E's customers will be able to purchase their utility services from multiple providers. Thus PG&E is intensely interested in its image in the mind of the customer. Effective competitive positioning requires a deep understanding of how customers currently think and feel. The results of ZMET research are helping PG&E to position itself competitively in a number of ways.

We turn now to the findings of PG&E's research and its application to PG&E's business problem.

Customers' Experiences with PG&E

A major "deliverable" for a project is a mental model, or consensus map—that is, a set of related constructs or ideas that are shared by most customers. PG&E's consensus map is shown in Figure 7-1. Besides being the mental "template" for the sorting and filtering of information about PG&E, the map identifies the relationships among constructs, showing which constructs, when activated, are likely to render other constructs salient.

This map also exists in multimedia form. "Clicking" on a construct displayed on the computer screen calls up a visual dictionary of that construct. In the dictionary are sample images containing the construct

FIGURE 7-1   Consensus Map for Pacific Gas & Electric

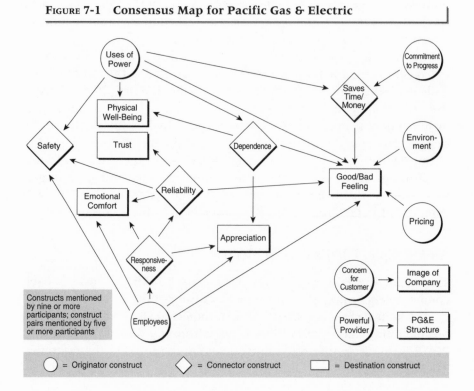

along with a description of the image's relevance to PG&E, recorded by a customer. This application preserves some of the richness of the raw data in an accessible format.

The map's constructs are bipolar: they may be important or unimportant, positive or negative, strong or weak, high or low. For example, the construct of reliability may be experienced favorably by some customers and unfavorably by others. Many constructs have multiple dimensions so that their full context is evident only in the visual dictionaries (see Exhibit 7-1: Visual Dictionary for the Constructs of Employees, Emotional Comfort, and Reliability). For some customers, reliability may manifest itself in a prompt or tardy response to problems; for others, it may manifest itself in the absence or presence of problems. Not only may the same construct manifest itself differently for different customers, it may have multiple and even conflicting meanings for a given customer.[3]

Construct Salience and Importance The constructs that appear in the map in Figure 7-1 are determined through the following procedure. First, all the constructs mentioned by all the customers interviewed were compiled. This list was then reduced to twenty-three constructs mentioned by nine or more customers. The requirement that a construct be mentioned by at least nine of the twenty people interviewed is an indicator of construct salience. The constraint was then added that each construct had to be directly connected to at least one other construct by a minimum of five customers during the interview probing procedures. That is, the same construct pair had to be mentioned by at least five customers. This constraint, which provides an indication of construct importance, reduced the list to nineteen key constructs. (These are constructs customers identified on their own, not their reactions to researcher initiated constructs.)

Direct connections between constructs represent the customers' thinking process, showing how one idea leads to another. Figure 7-1 understates the actual density of connections among constructs. For instance, three or four customers may have connected "responsiveness" to "safety," but a responsiveness–safety connection is not shown because it does not meet the cutoff point of at least five mentions. Furthermore, the indirect connections between responsiveness and other constructs through the safety construct would not have been shown in the map, if safety had not been mentioned in direct connection with those constructs at least five times.

EMPLOYEES

1. Dog (+)

This is my dog. I photographed her because she is always very eager and willing to please. And that's what I have found to be true of virtually every PGE rep that I've talked to on the phone and anybody that I can recall coming out to the house. Like other homeowners I deal with many other companies, telephone, cable TV. I would say that with all of the people I've dealt with on the phone and in person I am most impressed with PGE. you don't have to call them very often because there's not really any reason to, but you know when you do it's not going to be a negative experience, that they're going to take care of what you need.

The Color of PG&E is NOT...

2. Red (+)

Red. Red always somehow suggests alarm to me and being frenetic and they are not that. There's always a certain kind of calmness about the way they do go about their work which I appreciate.

The Emotion of PG&E is...

3. Guarded Concern (+)
(SEE ALSO: IMAGE OF COMPANY)

Guarded concern. In addition to that, there are individual employees that are just real decent individuals and I don't know if they, meaning the corporation spends a lot of effort in training the employees in how to deal with the public. I would presume that would happen. In addition to that, they're real good at screening people to get a good group of people that do an effective job of representing the company. Cause that's the part that helps them, meaning the company, look better. So that helps us to overlook some of the nastier associations with the company.

The Touch of PG&E is...

4. Cold (-)

Cold, their customer service is very cold and not particularly helpful.

EXHIBIT 7-1   **Visual Dictionary for the Constructs of Employees, Emotional Comfort, and Reliability**

EMOTIONAL COMFORT

1. GLASSES (+)

When you put your dishes in the electric dishwasher, how beautiful they come out, your plates are so shiny and clean and brings beauty to your home, beauty to your kitchenware, your table. If you want to entertain somebody. The beauty of the electric dishwasher that you can wash these by hand, but nowadays most people have dishwashers. I thought, how beautiful your dinnerware, sit down, invite people over, have them for dinner and be proud of your shiny glassware and your shiny dishes and can beautify not only yourself with the lighting for yourself, but for your dishes and everything thanks to PG&E.

2. ELECTRICAL STORMS (+)
(SEE ALSO: RELIABILITY)

Electrical storms, which cause a lot of damage, but that man is sleeping very peacefully. He's not even worried about it. Apparently he has faith in this electric company.

3. WOMAN ON THE BEACH (+)
(SEE ALSO: SAFETY)

When you have peace of mind you can go on vacation and enjoy yourself. You don't have to worry about somebody breaking into your home because you have the capability of security equipment. As long as I am quite sure that all my timers and yard lights are going to go on, I don't have to worry about my home or my personal things.

EXHIBIT 7-1   Visual Dictionary for the Constructs of Employees, Emotional Comfort, and Reliability (cont.)

EMOTIONAL COMFORT CONT.

4. FAIR (+)

We wouldn't be able to have a fair without PG&E because you need the electricity to ride all the rides and all the beautiful lights from the fair, the different colors. The lights, the rides, the beauty of all the colors, the fun times. You can go out and have fun and just forget all your troubles for one day. Just go do it.

The Taste of PG&E is...

5. COFFEE (+)

Coffee. Because I get up in the morning and it's something I welcome, it's very relaxing and it's my baby bottle in the morning. It's very comforting.

RELIABILITY

The Sound of PG&E is...

1. OCEAN (+)

The ocean. It rises and falls. Sometimes it's quiet and sometimes it's not. It is there constantly but it is not demanding of your time and your thoughts.

The Emotion of PG&E is...

2. FRIENDSHIP (+)

Friendship, the real close ones that I know are there. I don't see them all the time, but I know they're going to be there if I need them and if I think about the PGE, I feel the same way about the company. It's there, it's serving me, it's dependable, so it's a good friend.

The Sound of PG&E is...

3. A HUM (+)

A hum, like a computer running or a fan or a refrigerator. Like background noise, its always there and that's a comfort.

EXHIBIT 7-1   Visual Dictionary for the Constructs of Employees, Emotional Comfort, and Reliability (cont.)

All constructs in the map are important. The weakest link is in some ways the most important, since a breakdown at that weak point can cause the entire chain to become dysfunctional. Note that some constructs are classified as *originator constructs*; they tend to be the starting point in a thought process that leads to other constructs. The employees' construct is an example. Customer perceptions of PG&E employees affect both their perceptions of PG&E's responsiveness and their feelings of emotional comfort. In fact, customer perceptions of employees have both a direct and an indirect effect on feelings of emotional comfort, through the responsiveness, reliability, and safety constructs.

Other constructs tend to be *connectors* or *transmitters*: they affect and are affected by other constructs. Responsiveness, for example, is affected by employees; it is also a gate through which the employee construct affects other constructs, such as reliability. Finally, some constructs are *destination constructs*—end points in a reasoning chain. For example, appreciation is an end point in the safety reasoning chain.

Consensus Among Customers Another view of the mental map that is representative of customers' thinking is provided by a different analysis of the data. Files are selected at random, and the number of constructs mentioned in successive files but not in previous files are noted. This procedure is repeated several times. For example, with the PG&E data, in one run, fifteen of twenty-three core constructs (mentioned by nine or more participants) were mentioned in the first file selected; four more were added by the second file; three more by the third file; and one more by the fourth file. Repeated runs varied little from this pattern. On average, all key constructs were generated by the fourth file selected randomly, indicating strong consensus among the twenty participants about the salience of the twenty-three key constructs. Figure 7-2 shows the results in graph form.

On average, the twenty-three constructs represent eighty-seven percent of all constructs mentioned by customers. Figure 7-1 included seventy-three percent of the ideas of the person for whom the consensus map is *least* representative. It included one hundred percent of the ideas of the two people for whom it is *most* representative.

Technical Observations This pattern of rapid convergence on key constructs has been found in every ZMET application. In contrast to other techniques, it might be considered remarkable that so few people are required to generate a fairly exhaustive set of shared constructs, it is not surprising, however, given research in other contexts on expert judg-

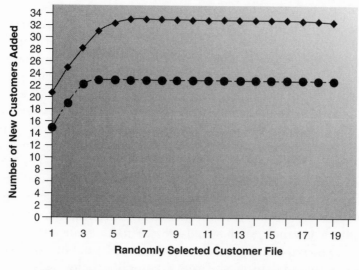

Figure 7-2   Number of New Constructs Added by Each Additional Participant

ments. In terms of identifying important ideas about an issue, the value of a third expert is significantly lower than the value of the first two. In ZMET research, each customer may be considered an expert on his or her own thinking about a company. The procedures that are used help customers to express their expertise readily, on a level of thought deep enough to surface socially shared cognitions.[4]

Though the constructs identified in this research would be unlikely to change had a larger sample of people been interviewed, we cannot generalize to a larger population concerning the numerical frequency of positive or negative feelings toward any construct. Knowing the incidence of positive and negative perceptions among specific market segments is important, but it is best addressed with survey research. ZMET focuses on the multiplicity of ways customers experience constructs, other than in positive or negative terms.

Digital Images of PG&E

In the final step of the interview, customers created a digital image of PG&E with the assistance of a computer graphics specialist. Representative of many of their important thoughts and feelings about PG&E,

the images were an opportunity not only to validate identified constructs but to bring to the surface others that might have been missed. Expressing their ideas visually using computer technology stimulated subjects' thinking in a different way, revealing previously unexpressed thoughts and emotions. Recall that subjects spent several hours prior to the interview thinking about meaningful images, and about one and a half hours discussing their ideas in depth with a skilled interviewer. Thinking about colors, shapes, object sizes, positions, layering, textures, location, and symbols to include in their composite images within the safe haven of a computer screen brought forth elements of their inner mental maps that had not surfaced in preceding steps. This result should not be surprising given that thought is image based, not word based, and that images have their origins in the motor, visual, and other sensory perceptual systems. The act of digital representation engages cognition and memory in ways that are otherwise impossible.[5]

Before subjects began, they received a brief description of the capabilities of the software and hardware and were told someone would handle the technology for them. (None of the participants had any appreciable prior knowledge of the technology.) They were also informed that they could augment the images they had brought to the interview by sketching or drawing from an image bank. Generally, however, participants used only the images they had brought to the interview.

The images were scanned into the computer and brought up on screen. The customer then directed the technician in the construction of a summary image. Participants varied widely in their comfort level and experience in working with computers and creating visual images. When the task was finished, the customer described (and audiotaped) the story or meaning of the completed image.

While the intent was not for participants to create visually pleasing pictures, the assistance of a skilled technician, together with sophisticated software, allowed participants to develop images unconstrained by their own skills. The use of computer technology to overcome limitations in their artistic skills encouraged the expression of their inner thoughts (images) more fully and deeply.

Some of the completed digital images encompassed most of the ideas discussed during the interview; others focused on a small subset of constructs. Not only did new ideas arise in this stage, but also original images were often used differently than they were in earlier steps. Different meanings were attached to them, or elements of a picture that a participant "hadn't noticed before" took on special significance. In fact, throughout the interviews, people often noticed aspects of pictures they had not been aware of when selecting them.

A question often raised about ZMET, especially the digital imaging step, is whether people vary in their ability to work with visual and other sensory images. Most people are highly skilled and fluent with images. Because thought is image-based, pictures are a natural means of reflection.

Image fluency is unrelated to formal education, occupation, or age, nor can one infer from a person's images anything about those background characteristics. In this sense, ZMET is very democratic. It establishes a platform in which people whose verbal skills may vary considerably can become more or less equal in their expressive capacity. (The screening criteria require considerable variation in ethnic origin, educational background, income, age, and place of residence.)

Most participants managed to find visual images which appropriately expressed their thoughts and feelings.[6] In those infrequent instances in which visual images are insufficient, sound, taste, touch, and smell images have proven powerful and effective sources of metaphor. Exhibit 7-2 contains a sample of participants' digital images of PG&E.

DEEP METAPHORS FOR PG&E

Many scholars consider the underlying structure of human thought to be metaphor based. From this premise flow two reasons to be attentive to customers' metaphors of a business. First, because metaphors create and shape thought, they are key to understanding customers' perception. Second, since metaphors also serve as vehicles for thought, they should be considered in the design of goods and services, delivery systems, and communications.

The specific constructs in the consensus map are metaphors for PG&E, as are the images which operationalize those constructs. Still more fundamental patterns of thought are the deep metaphors inherent in the constructs and images. Customers' deep metaphors with respect to PG&E were developed through content analyses of their multi-sensory images. They include:

- containers
- nature
- people and social relationships
- creation

DIGITAL IMAGES OF PACIFIC GAS AND ELECTRIC

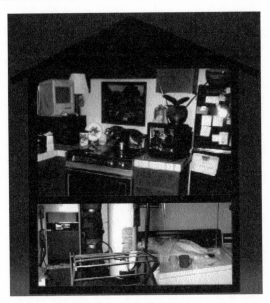

PGE05

So we're thinking about things on a time line and how history has more or less changed by the evolution of these things. You see the microwave which is an alternative cooking method right now but it leads you to what is it going to be next? Also entertainment is coming into the kitchen, instead of being the hearth of the family so to speak over the open fireplace or whatever the TV is actually taking the place of personal interaction. You see the computer that is going to allow that and where man is going to take his imagination and use these tools. Is it going to be good or is going to be bad, whatever are they going to do? It's just amazing. You think over there with the refrigerator that just shows a little bit that exploration was really caused by the necessity of buying spices for rotten meat. How much of this is going to be changed though in a hundred years? Because with the advent of the computer the possibilities are so amazing even what we're generating right now. Is it going to cause even more of the breakdown of a family? Does it get away from cooking as we know it with people really getting in the kitchen, yet at the same time I have to see this as allowing people to break away from traditional roles. You can have fathers who are now capable of raising kids because they can work, they can do it. You're not going to have the traditional mother. It's going to open up the horizons tremendously for women to be able to leave these tasks that have traditionally taken them forever and really more on. But I hope kids learn how to cook, I really do.

The basement level basically, in American everybody expects a washing machine, a dryer, whatever, I have my own, I live by myself, yet look at Rwanda. How do you juxtapose the amount of energy the American family or person is using? Also we expect to be able to have air conditioning, to have heat, to always have them on. To have hot water. To a certain extent we are living a very luxurious life. The tremendous amount of freedom we have compared to our parents even.

EXHIBIT 7-2   Digital Images of Pacific Gas & Electric

DIGITAL IMAGES OF PACIFIC GAS AND ELECTRIC

PGE09

I would choose a picture of a nice house as a background image, as the primary focus. I would add litter out on the curb to show my hesitancy about nuclear power. It would be at nighttime, and I would have at least some lights on in the windows. I would make it abstact-like; the one image I didn't have was of the spider, and I would make it look like it was a photograph, a created image or an artist's rendering, and I would have it walking across the page, not over the center of it because it's not a huge concern to me and the fear is not a big one, it's just sort of underlying. So I would have it maybe just walking across a corner, enough so you could tell it was there. You could shrink the dog and put him at the front door. Overall, these images show every thing I feel, more or less, about PGE. It shows expensive; the house itself is big and gives that feeling of power and wealth, obviously somebody has some control here. There's sort of a peaceful feeling with it being dark and the lights on in the house with people enjoying whatever they're doing at night in their home. The friendly aspect is the dog on the front step. The litter represents to me the beautifulness of what it's creating and the potential ugliness that might be a byproduct. The spider to me is fear - of, specifically, nuclear power but really more with the waste problem, the potential hazards to people and the environment; sort of the unknown.

EXHIBIT 7-2   **Digital Images of Pacific Gas & Electric (cont.)**

DIGITAL IMAGES OF PACIFIC GAS AND ELECTRIC

PGE 15

Well the dryer represents something that I do a lot of but it also represents, like I said, I can remember hanging clothes up and it just makes my life easier. By actually having it there and I do use it a lot. That's what the dryer represents, so I guess it would be ease. Making my life simpler since I have three small children and I work full-time. Moving to the picture with no power lines, it just makes the street nicer, it makes it a nicer place to live. That's what I like about that one. And of course, you always want to make sure that you leave the world a better place for your children so you hope that they [PG&E] take into consideration that there's a future generation coming, we don't spoil everything. And the fish, it just makes life nice in general to see that they are doing something that makes it a nicer place to live basically, having the fishery. The power lines brings back a lot of my childhood—back to the days when you'd have to wait for PG&E to come out to hook up the power lines. We lived basically, pretty much in the country back then. Of course the other one is the street light, of course I never grew up in a street that had lights but, it allows me, it allows my children the opportunities to stay outside a little longer but they like it because it looks like the moon. That's about it.

EXHIBIT 7-2   Digital Images of Pacific Gas & Electric (cont.)

DIGITAL IMAGES OF PACIFIC GAS AND ELECTRIC

PGE 18

The picture with my husband and his office—the typewriter and the computer system makes life easier on the job so it's comforting to know that they're there and they're available and it makes work easier. And then I'm going to move over to the collage picture of the house the front door, it's very comforting to have lighting, for safety in front of your home. And then you go into my son's room, the mess, where he has his toys, his pleasures, his electronic guitar, the TV, the luxuries. And then the top picture, relates comfort because of the softness of the clothes and the coziness of the towels and things that are made possible because of the electric dryer.

EXHIBIT 7-2   **Digital Images of Pacific Gas & Electric (cont.)**

Participants' images generally contained several deep metaphors. For instance, an image of a raging river could include two deep metaphors, nature and containers. The greater the number of deep metaphors a specific metaphor triggered, the more powerful was its impact. Images containing several deep metaphors were especially effective. An analysis of participants' deep metaphors and the more specific metaphors they contained sometimes revealed needs of which they were not fully conscious.

Some of the deep metaphors found in the PG&E research follow.

Containers One common deep metaphor involved the concept of a container. As protective devices or safe havens, containers may relate to basic security needs or the need for nurturance. Several participants created images of things that hold other things including buildings or parts of buildings; places or settings in which objects are made or sold; appliances in which clothing, food, and dishes are placed; and vehicles, shoes, and picnic coolers. Thus, the use of container metaphors in a corporate communication would be meaningful to PG&E customers.

Nature Nature was another deep metaphor that united many of the images created by PG&E customers. The need for control and autonomy may be associated with this metaphor, since nature is often perceived as being out of control or in need of taming. Associated metaphors included images such as waterfalls, trees, flowers, ground, sky, and weather conditions. These nature metaphors often stressed size and expansiveness. Also included were nature-oriented, but man-made, structures like a weathervane, a fish sculpture, a lighthouse, and a cemetery. Given the current importance of environmental concerns, the use of nature as a deep metaphor is not surprising.

People and Social Relationships People and social relationships were salient deep metaphors. Family members and friends were clearly evident in participants' images and interviews; pets and celebrities were also mentioned. Social relationship metaphors, such as parent-child relationships, often expressed feelings of power, especially those involving fathers, which evinced authority, dependency, vulnerability, and caring. Social relationships with PG&E were expressed by relating the people in an image to the size of a container. Customers were typically represented as being or feeling small in relationship to a tall building, tall trees, or an expansive sky. This deep metaphor may represent the basic need for affiliation and nurturance.

Creation One of the most pervasive deep metaphors in participants' images was creation. PG&E customers frequently referred to the diverse activities, events, and emotional or physical states of being made possible by gas and electricity from drying one's hair to the more dramatic instance of a child's being able to read at night to escape from the nightmare of physical abuse. Needs such as self-actualization, self-esteem, and achievement were likely to be involved in this deep metaphor. Hedonistic needs and the basic need for stimulation may also have been relevant.

Finally, deep metaphors may overlap. Both elements of nature and some containers, such as vehicles, have motion—another deep metaphor. Some containers, like rivers are expressive of nature; others, like power lines, may be perceived as intruding on nature. When represented by an expansive sky or a tall tree viewed from its base, nature also conveys the notion of a social relationship with PG&E.

A communications program that makes creative use of such ideas will facilitate what customers are prone to do anyway: perceive information in terms of deep metaphors. Using well-chosen metaphors enhances the likelihood that customers will make the interpretations a firm intends to convey. The next section details how PG&E used the results of the ZMET throughout its business.

PG&E's Experience with ZMET

WHAT PG&E GAINED FROM ZMET

ZMET research made several contributions to PG&E. It elicited a deeper level of information from customers than had other research methods, making more salient the complexity of PG&E's relationship with customers and the broad range of customer contact points that must be managed effectively. The consensus map indicated appropriate entry points and important constructs in communicating with consumers. The multimedia and written reports appealed to different audiences, broadening the reach of the research among various corporate users.

Deeper Level of Information PG&E conducts frequent research to determine what customers think about the company, its brand image, and its performance. The ZMET technique, however, elicited a deeper level of information from customers. Many of the issues customers raised involved personal and emotional needs. One person showed a photo of a bedside lamp: as a child PG&E's electricity had allowed her to read long into the night providing a spiritual escape from childhood abuse.

Another customer talked about how PG&E had enabled him to have deep personal friendships, because he could invite guests to a warm, well-lit house. Other customers talked about fear, dependence, emotional comfort, security, and vanity. In addition to the new information ZMET provided, its insights helped PG&E to interpret information provided by other research.

Greater Range of Brand Connections   PG&E's purpose in doing the ZMET study was to decide how to position and manage the corporate brand. The ZMET research reminded the company of the complexity of its relationship with customers, and the broad range of ways in which its image is projected. Customers described the impressions they had formed of PG&E from its advertising, phone representatives, service calls, and statements, as well as from the crews working along streets, the tone of a thank-you note, the greeting of a meter reader, the appearance of the power lines, and the personality of an acquaintance employed by PG&E. One customer summed it up by saying, "PG&E is like the air, it's everywhere." The ZMET results stressed the importance of managing each of these many contact points to achieve a positive brand image overall.

Key Constructs Map   One of the most useful outputs from the ZMET project was the map of key constructs shown in Figure 7-1. As PG&E interpreted it, it carried several important messages. First, the map has a limited number of "entry points" (origination constructs). By linking messages to those constructs, PG&E can connect with customers more directly. If PG&E's communications do not fit with one of the entry points, customers could misinterpret them.

The second message of the key-constructs map is its list of some of the more salient issues for customers. This list has been used on several occasions. For example, when PG&E staff began developing the architecture for its World Wide Web site, they looked at the constructs map to make sure they were addressing the issues customers had identified. The list was also used to help senior management think about brand positioning and corporate contributions' philosophy.

Finally, the key constructs map helped PG&E to understand which topics led to dead ends. Price is an originator construct that dead ends immediately in the destination construct "bad/good feeling." Usually the feeling is bad. Whether the company says it dropped prices or raised them matters little, if at all; most customer reactions to price messages of any kind are negative. This finding is consistent with the experience of the local phone company in San Francisco. When it announced a forty percent price drop, many customers responded negatively, saying that the price reduction implied the company had overcharged them before.

Multimedia Report The ZMET project provided PG&E with a written report and a CD-ROM that incorporated the pictures customers brought to the interviews with their "voice-over" comments. The CD-ROM also included thirty-second vignettes and summary digital "collages." The vignettes consist of imagined video or home movies expressing a customer's thoughts and feelings. The digital collage, in contrast, is a still image created on a computer screen. PG&E found both reports extremely useful. Market researchers and some of the managers found the written reports most helpful, whereas the "creatives" involved in designing PG&E's advertising and World Wide Web site found the visually-based results more useful. The creative director of PG&E's advertising agency exclaimed, "Now this is research I can really USE!" And during the early design of the web site, the project manager reported that the projects' creative director sat down with the CD-ROM for the better part of a morning. The manager doubted he would have even read a written report.

PG&E's Use of ZMET Results

Various uses followed directly from the knowledge gains just mentioned. Specifically, the information that was gathered was used in brand positioning, Internet communications, reflection on corporate philosophies, advertising, and the design of newsletters and brochures.

Brand Positioning Brand positioning was the primary reason PG&E was interested in ZMET. The results provided powerful imagery that has been particularly useful in the development and evaluation of PG&E's new positioning.

Internet Communications These ZMET results were used in the early stages of designing PG&E's World Wide Web site. They were helpful in developing the fundamental architecture of the site, creating navigation labels, and choosing the content and editorial style. The ZMET work is expected to continue to be useful as the company expands the information services it offers through the Internet.

Corporate Contributions PG&E is in the process of evaluating and revising its contributions' philosophy. The company used ZMET to assess different philosophies of giving and determine potential areas on which to focus.

Advertising Over the long run, the creative department at PG&E's advertising agency may be the greatest user of ZMET work. The thirty-second vignettes provide ideas and images for commercials. The visual dictionary is a resource for metaphors, pictures, and ideas for creative development. The deep metaphors identify images and concepts that are especially powerful or consistent with consumers' perceptions of the company. They may also help the agency to avoid overloading ads with powerful images that may inadvertently detract from the key message because of their metaphorical power.

Newsletters, Brochures, and Other Collateral Material ZMET research will be helpful to PG&E in the development of a broad range of customer communications. Its insights into which colors, images, and messages to avoid should be particularly useful.

CHALLENGES OF ZMET

While ZMET has been of great value to PG&E in providing background knowledge and guidance for specific tasks and decisions, it also poses certain challenges. The greatest is to understand how to use its results effectively. As an organization, PG&E is relatively new at using customer data to position and grow its brand and to design and market its products. Although the company is improving its ability to operationalize the results of more traditional linear research, it is not yet skilled in dealing with ZMET's multifaceted metaphor-based data. One senior executive noted that though the images were very powerful, and he could still see the digital images in his mind's eye, he was not sure how to make decisions based on the data or to communicate what he had learned to others. The general guidelines being developed by ZMET's staff should be helpful in meeting this challenge.

While ZMET identifies the key constructs that underlie customer thought and behavior, the small sample size does not permit an assessment of the relative importance of the key constructs. Neither does it provide a measure of the strength of association between constructs.

Relative importance and strength of associations are best explored using follow-up survey research. Survey research might also uncover associations among constructs not identified by the consensus map. A practical limitation of the technique is that it is also very labor intensive. Considerable time is required to encode the data following the transcription of the audiotapes and later to develop interactive materials involving customers' images and voices.

Conclusions and Future Directions

Firms often have great difficulty in learning about customers' deep thoughts, which are usually hidden and difficult to express. That is, they often encounter problems in getting what is inside the customer's mind out and into the mind of the manager. These problems are sometimes compounded by boundaries between the people who collect customer information and those who use it: the doers and users of research often have different frames of reference.

The firm–customer boundary is partly rooted in the limited capacity of traditional research methods. The ZMET helps to overcome that limitation. ZMET is founded on current knowledge in the social and biological sciences and the humanities, particularly the complex link between perception, memory, representation, and cognition.[7] It uses computer imaging techniques to empower customers to explore and express their ideas. The process of asking customers to locate visual images of their own prior to the interview, together with the probing procedures used during the interview, makes the use of digital imaging all the more effective.

Validation studies with clients indicate that this method surpasses others in providing useful insights (e.g., Greenspan et al. 1996; Lieber 1997; see also, Zaltman and Coulter 1995; Zaltman and Higie 1993). Validation studies typically involved comparing ZMET results with proprietary data already collected by the client using a standard research technique such as a survey, focus group, or in some cases, proprietary methods. The manner in which information is elicited from customers and the way in which it is presented to users helps to reduce the boundaries between researchers and clients. Still, ways of enhancing the technique's usefulness are being explored. They include the use of voice pitch analysis, further work with the vignettes, the development of nonvisual sensory images, the creation of digital images by managers, and the use of graphs to segment customers based on the reasoning chains in the consensus map. We are also experimenting with other multimedia formats.

ZMET is also being used in contexts other than market research. A basic social science research tool, it is useful in understanding myriad organizational issues and publics other than customers. We are also extending the technique to situations in which the group is the unit of analysis. Relevant groups include product management teams, cross-functional teams, boards of directors, workers, and others. Research can involve the surfacing of unspoken group maps, or the development of new ones.

Endnotes

1. It is not always necessary to go beyond surface thoughts and feelings. These, too, are important and can be sufficient for addressing some business problems.
2. Management science has stressed the role of logic and de-emphasizes and even tries to eliminate other qualities of thought. This tendency spills over into much research on customers.
3. A major failing of customer behavior models and research methods is their inability to acknowledge that a person may have conflicting thoughts and feelings, which are often important drivers of action.
4. In general, the deeper or more fundamental the thought/feeling that is elicited, the greater the likelihood is of its being widely shared by a defined group of people (Brown 1991; Kuchler and Melion 1991; Resnick et al. 1991), and the more likely it is to endure over time.
5. For more on the way in which memory, cognition, and representation interact, see Kuchler and Melion (1991).
6. Of the over 2500 people who have participated in ZMET projects, only one person ever failed to collect pictures. This happened in the PG&E project. In this instance, the interviewer prompted the individual about pictures in his mind's eye and drew them on index cards. The interview proceeded well.
7. For an extensive review of the supporting literature, see Zaltman 1997.

References

Vincent P. Barabba, *The Meeting of Minds* (Boston: Harvard Business School Press, 1995).

—— and Gerald Zaltman, *Hearing the Voice of the Market* (Boston: Harvard Business School Press, 1991).

Donald E. Brown, *Human Universals* (New York: McGraw-Hill, 1991).

Judee K. Burgoon, David B. Buller, and W. Gill Woodall, *Nonverbal Communication: The Unspoken Dialogue* (New York: Harper and Row, 1989) 155*ff.*

Antonio R. Damasio, *Descartes' Error: Emotion, Reason, and the Human Brain* (New York: G.P. Putnam's Sons, 1994).

Ronald de Sousa, *The Rationality of Emotion* (Cambridge, MA: The MIT Press, 1987).

Gerald M. Edelman, *Bright Air, Brilliant Fire* (New York: Basic Books, 1992).

Raymond W. Gibbs, Jr., *The Poetics of Mind: Figurative Thought, Language, and Understanding* (New York: Cambridge University Press, 1994).

Steven Greenspan et al., "Conceptual Experiences of Computer Mediated Communication: An Application of the Zaltman Metaphor Elicitation Technique," (working paper, Murray Hill, NJ: AT&T Labs, 1996).

Mark Johnson, *The Body in the Mind: The Bodily Basis of Meaning, Imagination, and Reason* (Chicago: The University of Chicago Press, 1987).

—— "The Imaginative Basis of Meaning and Cognition," in Susanne Kuchler and Walter Melion (eds.), *Images of Memory: On Remembering and Representation* (Washington, DC: Smithsonian Institution Press, 1991), 74–86.

Susanne Kuchler and Walter Melion (eds.), *Images of Memory: On Remembering and Representation* (Washington, DC: Smithsonian Institution Press, 1991).

George Lakoff, *Women, Fire, and Dangerous Things: What Categories Reveal about the Mind* (Chicago: The University of Chicago Press, 1987).

Ron Lieber, "Storytelling," *Fortune* (February 3, 1997) 103*ff.*

Michael Leyton, *Symmetry, Causality and Mind* (Cambridge, MA: The MIT Press, 1992).

Stephen McAdams and Emmanuel Bigard, "Introduction to Auditory Cognition," in Stephen McAdams and Emmanuel Bigard (eds.), *Thinking in Sound: The Cognitive Psychology of Human Audition* (Oxford: Clarendon Press, 1993).

Steven Pinker, *The Language Instinct: How the Mind Creates Language* (Cambridge, MA: The MIT Press, 1994).

Fernando Poyatos, *Paralanguage: A Linguistic and Interdisciplinary Approach to Interactive Speech and Sound* (Philadelphia: John Benjamins Publishing, 1993).

Lauren B. Resnick, "Shared Cognition: Thinking as Social Practice," in Lauren B. Resnick, John M. Levine, and Stephanie D. Teasley (eds.), *Perspectives on Socially Shared Cognition* (Washington, DC: American Psychological Association, 1991) 1–20.

Francisco J. Varela, Evan Thompson, and Eleanor Rosch, *The Embodied Mind: Cognitive Science and Human Experience* (Cambridge, MA: The MIT Press, 1991).

Judy Weiser, *PhotoTherapy Techniques: Exploring the Secrets of Personal Snapshots and Family Albums* (San Francisco: Jossey-Bass Publishers, 1993).

Robert C. Ziller, *Photographing the Self: Methods for Observing Personal Orientation* (Newbury Park, CA: Sage Publications, 1990).

Gerald Zaltman, "Rethinking Market Research: Putting People Back In," (working paper, Boston, MA: Harvard Graduate School of Business, 1997), 1–117.

—— and Robin Coulter, "Seeing the Voice of the Customer: Metaphor-Based Advertising Research," *Journal of Advertising Research* 3(1995) 35–51.

—— and Robin Higie, *Seeing the Voice of the Customer: The Zaltman Metaphor Elicitation Technique* (working paper 93-114, Cambridge, MA: The Marketing Science Institute, 1993).

PART THREE

Responding with Capabilities

8 | *Product Development on the Internet*

Marco Iansiti and Alan MacCormack

In 1993, a group of experienced design engineers from one of Silicon Valley's hottest workstation manufacturers met for the first time to define the concept for their next generation product, due out in 1996. To outline the specification, they turned their attention to the industries expected to represent significant target markets. In one of these, multimedia, most analysts were betting that video on demand would eventually take over and dominate. A lone voice at the meeting raised the issue of a small but growing global network called the Internet. But its potential market seemed limited—it was used mainly by scientists and the military. And anyway, serious software developers like Microsoft were "not in the online business," according to executives.

Three years later, video on demand was dead, and everyone, from IBM to your grandmother, had a web

Note: Earlier research on this topic was presented in Marco Iansiti and Alan MacCormack, "Living on Internet Time: Product Development at Netscape, Yahoo!™, NetDynamics, and Microsoft®," Case 9-697-052 (Boston, MA: Harvard Business School, 1996) and Marco Iansiti, *Technology Integration: Making Critical Choices in a Dynamic World* (Boston, MA: Harvard Business School Press, 1998), chapter 9.

site on the Internet. Netscape and Yahoo!, companies that didn't exist in 1993, were household names, in total worth over $5 billion. And in a stunning about-face, even Microsoft had radically changed its strategic orientation to focus on online computing.

Imagine running an R&D organization in this type of world. A world in which the pace is not expected to slow, as firms jockey for position to set the standards in emerging markets. Clearly, firms in these markets must adapt to constant changes in technical opportunities, markets, and customer preferences (Eisenhardt and Tabrizi 1995; Tushman and O'Reilly 1997). Yet developing this type of technology takes time. About three years are required for a major workstation development or software operating system release to move from conceptualization to market introduction. How can companies make such long-term commitments when customer preferences are continually evolving? Clearly, the traditional model of R&D—a sequential chain of steps comprising careful research followed by the development of a product concept that is rigidly frozen and then meticulously executed—simply does not work in such environments.

In response, leading firms operating in these types of industries have pioneered a new and more flexible process for product development. To achieve this, they have built skills in "technology integration," a mechanism for more closely matching technical choices made during design to the requirements of the environment in which a product operates (Iansiti 1997). In this approach to R&D, the concept design and implementation phases overlap, allowing product specifications to evolve gradually with the emergence of new information. Users are integrated into the development process, facilitating rapid and continuous feedback on a product's performance and its match with customers' preferences. And extensive use is made of experimentation, to generate knowledge of how a product's features interact with its application context.

This new model for product development emerged initially at Microsoft, one of the first firms to work at conquering the challenges of developing novel and complex products in a rapidly changing environment. Netscape, Yahoo!, and NetDynamics were among the firms that improved on Microsoft's approach, gearing it up for use on the Internet. Recently, Microsoft has responded by re-inventing its own development process to tackle this rapidly growing market.

This chapter tells the story of the changes that have swept through the software industry. It starts by developing a framework for a flexible model of product development. It then shows this model in action by examining the product development practices in four organizations that develop Internet software products and services. The examples are chosen to exemplify practice in diverse Internet software environments, and vary in both technical complexity and market risk. The accounts included summarize extensive field work conducted at firms competing in rapidly changing markets (MacCormack and Iansiti 1997, and Iansiti 1997 provide details on the field work methods employed). They highlight common patterns and important differences in approach, and illustrate the mechanisms that underlie their effective implementation.

Technology Integration: The Key to Flexible Development

Traditional models for R&D tend to emphasize the need to avoid unnecessary change and uncertainty during development. They are built on a structured process, with clearly defined sequential phases, through which a future product is designed and implemented (Cooper 1990; Ulrich and Eppinger 1994). A clear project-definition phase and stable product concept are the goal. The objective is a focused and efficient execution, achieved through strong project leadership, simultaneous engineering, and team-based organization.

In such models there is a distinct difference between concept development and implementation. Extensive efforts are first made to identify customer needs and assess the feasibility of new technologies. A detailed and thorough concept document is then developed and presented for approval. If approved, the concept is frozen, and attention shifts to its implementation. A good project is characterized by minimal changes at this point: if the early work has been done "right," later changes, which are inherently expensive, should not be necessary.

This model of R&D works well when technology, product features, and competitive requirements are predictable (Clark and Fujimoto 1991; Wheelwright and Clark 1992). If changes in technologies and markets can be forecast, delaying the concept freeze provides no benefit—the focus of the entire effort should be on completing all stages as quickly as possible. However, recent research in fast-moving technology-driven industries shows that leading firms embrace change rather than fight it. The new approach is characterized by its emphasis on flexibility (Iansiti 1995; 1997; Thomke 1996; MacCormack and Iansiti 1997). In essence, the concept development stage continues as long as the specification is evolving. Significant, systemic changes in a project's definition and basic direction are managed proactively in a process that starts without a precise idea of how the effort will end.

The key to the new approach is the ability to gather and rapidly respond to new knowledge about a technology and its application context on an ongoing basis, even after implementation has begun. As Figure 8-1 shows, this approach moves the concept freeze as close to the market introduction of a product as possible.

In the flexible model, concept development and implementation became tightly linked rather than separated. Project managers move back and forth between fundamental, architectural choices ("core concepts") and the detailed design. Work on the project is integrated and tested at regular intervals, and feedback from those tests integrated into the design. This "design-build-test" sequence repeats continuously as long as the concept development and implementation phases overlap. Finally, a stabilization phase follows, in which engineers focus on bringing the final product up to required levels of reliability. While some up-front design work is inevitably wasted with this approach, the need to respond rapidly to unpredictable changes in technology or market conditions make iteration essential.[1]

Speed is a subtle concept in this model. In a highly novel and complex environment, although total lead time is important, concept lead time and development lead time are critical measures in their own right. Concept lead time represents the "window of opportunity" for including new information and optimizing the match between a technology and its application. Development lead time represents the time during which that window is closed, the product's architecture is frozen, and new information cannot be taken into account. Although the total lead time is the same in Figures 8-1A and 8-1B, the project shown in Figure 8-1B is preferable to that shown in Figure 8-1A in a fast-changing environment. The shorter the development lead time is, the

A. Traditional Model

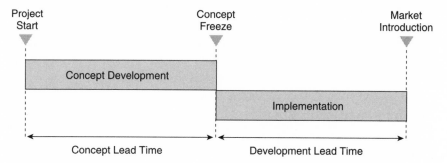

B. Flexible Model

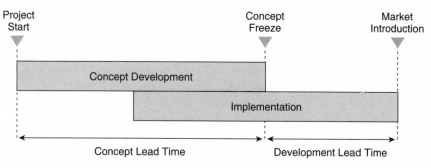

FIGURE 8-1   **Two Models of Product Development**

greater an organization's ability to respond to change will be. The most critical time-to-market measure is the time that elapses after the concept has been frozen.

Product development flexibility is rooted in the joint evolution of a technology and its application context. In traditional high technology industries, changes have been driven primarily by advances in the technical knowledge base. In semiconductors, for instance, the main customer requirements, processing speed and memory capacity, have remained relatively stable. The complexity of the application context has therefore been driven by manufacturing challenges. In emerging markets, however, much of the challenge is associated with applications that are external to the firm. In Internet software, for example, complexity arises from the evolving network architecture and user environments. In sum, while high-tech R&D has traditionally been "internally" driven, aimed at conquering technical and manufacturing challenges, effective development for emerging markets like the Internet must be as much "externally" focused, emphasizing the need to rapidly sense and then respond to turbulent market conditions.

The need to manage the joint evolution of a technology and its application context is illustrated by developments in the software industry. Traditional software development methodologies relied on an extensive specification phase, followed by a frozen product concept and a long period of detailed coding by software engineers. A troublesome integration phase, during which the product finally came together, ended the process. Severe delays resulted: products rarely shipped on time, and when they did, they were out of step with current market requirements. A way was needed to match the evolution of a product's design with changing market requirements.

Microsoft was one of the first companies to meet this challenge (Cusumano and Selby 1995). The evolution of its R&D process provides a good illustration of how skills in technology integration build flexibility into the development process.

Product Development at Microsoft

In the early 1980s, Microsoft's development process was informal, with little emphasis on schedule or process. Projects were driven by a few star developers, who had almost total control of a product's design. Like Bill Gates, most early Microsoft developers had little or no formal training in computing, though many had expertise in other fields, particularly math and science. Perhaps because of their lack of formal training, most of these "stars" (called technical leads) did not follow the highly structured software development methodologies created by the Department of Defense and large corporate MIS departments. Their exploits were legendary:

> There was one guy who could type at eighty words a minute. That's pretty impressive, but what's really impressive was that he actually wrote code at that speed. He'd write a ten thousand line application in two days, then if it didn't work, he'd throw it out and start again from scratch. He'd go through this process two or three times, until he ended up with a working program. Not only did it take him less time to do this than if he had sat down and tried to think everything out in advance, but the program that resulted was better too. Because he had implemented the same program several times before, he knew how to avoid all the pitfalls.[2]

Design and scheduling were equally idiosyncratic. One of Microsoft's early developers described his ideal audience:

I design user interfaces to please an audience of one. I write it for me. If I'm happy I know some cool people will like it. Designing user interfaces by committee does not work very well: they need to be coherent. As for schedules, I'm not interested in schedules; did anyone care when *War and Peace* came out?[3]

Not surprisingly given such attitudes and approaches, what a product would look like and when it would be released were frequently mysteries. Bill Gates was one of the few controls in the process, influencing developers through his attendance at intense project reviews.

During the late 1980s, Microsoft's software development projects, and the R&D organization needed to implement them, began to grow substantially in size and complexity, posing enormous challenges for developers. In the mid-1980s, a major application project might have included five developers; ten years later, it required more than fifty. The ad-hoc development process that had worked well for Microsoft to this point began to show signs of strain. Large application development projects increasingly fell behind schedule, often shipping years after the target introduction; and when they were finally complete, most had undergone major changes to the specification several times over.

In response to these problems, several proposals were made to improve Microsoft's development process. They were aimed at enhancing the quality and reliability of product development, and at increasing its flexibility and responsiveness. The new approach, detailed in a now famous "zero defects memo" written in 1990, was to let the specification change during the course of a project—the technological and market uncertainties were too great to allow accurate long-range predictions of final specifications. But rather than doing this in the haphazard manner of old, the new approach would achieve this in a controlled fashion, driven by frequent experimentation and daily integration of results into an "evolving" product design.

The process worked in the following way. After conducting considerable market analysis and several focus groups, product managers described the unfilled needs a new product should address. A "Program Manager" then translated these general market needs into broad project objectives, set forth in a vision statement and an "outline product specification." Developers then worked from the outline specification to bring the objectives to life. As they strove to code the desired features and optimize the software's performance, they discovered problems and potential improvements, which they discussed with the program manager. If necessary, the program manager changed the

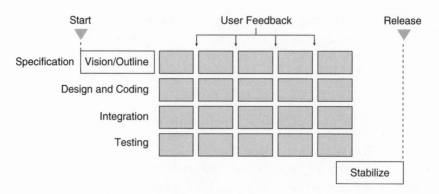

FIGURE 8-2   Microsoft's Flexible Development Process

specification. This cycle was repeated frequently until the project was finished (Figure 8-2).

At the start of a project, the features in the outline specification would be divided into bundles, each to be coded and tested separately. The product would progress from a simple (but functional) skeleton to a complete application in a controlled and testable fashion that program managers could closely follow. Programming tasks were split among the many team members and integrated as frequently as possible (often daily) into a functional prototype of the entire system. The ideal was to produce "a shippable product every day," adding desired features and product improvements according to priority. Developers worked on the most critical features first, and gradually expanded the product's feature set until it was time to ship it.

This new process allowed much deeper and more systematic customer feedback during development. Each of the major prototypes could be tested by customers in individual sessions or focus groups. This generated a substantial amount of knowledge within the project about the reliability of existing features, the potential of new technical options, and the product's performance in meeting customers' expectations. The feedback was incorporated as the project progressed, through the addition or removal of features in a controlled fashion. Thus, the product design evolved to match its application context.

Organizational and cultural changes at Microsoft complemented the new process. Developers and testers were assigned to work with each other on a one-to-one basis. This change promoted rapid feedback to developers; as a result, new parts of the code could be checked prior to their integration into the complete system. In addition, Microsoft's program managers became the primary drivers in a development project, exerting a strong influence on the company's future. One program manager described the role:

> The key is to be able to create and articulate a vision of the product. A good program manager must be comfortable with the technical aspects of the specification and know-how to change it, as the specification evolves. The ideal program manager would probably have a development background. The key, however, is to have the knowledge and ability to talk to developers in their own language. A program manager therefore needs strong design skills as well as good people management skills.

Program managers had responsibility for the entire specification, including the most critical tradeoffs. They had to take a holistic view, making sure that the component technologies being developed would work seamlessly at the system level, to create a well-integrated, reliable, and coherent product. They also made sure that the specification was updated to meet evolving market needs. Program managers at Microsoft had become the de facto technology integrators in a project.

Product Development on the Internet

With its new development process, Microsoft tackled a problem fundamental to all competitors in the rapidly evolving software industry. But even they did not recognize that the pace of technological change in some segments required even more innovative measures. By 1993, the program manager concept had evolved into a hugely successful method for managing large-scale development projects. However, several small organizations were experimenting with a networking technology developed by a group of Swiss scientists in the late 1960s. That technology was to become the Internet.

The firms that first chose to exploit the Internet were looking for radically new business models to exploit the disadvantages of their relatively small size. They used the network to distribute their products, saving the huge overhead associated with packaging and retailing. They used it to get early and rapid feedback on their products' performance, avoiding the need for internal testing. In essence, they turned size to their advantage, developing new product releases in incredibly short development cycles, often only a few months long. Their world was moving on "Internet time."

Three firms were among the leaders of this movement: Netscape, Yahoo!, and NetDynamics. As highlighted later in this chapter, the processes followed by all firms exhibit some striking similarities. However, there are also important differences, driven by the specific natures of their environments. Each competed in a different segment of "cyberspace," and faced different levels of technical complexity and market risk. For Netscape, the major challenge was coping with an increasing level of technical complexity, which motivated their use of their vast and often highly sophisticated customer base as an aid to experimentation and testing. For Yahoo!, the major concern was including feedback from users while managing the high degree of market risk in their service—they did not want the average user to be frustrated with trial versions, which explains their emphasis on internal testing. NetDynamics needed to tackle both types of challenges—a highly complex product and a high degree of market risk. Because it lacked any established user base, it could not afford to alienate potential customers with unreliable prototypes, and relied instead upon a few carefully selected lead users.

Netscape: Navigator 3.0

In mid-1996, Netscape Communications released the third version of its popular Internet browser "Netscape Navigator," which today commands the lion's share of the worldwide market. The company was founded on April 4, 1994, by Jim Clark and several University of Illinois students who had helped to develop the first graphical browser for the Internet, "NCSA Mosaic." Netscape improved on Mosaic with its Navigator application, which rapidly became the standard for browser software. When the company went public in August 1995, it quickly achieved a market value exceeding $5 billion. By June 1996, the firm had hired more than eleven hundred people, and was recruiting at a pace of forty new employees per week. Today, Netscape markets a whole range of Internet-related products, such as corporate intranet software, development tools, and software for managing Internet servers.

Netscape's development process is characterized by the early release of a product to interested users, long before product features have been established. The product goes through multiple "beta" versions, which are gradually and systematically improved through user feedback. In this way, the *customer base* helps the product to evolve until it is robust and complete enough for general release. A look at how Navigator 3.0 was developed will help to illustrate the process.

Navigator 2.0 was shipped in January 1996. Soon after, the development group began work on the next version, known as Atlas. The team assigned to Atlas included about twenty engineers who would focus on

Navigator's overall architecture and user interface. Other groups would work on designing program components common to other products ("plug-ins"), such as Java applications and security routines. The core team thus served as the technology integrator, working with other internal and external groups. While the development team included staff from other functions such as marketing, in the absence of a formal program management function, the project was driven by engineering.

The first system-level prototype was produced extremely quickly. By February 14, a "Beta 0" version had been put on an internal web site, for use by the development staff. Though the prototype was incomplete, it embodied the essence of the new design. On February 22, it was updated with a "Beta 1" version, again for internal use only. The first public release, "Beta 2," appeared on Netscape's web site in early March. Additional public releases were introduced every two or three weeks thereafter until the product's official release in August (Figure 8-3).

This sequence of beta versions was extremely useful to Netscape, because it enabled developers to react to feedback from users as well as changes in the marketplace. Because Beta users tend to be more sophisticated than Netscape's broader customer base, they are a valuable source of feedback. Most useful among them are developers from other Internet

FIGURE 8-3   The Development of Navigator 3.0

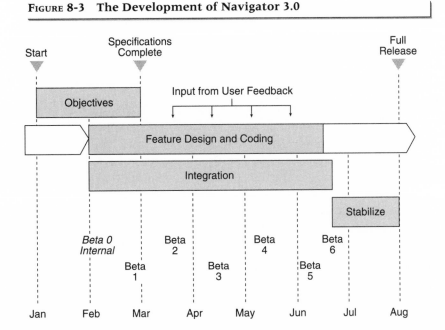

software companies, who tend to be the most vocal customers—especially those who use Navigator as part of the environment in which their own products operate. Another important source of customer feedback is "newsgroups," users' online discussions of the latest software releases and the bugs they contain. As an example, newsgroups alone were responsible for more than one hundred changes in Navigator 3.0's design over the life of the project.

To facilitate handling the vast amount of feedback obtained, an internal project web site was established on Netscape's intranet. This site contained the development schedule and product specification, which were updated as dates changed or new features were added. The site also contained bulletin boards for various parts of the design, and progress charts to track the completion of specific features or note bugs in existing code. These management tools were especially valuable when the product moved into the beta testing phase, since the amount of information to be received, classified, and processed grew significantly. Ultimately, they were especially helpful in determining when the existing beta version was thought stable enough for general release.

During the whole development cycle, the Navigator team also paid careful attention to competing products. As the largest and most powerful software developer in the industry, Microsoft's competing product, "Microsoft Explorer," is considered the most serious threat. Hence, engineers continually monitored the features and layout of the latest Explorer versions. Based on feedback from these trials, the Netscape team often added format and feature changes to their current Beta version.

Yahoo!: "My Yahoo!"

Yahoo!, an Internet service provider, operates search, directory, and programming services for navigating the increasingly complex environment of the World Wide Web. Founded in April 1995, the company went public one year later with a market valuation exceeding $500 million. In mid-1996, Yahoo! employed a staff of eighty, about half of whom were "surfers" whose job was to "travel the net," looking for new sites and classifying them for input to their proprietary database. The remaining employees focused on service development, advertising, and marketing.

Like many Internet-related firms, Yahoo! makes all its money from advertising revenues. For a potential advertiser, Yahoo!'s attraction is plain: as of June 1996, its web site received an average of nine million page views a day, from a base of approximately ten million users. The site was the second most popular site on the Internet (after Netscape). Yahoo!'s service philosophy is to minimize the amount of time users must spend at its site. According to the vice president of engineering "We know the user really wants fast access to other [home] pages, not ours. Hence we keep the graphics content of our pages low so that they will load faster."

In mid-1996, Yahoo! had a total of thirteen software engineers assigned to development. They were generally allocated full time to specific projects, with most projects carried out by small teams. Whenever a project neared completion, however, additional resources were often pulled from other projects to help get the product out the door. "We manage priorities, not projects," said the vice president of engineering. "Over the short term, we assume the number of people available to a project is fourteen, including me."

The firm's flexibility goes beyond the allocation of tasks. Given the nature of its product and the small size of its teams (which can be as small as a single person), Yahoo!'s engineers must possess a mix of skills. They must be broad enough to recognize the market requirements for the concepts they are developing, and deep enough to execute those requirements in software code. Engineers are also encouraged to be spontaneous in pursuing opportunities for additional services. For example, a few weeks before the "My Yahoo!" project (described later in this chapter) was due to go online, the chief developer, needing a break, spent the hours between midnight and 6 AM developing a new sports page to carry news and scores from the European soccer championships. By 9 AM, after a short demonstration to the first VP who had arrived, the service had been put online. Over the four weeks the competition ran, it became the most popular page on the firm's site with more than one hundred thousand visits per day. Indeed, when the Reuters news service automatic link went down one day, one of Yahoo!'s founders—the only developer with some spare time—jumped on a terminal and began typing in the scores manually.

Yahoo!'s development process is similar to Netscape's, in that it emphasizes the slow release of software to users as a product becomes progressively more robust. Early versions of new services are first put online internally. Given the development team's technical skills, these trials expose any major technical flaws and provide suggestions for ways in which the software can be improved. Once changes have been made the service is put online, but without links to highly frequented parts of Yahoo!'s web site, and without promotion. At this stage, only technically aggressive users are likely to find and use the service. The online trial exposes the service to rigorous external testing without revealing it to unsophisticated users, who might become frustrated by a slow, incomplete, or error-ridden prototype. Finally, at the official launch, the product is heavily promoted, normally through a direct link to the site from Yahoo!'s home page.

Scalability is a major technical challenge for development projects, given the uncertainty about potential usage. At present, Yahoo! meets its processing needs with a small number of inexpensive servers. Such low investment requirements mean that capacity can be scaled smoothly to meet demand. In the words of the vice president of engineering:

> We have to be really concerned about volumes. If we promote a service on our home page, it will be seen by five million people each day. Even if only a small number "click the button," we will get hundreds of thousands of hits. In a similar manner, too much early success can be bad. Overloads slow the system before you have a chance to build capacity. Then you lose the early adopters, who might migrate to a faster service. Structuring capacity in small chunks gives us flexibility. Our web site setup works just like a spigot valve. If we want to test out a product on several thousand users, we put it up on the home page on only a few machines.

Apart from enabling a quick response to fluctuations in demand, Yahoo!'s setup allows it to experiment with its software, running multiple versions with varying features on each server, and tracking response rates. Yahoo! can also influence which customers will try a new service. By promoting a new product from a specific page in the main directory, the company filters users before they gain access to the new offering.

Yahoo!'s development process can be illustrated by its My Yahoo! project (Figure 8-4). "My Yahoo!" is an individualized set of pages containing features, stories, and news items previously registered by a user. The project was formally started in January 1996, with a specification consisting mainly of a list of features drawn up by the company founders. One full-time employee was assigned to the project, who although new to Yahoo!, had previously spent five years developing and using CAD software. By early February he had produced a prototype of the product, comprising ten to twelve sample web pages. After its approval by the founders, he began coding, and by the end of March, the first partially working version was complete and available to Yahoo! employees.

During March and April, several competitors brought out similar products to the one Yahoo! planned. Yahoo!'s developers took time to evaluate them and compare them with their own. The marketing VP noted:

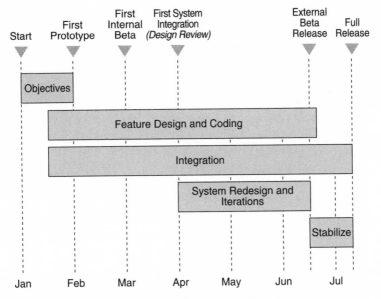

FIGURE 8-4   The Development of My Yahoo! Project

We thought they were rather dull and decided that they weren't really adding significant value over a basic search service. The problem was that they encompassed all the features that we had been planning to incorporate! We needed a major rethink. After a thorough review, we defined additional features, configurations, and content to make the product more aggressive and exciting.

At about the same time, the vice president of engineering decided to rewrite the original design using a different language, to allow it to scale up for higher volumes. Hence, the team was expanded to two full-time employees, responsible for both developing new features and recoding the original design. A target date of June 17 was established for a "soft" launch (an external release with no promotion). At the beginning of June, the team was increased to three people, and the first version of the new system, complete with new code and features, was integrated. This expansion of the team late in the project produced major changes in the software as the feature set was refined. For example, the team developed a completely new stock-quote system and a search engine that better matched the service's requirements. *The technical lead estimated that over fifty percent of the software was changed during the last four weeks of the project.*

After a month of monitoring feedback from beta users, My Yahoo! was officially launched on July 15, 1996, promoted by a direct link from the home page. Within six weeks, over one hundred thousand users had registered their preferences. But development did not stop. As the VP of marketing pointed out, "we already have a couple of thousand e-mails telling us how to improve the service. When you read five hundred of them telling you we need a link to the football scores or the weather in Canada, its pretty clear what the priorities are! We just wouldn't have got that from a focus group."

NetDynamics: Net Dynamics 2.0

NetDynamics provides development tools for the design of web pages that link to companies' internal databases. The product is extremely easy to use, and extremely "open": it supports Internet and database software from any vendor (e.g., both Microsoft's "Explorer" and Netscape's "Navigator" browsers). The company, originally called Spider Technologies, developed its first product for the UNIX operating system and launched it in August 1995. The rapid growth of Microsoft's "Windows NT" operating system soon made it clear, however, that this product would have to run on the NT platform as well. Late in 1995, it was decided that rather than trying to port the original UNIX design to the Windows system, it would develop a completely new version for both.

Design work began on December 1, 1995. Seven engineers were recruited, each of whom had a background in developing software for Windows-based systems. They joined the two engineers who had developed the original product. The initial target was to have a new product ready by the end of February 1996.

During December, the team defined the basic system architecture and developed a simple prototype of the product, comprising a mock-up of potential web pages. Existing customers were shown the prototype, then given a list of potential additional options and features and asked to rank them in importance. The results of this exercise were tabulated and used to inform design trade-offs. For example, as a direct result, the new product was designed to emphasize security, a major concern of users, given the access the tool provides to internal data. In addition, as the schedule did not allow enough time to develop a full web page editor, it was decided to make the program general enough that users could employ any commercially available editor to develop their applications with.

The single most important technical decision made during this period was the choice of a scripting language. By the end of December, the company had reviewed five alternatives: their own proprietary language (code named "E"); Visual Basic (a popular and simple language); C++ (a popular more sophisticated language); Python (a specialized language); and Java. The choice was eventually reduced to either "E" or Java, the two that would offer the maximum speed and greatest simplicity for users. Making such trade-offs was accomplished by referring to the vision for the original product—an emphasis on ease of use, emerging standards, and an "open" platform. Hence, Java, the emerging standard for Internet application programs, was finally chosen.

To make the decision, NetDynamics engineers spent time experimenting with various options to identify the potential and risks of each one. Because they were experienced with other approaches, they spent most of their time familiarizing themselves with Java, writing simple routines, then gradually moving to more complex programs. While ultimately, they chose Java, there was significant controversy over the choice given its relative immaturity at the time of the decision. In the words of the chief engineer:

> We knew Java was going to be big, but it was still only available as a beta version. The development tools which went along with it were either terribly buggy, or nonexistent. Consequently, we had to develop many of our own development tools.

Working with other companies' beta software was a continual problem. Much of the work carried out with Java unearthed bugs that even Sun Microsystems had not known about. But to demonstrate that the bug was in Java rather than their own code, engineers often had to develop small test programs to "expose" the bug. On another occasion, when the team was using a fast beta version of Navigator, all the engineering systems suddenly crashed. After several hours of investigation, the chief engineer traced the fault to a "time bomb" installed in Navigator, meant to stop unauthorized use past a certain date.

In January 1996, with the major design decisions made, the team had to commit to a schedule. They developed a project plan based on an analysis of the time required to bring together the two components of the new product: "Studio" the development environment, and "Runtime," the application program that handled the data flow between the Internet server and the database. The team divided in two; five engineers went to work on Studio and four on Runtime plus the networking software.

By January 15, the Studio team had begun coding. The Runtime team required a little longer to work out design issues and began coding around the beginning of February. The decision to start coding, however, was a controversial one. The chief engineer wanted another month to make the design more robust. Heated discussions ensued, most of them over the list of fifty to seventy "open issues" that were still unresolved. While the majority were minor details that could be tackled later, about ten involved major design trade-offs that had not yet been addressed. Despite the engineers' objections, however, the CEO pushed for an early start. As he put it, "Time is more important than being perfect."

By the end of February, the Studio team had a basic program framework up and running. The team started usability testing, by developing a suite of regression tests to simulate the impact of general use. Just before March 10, the two components of the system were integrated for the first time. The pressure for integration came from the CEO, who had scheduled a demonstration of the product to analysts in New York. The team programmed the demonstration version to work only with a Netscape browser and a Microsoft database. While this initial version was a little shaky (and some features, such as networking, were not complete), it did show off the product's capabilities from end to end.

Once this first working model had been built, the software was integrated on a daily basis (Figure 8-5). Each morning a "daily build" was performed and everyone who needed the most recent version received a copy. When bugs were found in the daily build, they were reported, and a centralized system was used to track and allocate them to the design team. By the end of the project, over six hundred and forty bugs had been found and fixed.

On April 8, NetDynamics announced that the product would be shipped within thirty days. Even though the product was not yet complete, marketing pushed for a training program in early April, which was run by the engineers developing the product. At the same time the team was working with twenty beta customers to bring the product up to required levels of reliability. Some features were still in a state of flux, as well as some major design issues. But last-minute changes had been expected, as the market was evolving rapidly. As the chief engineer pointed out, "We have to expect things to change, as do our engineers. They have to be prepared to retro-fit their work as we determine the feature set has to change."

During late April, the engineers realized that the product would not be fully stabilized, nor its features complete, by the end of the month, so they decided to delay the release. During May they worked to fix bugs, train major customers, and perform another round of acceptance tests with "gamma" customers. In this period, NetDynamics learned to embrace those users who stretched the product to the limit, since that was often the only way they learned where those limits were. One user even slept at the

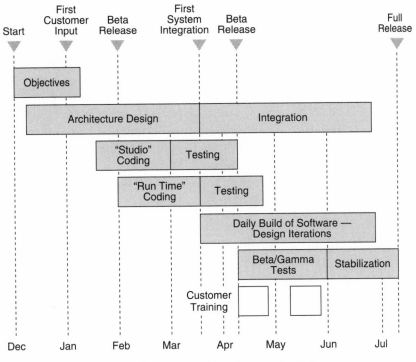

FIGURE 8-5   The Development of Net Dynamics 2.0

NetDynamics offices for a week to maximize his interaction with the emerging product! Customers like this would often detect design flaws that the team would never have found until much later in the process.

As the Net Dynamics project approached release in July 1996, the team began to move to focus on new development projects. The chief engineer described the challenge for the future:

> Development is a never-ending cycle of integrating new features and standards. Given the rate of change in the industry, we cannot rest. HTML is dying now, and Java applets are taking over. As soon as this product is released, we have to start developing again. It's worse because we are so "open." We have to support everything.

MICROSOFT'S RESPONSE

Microsoft was late in entering the Internet environment. Its senior management team was slow to recognize the opportunities offered by the World Wide Web. Not until the end of 1995, did Microsoft begin to focus on developing critical Internet products, like a browser to rival Netscape's Navigator. When Microsoft did enter the browser market with its first release of "Explorer," Netscape already had a dominant market position and its product was far ahead of Microsoft's in terms of features.

Though Microsoft appeared to have missed an opportunity, it recovered from its strategic mistake with incredible speed. In six months—from the end of 1995 to the middle of 1996—it went from having no presence in the critical browser market to offering a product several industry experts claimed was comparable with or better than Netscape's Navigator. By August 1996, Microsoft had only a small share of the browser market, but its Internet business was gaining momentum. A Microsoft employee exulted:

> Think of how far behind we were a year ago. It's true that we missed an opportunity to put our name out in front. But within a year we put out something that was better, and integrated from beginning to end. Imagine what someone else would have done. This is what we are good at [at] Microsoft. We will argue with each other and procrastinate until someone on the horizon paints a target on their chest, like Netscape. Then we go for the kill.

Microsoft was able to come from behind because it had the right product development philosophy in place. When Gates and the rest of Microsoft's senior management team finally acknowledged the need for a strategic shift, Microsoft's R&D groups were ready for action. Its applications development process shared many similarities with Netscape's and Yahoo!'s, including the rapid iteration of prototypes, early beta releases, and a flexible approach to the product architecture and specification. It was, however, more internally focused, driven to a greater degree by internal releases than by external customer feedback. Microsoft went through about half the number of betas as Netscape—two or three, rather than six or seven major releases. Instead, it relied heavily on extensive testing through its own intranet. As one of their program managers explained:

> We try and be a bit more careful about staging betas than Netscape—we need a clear reference point for feedback, things get confusing if you release too many different beta versions in a short period of time. However, we build everything as frequently as possible. Then we release it for internal testing. Everyone around Microsoft is encouraged to play with it. Internal testing on our intranet means that we can release it to thousands of people that really hammer away at it.

We use the product much more heavily than the average web user. By the time we ship a version of Explorer it will have had much more test time than Navigator.

Microsoft's rapid recovery was also facilitated by its large reserves of skill and experience. The company has an incredible depth of talent—a vast pool of individuals good at problem solving under pressure. Once Gates decided to go after the Internet, the organization dedicated its best resources to the effort. One employee recalled a job listing on Explorer:

I still remember the internal job listing for a program manager spot on Explorer. The requirements were incredible. You had to be a level 12, one level below business unit manager. You had to have at least a 4.0 average for reviews, which is almost impossible. You had to have shipped at least four products, and had to have been at least five years at Microsoft. The amazing thing is that these positions were staffed almost immediately! This is one of our greatest advantages. We have those kind of people floating around here. We are out to kill, and we have people here that can do it.

Microsoft adapted rapidly to the turbulence of the Internet, releasing three major versions of Explorer in just nine months. By the middle of 1996, the company had begun to threaten Netscape's dominance.

Emerging Patterns in R&D

We have described R&D at four different firms, yet the similarities between their development processes are striking. In each, concept development and implementation overlap. Team members quickly translate a product's features into a functioning prototype. User input, both internal and external, is continuously integrated into the design process, through a series of rapid iterations. And firms strive for an early integration of the components into a system, which once achieved, is "built" on a daily basis to allow the product (and specification) to evolve.

The reactive nature of these projects is useful however, only because there is good information to react to. The value of flexible R&D therefore hinges on the quality of the process through which knowledge of user needs and market requirements is generated. Unlike traditional development projects, in which research on user needs provides occasional bursts of input to the development process, these projects require continuous feedback on critical features. One of the most significant patterns to emerge has been the emphasis on generating such feedback.

Simultaneous Feedback on Technology, Market, and Customers

Nowhere is customer feedback more important than at Netscape, where the release of up to six beta versions of a new product means that users have a large role in "evolving" the product. Significant amounts of the new code, features, and technology that were integrated into the Navigator 3.0 release were developed *after* the first beta version had been released. Netscape therefore had considerable flexibility in responding to market changes *within* its development cycle.

At NetDynamics, once the initial prototypes were completed, lead users were brought in to evaluate the concept. Soon after the design was first integrated, the development team began working closely with handpicked beta customers who stretched the limits of performance. Running the training program simultaneously with design work also gave the team additional experience with user problems and requirements.

At Yahoo!, external users were integrated into the development process at a later stage. Being a service provider, Yahoo! believes that before a service is released to the outside world, it needs to be more robust than the typical Internet beta. Users who try a service once and have a poor experience with it are unlikely to return to that service. To mitigate the potential disadvantages of later testing, Yahoo! relies on its internal staff to adopt the position of lead users. And once a service has moved to external testing, it receives a significant amount of exposure over a very short period. Over thirty thousand Yahoo! users have volunteered to be beta testers. My Yahoo! was tested by over five hundred of them before its "soft release."

Microsoft similarly obtains rapid, high-quality feedback through its employees. Its engineers are expected to be extensive users of the technologies they are developing. They are also expected to be up-to-date with the functions and features of all competitors' offerings. Combined with carefully staged external beta releases, their approach limits the risk of imperfections in early releases damaging the company's reputation.

Overlapping Conceptualization and Implementation

To be effective, customer and market feedback must be rapidly translated into new technologies and product features. These changes must be made *within* the development cycle. The My Yahoo! project illustrates this dynamic well. After three months, a partially complete version of the service had been developed, but several competing products had been launched. In addition, the phenomenal growth in the popularity of the Internet, had cast doubt on whether Yahoo!'s existing software could support the anticipated usage. Thus, Yahoo! decided that major revisions were necessary. A new set of features and functions was developed to better differentiate the product from competitors. And the software was rewritten to support the expected increase in volume. By launch, estimates were that the new service had been rebuilt almost *three* times during the development cycle. In a traditional industry, My Yahoo!'s project manager would probably be looking for alternative employment! In the Internet world however, he saved the firm from introducing a weak product into a market where preferences had long since evolved.

At NetDynamics, concept and implementation overlapped considerably, as so much uncertainty existed over the evolution of the Internet. When coding started, some fifty issues still needed to be resolved, of which ten were major design trade-offs. The decision to begin coding was taken not because those issues were unimportant, but because the next few months were expected to bring additional information with which to make those choices. Similarly, although the decision to use Java was informed by the product's open philosophy, if the ground had shifted mid-project and Java proved undesirable, the development team would have had to shift with it, and rethink the basic concept.

Leveraging Experimentation and Experience

Good decision making is built on knowledge generated through experimentation and accumulated in experience (Iansiti 1997; Thomke, Von Hippel, and Franke 1997). In the world of the Internet, the rapid obsolescence of knowledge makes experimentation central to the development effort, hence the emphasis on building a working model or prototype early in each of the projects, which becomes the focus for ongoing experimentation. While these early prototypes do not have to be fully functional, they have to lay the foundation for the product's architecture, setting priorities for the development of features and creating a vehicle for user feedback. As new functions are added and user feedback is obtained from external beta tests, these prototypes are updated, evolving the product design until it is robust enough for release.

Experimentation alone, however, does not guarantee a project's success. When we asked project members at each company about the ingredients most critical to a successful project, they consistently noted the experience of their software engineers and managers. Experience was deemed crucial to deciding *which* experiments to conduct while navigating the complexities of the technological and user environments. Yahoo!'s chief engineer underscored the point. "Experience is essential. It is the only thing that lets you see how the whole system works. It is critical to making the right tradeoffs as a project evolves." Ultimately, Microsoft's speedy recovery was due largely to the incredible depth of experience and skill of its staff. Once the company's strategic shift towards the Internet had been made explicit, the collective talent of its employees was turned loose on the Internet, with impressive results.

Integrating New Technology with Market Preferences

The vast uncertainty of the Internet environment has deeply influenced the nature of research and development in the firms we have described. Gone are the days of clear objectives, frozen specifications, and "proven" technologies. If firms wait until all uncertainties have been resolved, the market opportunity will be gone. Thus, leading firms have acknowledged the need for more flexibility and have developed processes characterized by the rapid integration of a variety of technical possibilities with the evolving application context.

At the core, the responsiveness of the new product development models is driven by integration. The integrative challenges go well beyond the traditional boundaries of the project, however. First of all, given the requirement to adapt to new information as development progresses, there is a need to tightly integrate with customers. Given the rate at which market requirements change, the manner in which the project–customer interface is structured will to a large extent dictate the value which can be extracted from a flexible development process. In the projects we described, customers became "partners" in the process, rather than a passive source of ideas. In each, the process involved sensing customers' needs, responding with a technical solution, then rapidly gathering feedback about the merits of this solution. During a development cycle, this transition was made several times, whether through broad beta testing, or intense interactions with a few lead users.

Secondly, this new model of development requires the ability to rapidly integrate technologies across networks of development organizations. Technological possibilities at the disposal of developers reach well beyond those developed within their own firm. Networks of third-party firms have emerged, each of which provides complementary technologies that add significant functionality to any core product offering (e.g., browser "plug-ins" or Java applets). This adds significant integrative

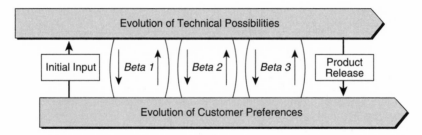

FIGURE 8-6 Integrating New Technology with Customer Preferences

challenges at the project level and motivates the creation of alliances across firms, joint development agreements, open product architectures, and modular product designs.

Finally, there is a need to integrate across projects. Developing products for the Internet is more like managing two parallel streams, one representing the evolution of technical possibilities and the other, the evolution of customer preferences. As shown in Figure 8-6, the challenge is to decide when a given set of technical options should be taken from the first stream, integrated into a "product," and offered to users in the second stream. This bundling can be done either as a beta version or a final release. In both cases, the product is simply the next step in the interaction between two rapidly evolving streams, rather than a final outcome.

Viewing the process of product development as streams of innovations linking a variety of organizations and customers across space and time requires a major shift in thinking. It dictates a focus on generating and integrating knowledge rather than on accumulating concrete assets, which are subject to frequent obsolescence. Knowledge generation mechanisms are a firm's most flexible assets, retaining value even in turbulent settings. The ideal development process may be one that accumulates knowledge continuously, commits to product specifications, and completes product design only a moment before shipping each product version. As the Internet companies have shown us, this model is not as far from reality as we might have thought.

Endnotes

1. The flexible model goes beyond concurrent engineering or integrated problem-solving. While concurrent engineering fosters the joint resolution of different functional tasks at each stage of a project, flexible development implies overlapping of the stages.

2. Source: Microsoft Corporation: Office Business Unit; Harvard Business School Case #9-691–033.
3. Ibid.

References

K. B. Clark and T. Fujimoto, *Product Development Performance* (Boston: Harvard Business School Press, 1991).

Robert G. Cooper, "Stage-Gate Systems: A New Tool for Managing New Products," *Business Horizons* (May–June 1990).

M. Cusumano and R. Selby, *Microsoft Secrets* (New York: Free Press, 1995).

K. M. Eisenhardt and B. N. Tabrizi, "Accelerating Adaptive Processes: Product Innovation in the Global Computer Industry." *Administrative Sciences Quarterly* 40:1 (1995).

M. Iansiti, "Shooting the Rapids: Managing Product Development in Turbulent Environments." *California Management Review* 38:1 (1995).

—— *Technology Integration: Making Critical Choices in a Dynamic World* (Boston: Harvard Business School Press, 1997).

A. MacCormack and M. Iansiti, "Product Development Flexibility" (working paper, Boston: Harvard Business School, 1997, 97–072).

S. Thomke, E. A. Von Hippel and R. R. Franke. "Modes of Experimentation: An Innovation Process Variable," (working paper, Boston: Harvard Business School, 1997, 97–052).

—— "The Role of Flexibility in the Development of New Products: An Empirical Study." *Research Policy* 26;1 (1997) 105–119.

M. L. Tushman and C. A. O'Reilly, III, *Winning Through Innovation.* (Boston: Harvard Business School Press, 1997).

K. T. Ulrich and S. D. Eppinger, *Product Design and Development* (New York: McGraw-Hill, 1994).

Steven C. Wheelwright and Kim B. Clark, *Revolutionizing Product Development* (New York: Free Press, 1992).

9 | The Emergence of Internetworked Manufacturing

David M. Upton and Andrew P. McAfee

THE RECENT CONFLUENCE of communications and computer internetworking technologies, together with the competitive imperatives for rapid and dense information flows between firms, have combined to create a new business environment for all companies, particularly manufacturers. The World Wide Web (WWW), whose explosive growth has been well-documented[1-3] is the most visible manifestation of this technological convergence. The web has grown so spectacularly because it builds on two other recent developments: increases in the bandwidth, or carrying capacity, of telecommunications channels and internetworking, or the connection of physically separate computer networks.

Beginning around 1995, these same advances were put to another, closely related use: the construction of Intranets, or internal networks that make use of Internet protocols. While much of the publicity surrounding the

Note: Figures 9–1, 9–2, 9–3, 9–4, and 9–6 are adapted and reprinted by permission of *Harvard Business Review.* From "The Real Virtual Factory" by David M. Upton and Andrew McAfee, July–August, 1996. Copyright © 1996 by the President and Fellows of Harvard College; all rights reserved.

201

business use of Internet technologies has focused on consumers, intrabusiness use has been a less visible but equally important application. Here again, growth has been spectacular: an April 1996 survey of five hundred firms that owned large computer networks of any type found that seventy-three percent were using WWW-like Intranets to distribute information internally, and nearly ninety percent planned to implement a specific Intranet strategy within twelve months.[4] Companies have found that abundant bandwidth and powerful, flexible, and open Internet protocols allow their employees to collaborate electronically with great efficiency.

Between such company Intranets and the global Internet, however, lies a large and important gap. Neither of these networks addresses directly the question of how to allow a *group* of firms to work together securely, a critical issue for manufacturing firms, for three reasons. First, manufacturers are heavy users of information technology (IT); all the activities in a modern production supply chain, from design through production to distribution, are supported by IT tools. Second, most manufacturing sites interact continually with a large number of partners, including suppliers, customers, and subcontractors. Typically, these partners are spread over a wide area: most are external to the firm. Finally, many trends in the organization of production suggest that, in the future, information sharing will become increasingly important: joint ventures, outsourcing, and the rise of the "virtual corporation" all require richer communication among more partners and more locations. To remain competitive, producers will need to share information seamlessly among a group of partners with varying internal technologies. In other words, they will need to internetwork to form a manufacturing community.

Multicompany internetworks have come to be called "Extranets," and many firms have begun to experiment with them. Fully functioning Extranets, however, are still rare, and many operations remain unaware or unconvinced of their benefits. This chapter describes a promising approach to internetworked manufacturing, using a currently operating large Extranet as a case study. We begin by reviewing three current technologies for information sharing across sites. We then present a framework for understanding the information-sharing requirements of internetworked manufacturing, show where current approaches fall short, and discuss a new model that is currently unfolding. A case study of the AeroTech Service Group, which has integrated McDonnell Douglas Aerospace and many of its partners into a low-cost internetwork, follows. The chapter concludes with an analysis of how the transition to electronic collaboration is likely to be accomplished.

Current Internetworking Technologies

Internetworked manufacturing may be defined as a collaborative environment in which several partners share information and IT functionality around a product, process, or project (e.g., a new product development effort). The partners may be producers, suppliers, customers, subcontractors, consultants, government and regulatory agencies, or other relevant entities. They may be clustered in one area or widely dispersed. To borrow Negroponte's concept, the point of internetworked manufacturing is to transmit and transform the *bits* (information) instead of the *atoms* (materials) related to production.[5] In many cases, much (if not most) of the delay, waste, and inefficiency in production can be traced to poor bit handling, rather than to problems with atom movement or processing. If internetworked manufacturing can reduce bit-based delays and costs, it will become both extremely powerful and widely used.

Until very recently, three methods for achieving the goals of internetworking dominated: Electronic Data Interchange (EDI), groupware, and Wide Area Networks (WANs). A comparison of these three technologies is not an apples-to-apples comparison, since they occupy different levels in the networking hierarchy.[6] However, these are frequently the categories manufacturers cite as the strategic focus of their internetworking efforts, so it is appropriate to consider them together.

ELECTRONIC DATA INTERCHANGE

EDI grew out of a need to standardize the paperwork relating to the Berlin airlift. Modern EDI is a collection of standard formats for communication between computers. It includes interchanges of commercial data like purchase orders, electronic funds transfers, database queries like those made to book airline reservations, and graphical data such as Computer-Aided Design (CAD) drawings. EDI standards specify exactly how each of these interchanges should be structured, so that any firm that implements an EDI system can accept transmissions from any other and be confident of the location and format of each data element.

EDI standardization has been a valuable first step for many companies interested in creating electronic communities. EDI formats are rigid, however, and often do not cover the range and type of information firms need to share. Also, because EDI can be expensive and time consuming to implement, it remains beyond the reach of many small firms.[7] More fundamentally, this technology is of limited use for internetworked manufacturers, because it can be used only to transfer discrete bundles of information. An EDI link serves simply to shuttle information back and forth; it cannot be used to access a remote computer and use its applications, or even to download a file from another computer.

GROUPWARE

The class of software known as "groupware" addresses some of EDI's drawbacks. Groupware applications like Lotus Notes can help to coordinate group work in three ways.[8] First, they make a common body of information available to a widely dispersed group, so that a sales force, for example, can check the in-stock status of orders. Second, they track work flows so that group members can collaborate remotely on documents and projects; all members of a design team, for example, can use Lotus Notes to make sure they are working on the most recent version of a drawing. Finally, the software provides a platform for communication and interactive discussions, from e-mail and bulletin boards to on-screen video.

Although groupware is a powerful tool, it can be expensive to install and maintain. Each user must purchase a copy of the groupware application, and training and administration expenses are high. Lotus Notes, for example, costs between $1,000 and $5,000 per user over a three-year period, according to one estimate.[9]

Another drawback is that Lotus Notes and its relatives cannot be used to gain access to remote computers, which are not linked to groupware servers. For example, Notes generally cannot be used to connect to a partner firm's network and use its manufacturer's requirements planning (MRP) or CAD programs, or to access inventory data stored on a mainframe.[10] These abilities are important in collaborative manufacturing, in which a wide variety of data formats and applications should be available, and installing a particular brand of groupware at each site and on each relevant machine generally is not feasible.

WIDE AREA NETWORKS

To make information and programs more widely available, and to facilitate collaboration among several sites, many manufacturers have installed WANs, across which they usually run proprietary protocols and custom applications. WANs are typically dedicated high-speed links that interconnect individual local area networks, or LANs. Unlike EDI or groupware links, WANs exist permanently, providing universal access to all data and applications resident on member LANs. WAN construction, in other words, *is* internetworking.

However, WANs typically exist only within firms; they are rarely extended to partner companies because of the expense of dedicated telecommunications lines. Monthly use of a high-bandwidth T1 line, for example, can cost more than $1,000 for each link.[11] In addition, administration of a dispersed network is complicated; a group needs a relatively high degree of IT sophistication to participate in such a network. For most manufacturers, then, WANs exist only among a few large sites. Small companies in particular are excluded from this type of interconnectivity, and so are left out of most current manufacturing internetworks.

The Requirements of Internetworked Manufacturing: A Framework

Though implementations of the three current approaches to internetworking have shown the potential of electronic collaboration, they have been accompanied by frustration and unmet expectations. EDI often serves only to automate document flow, groupware stops short of opening up all the power of member computers, and WANs cannot be extended to all desired sites. Firms that have adopted these approaches, or combinations of them, often find they and their partners are still not able to share resources as effectively as they would like.

We believe that the key to understanding this issue, and to conceptualizing the shortcomings of current approaches, lies in an understanding of the fundamental information-sharing requirements of multipartner manufacturing networks. There are many such requirements, but they can be divided into three categories, or performance dimensions. An effective internetwork will be extendable to partner firms at any *stage* of a relationship, will accommodate companies at all *levels* of IT sophistication, and will provide all required *functionality*.

STAGE

Manufacturing partners typically convert to internetworking in *stages*, moving from exploratory relationships to collaboration and in some cases to full integration. Companies in the exploratory stage exchange information about potential joint efforts and establish bases for further interaction. Common exploratory activities include requesting and sending information about products and services, distributing requests for bids and receiving quotes, and establishing contracts and purchase orders. Once the two parties have decided to collaborate, they begin to engage in sharing and planning. Firms at this stage exchange and review more detailed data, such as CAD/CAM files and supporting documentation, about their joint activities. Collaborating firms may also want to use the applications that reside on each other's machines, for example, to use a specialized application that only one partner possesses. The final stage, integration, implies that the sites expect a continuing relationship; they may be separate locations within the same company, or joint venture partners. Activities at this stage include sharing detailed production and financial data, and routinely accessing the information and applications resident on each other's machines.

Firms also move backward through these stages, collaborating on a single project or contract and then detaching themselves from each other. Under these circumstances, it would be impractical to build a costly information-sharing infrastructure—and one of the common drawbacks of EDI, groupware, and WANs is that they require a significant initial level of investment, as well as ongoing expense.

LEVEL

Regardless of the stage of their relationship, potential participants in an electronic manufacturing community will embody varying levels of technological sophistication. The determinants of this level include the type and power of installed hardware and software, the average and highest levels of computer expertise among site personnel, and the degree of connectivity of the local area network. Most large manufacturing firms are patchworks of computing ability. A design group, for example, may possess a cluster of linked workstations running advanced drawing and modeling software, while production control uses dumb terminals to access mainframe MRP software. The two functions may not be able to interact electronically, nor communicate with a sales manager's lone PC.

Smaller firms tend to be more homogeneous in their level of sophistication, though there is a large variation across companies. A subcontractor specializing in Finite Element Analysis or other modeling techniques is likely to have an advanced computing environment, while a supplier of packaging materials may have only rudimentary systems.

Any attempt to link disparate partners in internetworked manufacturing must allow for different levels of technological sophistication. Two approaches are possible: accommodating all levels, or bringing the least sophisticated users up to a minimum level before or during interconnection.

FUNCTIONALITY

An effective internetworked manufacturing community must allow all its members, regardless of their stage and level, to carry out a common set of information handling tasks; in other words, it must provide universal functionality. Three capabilities make up the core of this requirement: *transmission, data access,* and *telepresence. Transmission,* the most straightforward, is the simple transfer of data. Partners need to exchange information, from e-mail, to purchase orders, to numerical control programs.

Data access means the sharing of common pools of information. Through virtual file cabinets and bulletin boards that can be visited by authorized users, firms can make sure that all participants in a project are working to the same schedule, that updated CAD files are always available to suppliers, or that regulators and other concerned groups can monitor emissions levels. To clarify the difference between transmission and data access, consider the difference between sending an electronic bid request to potential suppliers and posting the same information to a freely accessible directory.

Telepresence is the ability to access a remote machine and use it as a local operator would. It permits all authorized users to employ the programs and data on a given computer, whether these people are on-site or remote, inside or outside the firm. Telepresence is one of the key characteristics of the Internet, which enables users to access information and applications on machines around the world. It is especially useful in internetworked manufacturing. With this capability, small firms can do computationally intensive simulations on a large partner's machines, or customers can check inventory and delivery status by logging onto a supplier's DRP system.

Current Approaches to Internetworked Manufacturing Compared

A manufacturing community is effectively internetworked when it provides the *functionality* just discussed to all member firms, regardless of the *stage* of their relationship or their *level* of sophistication. Figure 9-1 shows a diagram of these requirements in the form of a cube. The *stage* of a relationship is shown as the width of the cube, with the exploratory stage farthest to the right. IT *functionality* is shown as the height of the cube, starting from mere transmission at the bottom to telepresence at the top. The lowest *level* of sophistication among participants is shown as the depth of the cube; an internetwork that includes very naïve partners would be placed far back. Note that the harder the internetworking task, the further it is from the front corner of the cube. An integrated community of sophisticated IT users who only wanted to transmit information would be situated very close to this front corner. A group of diverse parties who want high functionality, on the other hand would be placed at the far corner of the cube.

Existing approaches to internetworked manufacturing, including EDI, groupware, and WANs, can be judged by how well they fill the cube in Figure 9-1; that is, how close they come to enabling effective internetworked manufacturing among any group of partners.

As Figure 9-2 shows, EDI fills very little of the cube. It does not supply most of the required functionality, is not useful for unsophisticated

FIGURE 9-1   The Requirements for Internetworked Manufacturing

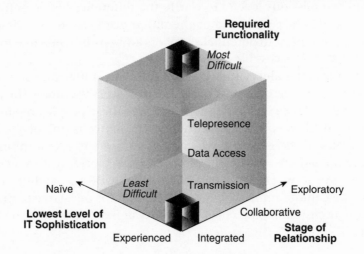

Required Functionality

Most Difficult

Telepresence

Data Access

Naïve

Least Difficult

Transmission

Exploratory

Lowest Level of IT Sophistication

Collaborative

Experienced

Integrated

Stage of Relationship

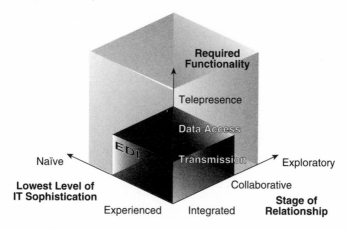

FIGURE 9-2   EDI and the Requirements Space

users, and is typically established only after firms are already collaborating with each other.

Groupware, shown in Figure 9-3, is a much more complete solution that supports two of the three necessary functions and is available to all users comfortable with PCs. But because groupware entails a significant amount of administration and overhead, and often an agreement on a proprietary standard, it may not be adopted until it is clear that the relationship among firms will continue.

FIGURE 9-3   Groupware's Fulfillment of the Requirements of Internetworked Manufacturing

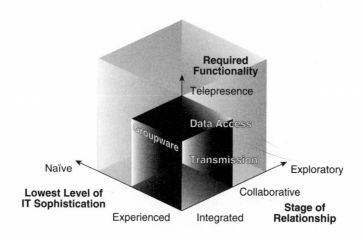

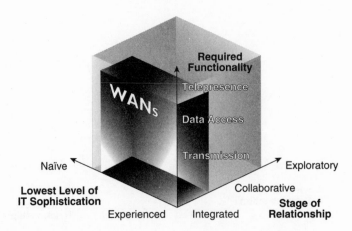

FIGURE 9-4 **WAN's Fulfillment of the Requirements of Internetworked Manufacturing**

As Figure 9-4 shows, dedicated WANs and their associated software can often provide all the needed functionality. But WANs are built only by higher-level users, and only in support of well-established and long-standing relationships. Rarely are they built by firms that are only exploring or collaborating on a single effort.

A New Approach to Internetworking

As these figures show, none of the three existing approaches to electronic collaboration is fully satisfactory. Powerful needs are driving the search for better internetworking solutions. For instance, some large customers, like the Department of Defense, are demanding that product information be delivered digitally. Military Standard 974 mandates a "contractor provided service for electronic access to and delivery of contractually required digital data."[12] Faced with a choice between creating a database from a mountain of paper or building it through electronic collaboration, prime contractors are understandably opting for the latter. Less extreme examples of this trend are found in retailing. Wal*Mart and other powerful discount chains require suppliers' systems to interface with their own in order to simplify inventory management.[13]

Subcontracting, outsourcing, and temporary alliances also appear to be on the rise both in manufacturing and other industries, to the point that "virtual corporations" and the "company in a box" are becoming a reality.[14] These new entities require collaborative capabilities far beyond what the telephone and fax machine can provide but are unwilling to commit to a hard-wired IT infrastructure. Existing solutions do not fit their internetworking needs.

Fortunately, the technological components to make possible a new approach to collaborative manufacturing (the "supply" to meet these demand drivers) now exist or are falling rapidly into place. Communications bandwidth is increasing and becoming cheaper. Though technical hurdles and issues of standards remain, the deployment of fiber optic cable and increased competition in and deregulation of the communications industries are fueling this trend. Indeed, some observers predict a coming bandwidth "tidal wave," which will drive transmission costs down until they become negligible.[15] In the meantime, older technologies are being revitalized. ISDN, a thirteen-year-old alternative to standard phone lines, provides enough bandwidth for modern desktop videoconferencing applications; over one million ISDN products were shipped in 1995—a thirty percent increase over 1993.[16]

To be useful, the information that is transferred through these ever-larger pipes must be readable and usable when it arrives. The widespread convergence of standards in recent years will ensure that it is. Protocols developed for the Internet are now appropriate for communication among virtually all platforms. De facto exchange standards exist for applications such as PC word processors and spreadsheets and CAD drawings. This growing interoperability means that firms will be able to share a great deal of their information without prior agreement on hardware and software, and without "shoehorning" their systems into clumsy configurations.

The World Wide Web has emerged as one of the most important of these *de facto* standards. Web browsers (e.g., Netscape's Navigator) and servers combine to bring huge amounts of information, in a range of formats, to users. Information providers on the web can make use of technologies such as CGI software, server-based Java, and client-based Java applets to move far beyond static web pages. The browser has become a widespread and powerful information presentation device, and more firms every day are adopting it as a standard.

In summary, high bandwidth and widespread agreement on standards now permit a new approach to collaborative manufacturing, one that addresses the shortcomings of existing models and meets unfulfilled demands. This new model provides broad functionality across all stages and levels. Furthermore, it is relatively inexpensive and only minimally centralized and hierarchical.

The AeroTech Extranet

AeroTech Service Group, Inc., is a startup firm that maintains an inter-networked environment for McDonnell Douglas Aerospace (MDA). The product at the heart of this environment is known as the Contractor Integrated Technical Information Service, or CITIS. MDA developed CITIS in the early 1990s to respond to Military Standard 974, which requires prime contractors to make contractually required information available electronically.

After CITIS was put in place, MDA decided to outsource its maintenance, improvement, and continued expansion. The company had turned over many of its other IT tasks to outsiders and had a general preference for using computer systems over owning them. AeroTech assumed management of the system in May, 1994.

System Operation

CITIS's function was to serve as a gateway to other information resources. Those resources fell into two categories: information pools and applications. An information pool is a collection of data stored electronically—for example, a purchased parts database, a computer directory of CAD drawings, or a file of suppliers qualified to manufacture certain parts. An application is a computer program, such as a word processor, software for MRP, or a three-dimensional CAD package.

CITIS's main contribution was to make available information pools and applications that were not resident on a user's machine. In other words, CITIS freed users from the requirement that they be sitting in front of the computer that contained the data or program of interest. Thus, geographic distance and organizational boundaries were no longer constraints on CITIS users; at any time they could access the information and applications on any computer they were authorized to use—even if that computer resided in another time zone, country, or firm.

Protocols

To enable remote access to information and applications, CITIS used protocols developed for the Internet. By the mid-1990s, those protocols were well developed and could be implemented on virtually any hardware. Table 9-1 lists them in increasing order of sophistication, along with examples of how MDA and its partners used them.

TABLE 9-1   **Internet Protocols Used in CITIS**

Protocol	Purpose	Examples of Use
Mail protocols (pop, smtp)	Allowed users to exchange messages.	MDA engineer in St. Louis notified a machine shop manager in Los Angeles that a new version of a Computer Aided Design (CAD) drawing was available.
File transfer protocol (ftp)	Allowed users to access files on a remote machine and transfer them to a local hard drive.	Machine shop manager accessed CITIS to establish a link to a St. Louis mainframe, then downloaded an archived CAD file to her PC.
Telnet	Allowed users to access/log on to a remote machine and use the applications resident on it.	Department of Defense employee in Washington, DC logged onto a mainframe in St. Louis to access program schedule information.
X-Window	Allowed users to display 'windows' of text, graphics, or applications that reside on a remote machine.	Machine shop manager used CITIS to access a computer in Phoenix and view drawings created with a UNIX-based viewer.
Hyper text transport protocol (http)	Allowed users on the World Wide Web to transfer and integrate information in many formats (text, graphics, sound, video, client-based applets).	Later versions of CITIS made use of the web and http protocols to deliver information to authorized users. MDA and AeroTech satisfied themselves that http transmissions could be sufficiently secure (using the secure https standard), and began using web browsers. These browsers also accommodated earlier IP-based protocols, such as ftp and pop.

Internet protocols were not the only choice for enabling the tasks described in Table 9-1, but they were particularly attractive because they were "open" standards. That is, they were not owned by any one entity or company, the details of their operation were widely available, and they could be incorporated into any software or system without incurring licensing fees. Internet protocol bundles were available for almost any computer. Because CITIS participants were using many different hardware platforms and operating systems, this universality was important.

AeroTech's effort in building the system demanded more than simply distributing software to users and then troubleshooting during installation. To satisfy MDA and all its partners, including the U.S. government, two significant challenges remained: guaranteeing the system's security and ensuring sufficient speed.

SECURITY

The Internet protocols just described were developed under the assumption that all connected computers would share information freely. That was emphatically not the case for an aerospace and defense firm like MDA, whose computers contained large amounts of Department of Defense data. This fundamental incompatibility between the technology underpinning CITIS and the project's security requirements had to be resolved. MDA would not build any internetwork that allowed its computers to be accessed by outsiders.

AeroTech addressed this concern in two ways. First, it did not replace or alter the existing protection on any member computer. Log-in procedures, User ID names, passwords, and all other safeguards remained unchanged. In other words, CITIS simply delivered users to a computer's "front door"; users still needed the appropriate keys to enter it.

Second, AeroTech kept track of which "front doors" each user was allowed to visit. CITIS included a database that listed all users and the files, directories, and computers they were authorized to use. Before allowing access to a remote machine or information pool, CITIS first verified that the user was authorized for that activity. Authorizations were granted by a group within MDA and maintained by AeroTech.

BANDWIDTH

An important concern in designing the CITIS system was making the system as "fast" as possible for all users. The speed and responsiveness of any internetwork is largely a matter of bandwidth, or the information-carrying capacity of the links among computers. A system that uses only modems and normal telephone lines would be slow, while an internetwork based on other networking technologies, like Ethernet, FDDI, or ATM would be much faster, but also more costly to implement and maintain.

AeroTech realized that not all CITIS users would require the same bandwidth. A machine shop that connected to CITIS only to download electronic drawings would probably be satisfied with modem speeds. A large aerospace firm that was collaborating with MDA for videoconferenced design reviews, meanwhile, would need much more bandwidth. AeroTech used its telecommunications expertise to build a variety of communications links, creating a bandwidth "patchwork" among users. Those with minimal or sporadic needs accessed the system with modems, while more permanent participants (e.g., distant MDA sites, customers within the government, and other large aerospace firms) used dedicated high-bandwidth links.

ECONOMICS

The contract for CITIS management and administration provided for variable weekly expenditures against a yearly budget. AeroTech typically charged a flat weekly fee and billed MDA for unexpected support requests. The firm did not charge based on the number of users added or traffic on the system, because such increases did not increase the cost of running the system. It did charge for special projects, such as connecting a large partner with high-bandwidth requirements, if significant amounts of time were required.

MDA estimated that by mid-1995 the CITIS system was paying for itself, taking into account only the time savings realized from distributing bid requests electronically rather than manually.

GROWTH IN USE

CITIS, then, was essentially a security and authorization system that presided over an internetwork of computers, all of which used Internet protocols to share information. The only dedicated physical manifestations of the system were two small networks of computers, one at AeroTech and the other at MDA, and some dedicated communications links. Beyond this equipment, CITIS was purely a method of exploiting the information resources of a large number of geographically dispersed partners.

In mid-1993 fewer than fifty people, all of them within MDA, were authorized to use the CITIS system. By the summer of 1994, after AeroTech had taken the CITIS contract, that number had grown to two hundred internal and external users. Within a year, there were thirteen hundred users and by the summer of 1996, the system linked thirty-four hundred people. Figure 9-5 shows the increase graphically. 1996 has seen the expansion of the AeroTech membership base to Europe and Asia.

By mid-1996, CITIS had reduced the cost of transmitting information among MDA and its partners. It had also eliminated needless travel and time lost searching and waiting for information. Both AeroTech and MDA

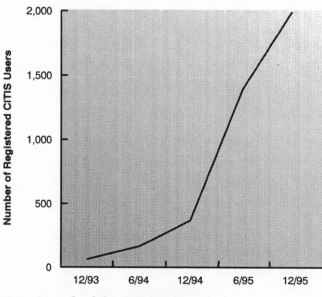

FIGURE 9-5   **Growth of the CITIS System**

anticipated that as more applications were discovered and more users added, CITIS would continue to grow in both size and importance.

CITIS largely solved the problem of providing the required functionality for an electronic community across all stages of relationship and

FIGURE 9-6   **CITIS's Fulfillment of the Requirements for Internetworked Manufacturing**

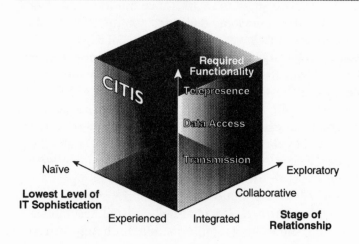

levels of sophistication (Figure 9-6). Because its software was easy to install and use on computers as small as PCs, it was available even to the least computer-literate groups and firms. The system's ease of use, together with the fact that it was free, meant that companies that were only exploring a relationship with MDA could benefit from it. Collaborating and integrated parties also found the system useful because of the high functionality it provided.

FUTURE DIRECTIONS

AeroTech will continue to provide consulting and special projects services in support of the system but is exploring ways to leverage its experience with CITIS in new business areas. One strategy is for the firm to become an "information broker" for manufacturers. Such a broker helps members of the manufacturing community become aware of the value of their information resources and then assists them in extracting that value. This role will require many skills AeroTech already possesses, particularly a knowledge of the industry and the ability to control and monitor each user's access and activity. Deep familiarity with the industry is required to determine which information has value to which parties and how much it is worth; control and monitoring capabilities help to assess information charges.

An example shows the potential importance of an information broker. MDA's aircraft are in use all over the world and must be serviced frequently. Spare parts manufacturing, then, is a large and lucrative international industry. Because MDA originally developed or purchased all the components and subassemblies, it possesses many of the blueprints, process details, and all the other information required for production. Even if the company does not want to monopolize the business (and it probably does not), it can generate revenue from spare parts manufacturing by charging for access to production data. Spares producers, wherever they are located, would join the internetwork, and AeroTech would enable and monitor their access. As the information broker AeroTech would also implement the billing system. AeroTech is currently working with MDA to identify such opportunities, and to develop pricing schemes.

The Future of Internetworked Manufacturing

The AeroTech case study raises many interesting questions about the future of electronic collaboration. Two of them are considered here. First, if the internetworking solution epitomized by MDA and AeroTech really is superior to other approaches to collaborative manufacturing, how will it spread? Which firms or industries will be first to use such secure Extranets, and which will lag? Second, what are the main obstacles faced by those who would build these communities? Insight into these two questions will help both manufacturers who are looking for better ways to work together and the information brokers who assist them.

Prospects for Implementation

The AeroTech model will probably be replicated most quickly in environments that resemble MDA's. Three factors in particular make a firm or industry highly suitable for this approach: the presence of one large partner, a high degree of required functionality and intercommunication, and low levels of commitment among many players.

The presence of one large partner seems critical. MDA provided both the impetus and the funding for the CITIS project; on their own its smaller partners probably would not have seen a need to build an electronic community, or been able to pay for it. And because MDA had a clear idea of its requirements, it was willing to assume all the costs of filling them, even though others would reap the benefits as well. One of MDA's requirements was that partners have access to one another's information, machines, and applications. This high level of required functionality precluded the use of existing groupware and other schemes, forcing a new approach. If MDA and other firms had needed simply to exchange data, there would have been no need to build a new set of methods.

Because so many partners were involved in CITIS, and because any subset of them might need to interact, CITIS needed both a highly flexible structure and detailed authorization and record keeping capabilities. If only MDA and one or two other firms had needed to collaborate, they could have simply made dedicated connections among themselves and assigned passwords. Finally, the environment had to include firms at all stages of a relationship, from MDA's collaborators on large procurement projects to small potential suppliers. For a community to span such a wide range, it must entail a minimum commitment that is quite low. If participation is expensive, or the tools involved difficult to learn and use, many partners will opt out.

Obstacles to Implementation

The constructors of internetworks face several hurdles. Security is a widespread concern given the well-publicized break-ins at firms such as GE.[17] A recent *Business Week* survey portrayed electronic commerce as an essentially lawless frontier populated by clever criminals.[18] But while security is a valid concern, powerful safeguards are available. Tools such as network firewalls and "hard," or virtually unbreakable, data-encoding schemes provide great protection when well-implemented.[19,20] Security concerns will never completely vanish, of course, but they can be adequately addressed.

Bandwidth, or the information-carrying capacity of the channels used, is another obstacle to implementation. Many firms, especially small ones, have only low-bandwidth access to internetworks, and so find participating inefficient. Traffic over the Internet, the largest of all internetworks, is increasing geometrically and may soon strain the Net's capacity.[21] Significant improvements in bandwidth are becoming available, however. Many telecommunications providers are lowering the price for ISDN lines,[16] which improve current phone-line rates by a factor of five. ADSL technology (for phone lines) and cable modems now deliver speeds as high as those available from LANs,[22] and will soon be widely available. These technologies will render information sharing and remote access almost transparent, at a price that will be economical for all firms interested in collaborative manufacturing. At the same time, significant improvements are being made in the already massive capacity of fiber optic cable. Some technology-watchers predict that bandwidth will soon become an essentially costless commodity.[14]

A lack of required skills is likely to remain a serious obstacle much longer than security concerns or bandwidth scarcity. To create the CITIS internetwork, AeroTech's personnel had to combine expertise in telecommunications, database design, construction, administration, computer security, Internet protocols, and real-time troubleshooting and customer service. This skill set is in many ways very different from that of most IT contractors and integrators and will not be replicated quickly.

While all these issues are important, the single largest impediment to the spread of electronic manufacturing communities like CITIS is a lack of awareness among potential users. As viable (i.e., economical and safe) options for sharing information resources among partners, Extranets are a relatively recent phenomenon. This situation is changing rapidly, however, as more companies discover the potential value of the Internet for business-to-business use.

AeroTech and MDA have just begun to explore ways to extract value from internetworking. These firms face two main challenges: determining which information is most valuable to partners, and developing a viable pricing model for information brokerage. If they can meet these challenges, and if the results are generalizable, they will have created another powerful incentive for manufacturers to build collaborative internetworks.

Endnotes

1. C. Anderson, "The Internet: The Accidental Superhighway," *The Economist* 336 (1995), s3–s18.
2. MIDS, "Third MIDS Internet Demographic Survey," MIDS, Austin, TX. Web site http://www2.mids.org/ids3/index.html (October 1995).
3. Network Wizards, "Internet Domain Survey," Network Wizards, Menlo Park, CA, Web site http://www.nw.com/zone/WWW/top.html (January 1996).
4. Network World, "Internet and Intranet Growth," Network World http://www.nwfusion.com (April 3, 1996).
5. N. Negroponte, *Being Digital* (New York: Alfred A. Knopf, 1995).
6. K. Siyan, *NetWare Training Guide: NetWare TCP/IP and NetWare NFS* (Indianapolis: New Riders Publishing, 1994).
7. R. H. Baker, *EDI* (Blue Ridge Summit, PA: TAB Books, 1991).
8. M. Frank, "Building Notes Applications," *DBMS* 8 (1995) 62–67.
9. P. Rooney, "Lower-priced Notes Clients Spur Momentum, But the Total Cost of Ownership Remains High," *PCWeek* 12 (1995) 1–2.
10. The most recent versions of groupware, such as Lotus's Domino do incorporate some of this fuctionality. They do this, however, by adopting the open standards described later in this chapter; in particular, groupware clients are becoming more like WWW browsers.
11. J. E. Gaskin, "Unclogging Your Web Site," *InformationWeek* (1996) 60–63.
12. D. I. S. Agency, "MIL-STD-974 Contractor Integrated Technical Information Service (CITIS)," Defense Information Systems Agency (August 20, 1993).
13. A. Safer, "Electronic Commerce Takes Atlantic Canada by Storm," *Computing Canada* 21 (1995) 54.
14. R. T. King, "The virtual company: when is a company not a company? When it's in a box," *The Wall Street Journal* November 14, 1994, p. R12.
15. G. Gilder, "The Bandwidth Tidal Wave," *Forbes* 154 (1994) 162–173.
16. A. Schurr, "Lower Prices, Desire for Digital Spur ISDN," *PCWeek* 12 (1995) 1–3.
17. J. Sandberg, "GE Says Computers Linked to Internet Were Infiltrated," *The Wall Street Journal* November 28, 1995, p. B5.
18. J. W. Verity, "Hacker Heaven: So Many Computers, So Few Safeguards," *Business Week* 3430 (1995) 96.
19. B. D. Chapman and E. D. Zwicky, *Building Internet Firewalls* (Sebastopol, CA: O'Reilly & Associates, Inc., 1995).
20. S. Garfinkel, *PGP: Pretty Good Privacy* (Sebastopol, CA: O'Reilly & Associates, Inc., 1995).
21. H. Brody, "INTERNET@CROSSROADS.$$$," *Technology Review* 98 (1995) 24–31.
22. A. Knowles, "Internet Tunes In to Cable Reception," *PCWeek* 12 (1995) 105.

$\underline{10}$ | *Virtual Value and the Birth of Virtual Markets*

John J. Sviokla

INCREASINGLY, THE WORLD OF BUSINESS is competing in both the physical world—the marketplace—and the electronic world—the marketspace.[1] There are many different types of marketspace: some are communities of knowledge, others transaction environments.[2] This chapter explores in detail several marketspaces for tangible goods; in particular, electronic markets and market facilitators. An *electronic market* is a system that brings together buyer and seller and provides the operational context in which to consummate a sale. The electronic market "opens the envelope,"[3] providing the rules and means of exchange between buyer and seller. A *market facilitator* is an organization that collects information about buyers and sellers, but does not "open the envelope"; instead, the buyer and seller arrange the exchange. We then explore some new emerging intermediaries, and conclude with a model of how these new marketspaces evolve from a social and technological perspective

In the marketspace, three components of the value equation are critical: content, context, and infrastructure.

Content must be trustworthy, its context easy to use, its infrastructure fast and efficient. Providing this kind of value poses some significant managerial and economic challenges, including the building of consumer trust and the attainment of an economically viable scale.

Not surprisingly, the coming of marketspace has rendered traditional value equations and value propositions vulnerable to change. For the manager, it has created three related challenges. First among them is to learn how to use the virtual value chain to lower costs. Second is to learn how to differentiate one's organization by turning raw data into value for customers. Third is to understand the economics of the marketspace, and how different they are from the traditional "linear" economics of the marketplace.

Traditional business strategy has used notions of economics to show how companies create value through a "value chain"—that is, a sequence of value adding steps.[4] In this established mode of thinking, information is a support function to the central value adding process. This chapter presents four examples of companies directly managing their virtual value chain as a central, not peripheral, value adding process. They show that maximum value is extracted when managers understand how the virtual value chain is different from traditional, physical value chains.

The first case is Pacific Pride,[5] a company that sells commercial gasoline—a tough, low margin industry—in which this successful company uses information to lower costs and add value. The second example, Edmund's, is the most popular automobile price guide on the World Wide Web (WWW). The third example, American Gem Market System, which is a failed information business, helps to suggest what makes for failure as well as success. The final case describes AUCNET,[6] an electronic market for used cars in Japan. The data on these companies can be used to articulate factors for success and failure, as well as the new rules for value extraction in the marketspace.

Pacific Pride: The Power of a Well-managed Virtual Value Chain

When a company can unlock the potential of its virtual value chain, the resulting impact on its profit margin is striking. Take the case of Pacific Pride,[7] a franchised gasoline retailer specializing in commercial refueling. Pacific Pride's target is the commercial customer with a small to medium fleet of vehicles. A pioneer in unmanned gas stations, Pacific Pride offers the customer convenience, control, and credit through a simple ATM-like interface. The company aggregates information about gasoline purchases for the customer in the form of control reports broken down by vehicle, time, and driver.

PREMIUM PRICE FOR ADDED VALUE

When Pacific Pride first implemented its control reports in the late 1980s, management's inclination was to lower the price of fuel to customers. Its investment in unmanned gas stations, and the superior information that investment provided, had lowered the company's costs. Savings arose from more productive use of labor, as well as better control of credit. In fact, Pacific Pride had one of the lowest credit loss ratios in its industry, a fact management attributed to daily reviews of all credit transactions.

Just before implementing the intended price cut, however, one of the company's executives visited a franchisee who was charging a premium price for gasoline. He had convinced his customers that the value added by Pacific Pride's control system should command a premium. In the cutthroat market of commercial refueling, Pacific Pride's customers were paying four to eight cents more per gallon for the extra information. Given that net margins in this segment of the market were usually one to four cents, this price premium was huge. Figure 10-1 illustrates the relative increase in margin Pacific Pride enjoyed.

Pacific Pride's story illustrates the value of the information generated by a core business. In managing its virtual value chain, Pacific Pride unlocked significant margin. Though management had originally invested in information technology in order to lower costs and increase control, the unintended by-product of increased value for consumers proved even more profitable. From a competitive standpoint, their offering is unmatched. Though any major competitor should be able to copy Pacific Pride's innovation, none has yet done so.

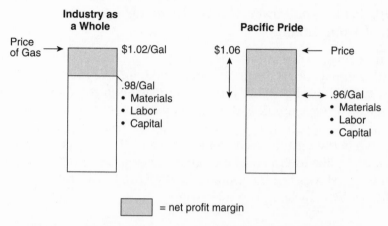

FIGURE 10-1   **Marginal Profit in Commercial Refueling Industry**

SWITCHED VOLUME: A NEW SOURCE OF REVENUE

As a franchiser, Pacific Pride receives two types of revenue: franchise fee income and "switched volume" fees, an invention of Bruce Douglas, CEO of Pacific Pride. Franchise fees are fixed annual fees paid by franchisees. The revenues from franchise fees and the costs associated with the company franchises both vary directly with the number of franchises (Figure 10-2 left).

The switched volume fee proceeds from transactions among franchisees. Pacific Pride licenses franchisees by territory, encouraging the creation of many small (one- to three-unit) franchisees. Though each franchisee signs up its own accounts, customers with fueling needs in more than one area can go to any Pacific Pride station. If one franchisee's customer goes to another franchisee's station, money is transferred from the owner of the account relationship to the other ("foreign") franchisee, to pay for the gas that was pumped. On each of those transactions, Pacific Pride levies a small "switched volume" fee, about 2.5 cents on an average forty gallon purchase.

As the network grows, the switched volume grows, and Pacific Pride earns increasing revenue—not unlike a phone company. The larger the volume of transactions is, the more money the company makes. Because the marginal cost of adding another transaction is trivial, costs do not rise proportionally; almost all the extra marginal revenue drops directly to the bottom line (Figure 10-2 right).

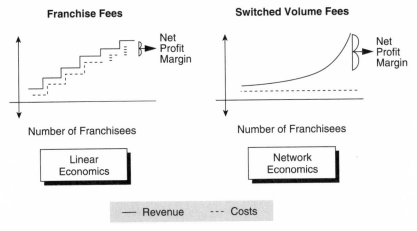

FIGURE 10-2   Franchisee Fee and Switched Volume Fee Revenues and Costs

INCREASING RETURNS TO SCALE

Like many companies, Pacific Pride has used the Virtual Value Chain to lower costs and gain better control over its business. This is the familiar story of *technology substituting for labor* and lowering costs in the process. It is and can continue to be a major motivation for exploiting the virtual value chain. Pacific Pride has also turned the data gathered by its new technology into information, using the basic steps in the virtual value chain model: gather, organize, select, analyze, and distribute.[8] In the process, the company created enough value to convince customers to pay an additional four to eight cents per gallon.

In this respect, Pacific Pride illustrates the difference between marketplace economics and marketspace economics. Marketplace economics encompasses both economies of scale and diseconomies of scale (Figure 10-3). From point a to point b, per-unit costs are falling, creating economies of scale. Point b represents the lowest marginal cost. From point b to point c, unit costs are increasing—that is, rising with volume—and diseconomies of scale are developing. At point c, marginal costs equal marginal revenue—the point of profit maximization for the firm.

Marketspace economics, in contrast, offers increasing returns to scale (Figure 10-4).[9] As in Pacific Pride's case, costs rise very slowly, if at all. To a prospective customer, the marginal cost of becoming a new member of the Pacific Pride network is trivial. Moreover, once the network

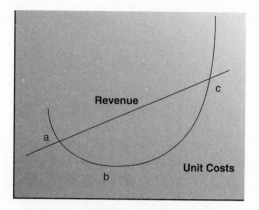

FIGURE 10-3   **Marketplace Economics**

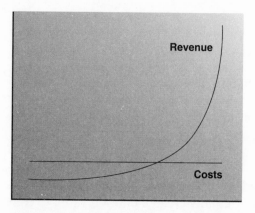

FIGURE 10-4   **Marketspace Economics**

reaches a critical mass, each additional node that joins the network receives tremendous benefits. The telephone network is a common example; one simple device gives a new customer access to the entire world through the global telephone network. The same is true of Pacific Pride: each new franchisee receives access to the company's entire network of stations. Meanwhile, Pacific Pride receives incremental revenue at very little cost.

What lessons can be drawn from this case? Pacific Pride is a company that has used "low tech" management of its information to create value for its customers, by thinking of those data as more than a means of cost control. In the process, it has increased its profitability resoundingly. Its cost control network became the managerial infrastructure on which was built a franchise business, enhancing the company's value. Thus, there are at least three ways to add value through the virtual value chain: lowered cost, added informational value, and increased network fees.

In short, Pacific Pride has a very lucrative information business. It has effectively used information to differentiate a tangible product and create an entirely new business within a business.

Edmund's: From Marketplace to Marketspace

This chapter began with Pacific Pride to show that the virtual chain has implications for businesses with tangible output, like gasoline. Obviously, the virtual value chain is important to businesses whose core value proposition is information, like publishers. For years, leading houses like Simon and Schuster have been putting their content into digital form. Yet even in these businesses, the business model for making money from digital content and for serving the end customer are not that well understood. The example of Edmund's Publishing shows how the virtual value chain turns the traditional economic model inside out.

Over the years, Edmund's *Automobile Buyers' Guides*, first published in 1966, have achieved substantial distribution nationwide, on newsstands and in the automotive section of most large bookstores. By 1995, the company was selling a total of about five hundred thousand units annually. The three main titles in its product line were *New Car Prices & Reviews* (one hundred thirty thousand copies), *New Truck Prices & Reviews* (one hundred twenty thousand copies), and *Used Car Prices & Ratings* (two hundred fifty thousand copies). The company worked hard to keep the customer's trust, accepting very little advertising and maintaining strict separation between its editorial and business departments.

The electronic portion of Edmund's offering was launched in the fall of 1994, when the company's president, Michael Samet, created the firm's first Internet site, featuring free access to comprehensive automobile information, including reviews, specifications, equipment, manufacturers' suggested retail prices (MSRPs), and dealer invoice prices. Since its launch, traffic has grown from approximately fifteen hundred hits by fifty to one hundred users per day to more than seven hundred thousand hits by at least fifteen thousand to twenty thousand users a day. Though the growth rate is hard to measure, by July 1996 volume was increasing at more than ten percent per week.

REFERRAL-DRIVEN ECONOMICS

Although the content of Edmund's web site[10] was very similar to the content of its books, the economics of the two ventures were totally different. The book business was driven by consumer purchases of information; the web business was driven by customer referrals. Edmund's strategic partner in providing automobile referrals was Auto-By-Tel, a Los Angeles-based service started by Pete Ellis, a former automobile dealer. At the Edmund's site, a serious shopper could fill out an Auto-By-Tel form indicating the car make, model, and options desired, as well as the trade-in, lease or purchase, and financing arrangements. Edmund's captured these data and shipped them to Auto-By-Tel, which alerted dealers to the customer's requirements. The customer and dealer were responsible for cutting the deal.

Auto-By-Tel made its money by selling "subscriptions" to its service to the dealers. Every time a customer filled out an Auto-By-Tel (ABT) form at Edmund's site, Edmund's received a "finder's fee" of several dollars, regardless of whether a deal was consummated. The business model for this service is shown in Figure 10-5. Early in the company's history, Edmund's customers were completing approximately one thousand forms a day, generating approximately $1 million profit per year for Edmund's. The quality of the leads generated by Edmund's site was striking. According to ABT's management, the lead-to-sale ratio was fifty percent or more.

The Edmund's brand had been on the market for almost two decades before its launch in cyberspace. The trust in its consumer-oriented price guide helped the company to leverage its existing customer relationships in its new business as an electronic market facilitator. It must be remembered that Edmund's has no direct connection to the dealers. The customer comes to Edmund's for high-quality content and receives the option to fill out a form for the ABT service. Furthermore, Edmund's is not the only means of referral to ABT. ABT advertises its own web site, to which the customer can go directly. Nevertheless, Edmund's forwards the majority of ABT's leads.

BRAND EXTENSION: GEICO REFERRALS

As a market facilitator, Edmund's offers an *inventory of opinion* on cars and their ratings. Just like *Consumer Reports* or *Moody's Bond Rating Service*, Edmund's has a brand name that is respected in the marketplace. When the company brought this name to the Internet, it was able to

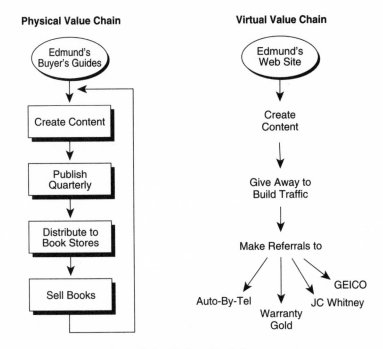

FIGURE 10-5   Inversion of the Value Model

build a critical mass of users in a very short time, due not to a lack of competition—dozens of car rating and car shopping services inhabit the Internet—but to an easy-to-use design and trusted content. Edmund's is now struggling with the question of how far to go in recommending a particular product or service, since maintaining independence on the issues is critical to the company's brand name.

Another issue is whether Edmund's brand can be extended to related, and perhaps even some unrelated goods and services. At its web site in 1996, the company had considerable success in selling insurance through GEICO, a price-oriented direct insurance company. It also tried out pilot programs with JC Whitney, a parts reseller, and Warranty Gold, which offers extended warranties. This combination of insurance, an extended warranty, and a parts program begins to mirror what is available to customers in the physical marketplace. More important, all these sales referrals are achieved without the usual "brick and mortar" necessary to open an automobile dealership. The store and the referrals are real; the only cost is the information.

From Tangible Product to Virtual Service

Edmund's entire value proposition is based on what the customer wants, not what the supplier supplies. That is to say, in the physical world, used parts are typically distributed separately from used cars, despite the fact that the consumer may want the two items together. Meeting all the customer's needs in one context adds value to the relationship, altering the company's positioning from a product or service provider to an experience or solution provider. Not only has Edmund's value equation been turned inside out, then, in that the firm first gives away its content and gets paid later; its books have become more of a service than a tangible product.

Managers at Edmund's are now focusing on shorter and shorter timeframes for revision of its data, moving from quarterly to monthly updates. Soon they will be able to offer weekly or even hourly updates. They also plan to classify the data by city or town, lending even more precision to the service. As they concentrate on managing the virtual value chain more efficiently, the shape of the company's offering evolves into a real-time, online source of data on auto prices and trading opportunities.

In the move from a tangible product distributed through physical distribution channels to a virtual service distributed online, the economics of Edmund's business has changed radically, expanding in the process. Rather than simply selling books, Edmund's now wants to penetrate the auto market as deeply and completely as possible. The ultimate goal is not a single transaction, but multiple referrals covering the entire car-buying, repair, insurance, and warranty process.

So we see that effective management of the information value chain can both create value and change the company's outlook from a supplier-focused mentality to a problem-solving, buyer-focused mentality. This statement is true of all types of products and services. To effectively manage the virtual value chain, managers must begin to think of products and services as *information*. That is, a physical value chain can be described and thought of in terms of information. Once one begins to conceive a product or service in this way, it becomes a "vessel" of value, a bundle of information to be managed for the customer's benefit. Gradually, it becomes less like a product and more like a service. When Pacific Pride added information to the gas it sold, it became more of a service provider than a product provider. When Edmund's began to give its product away online, it became more of a service company.[11] Edmund's and Pacific Pride successfully managed their virtual value chain. However, some companies such as the American Gem Market System, have been unsuccessful in doing the same thing.

American Gem Market System: A Failed Electronic Market

In the mid-1980s, Tony Valente founded American Gem Market System (AGMS) to promote his computer-based gem-grading program.[12] By 1987, he had begun to offer the product online. Valente saw a market opportunity in the over thirty-seven thousand domestic jewelers, with sales of $50 billion in the United States and $125 billion worldwide. He hoped to increase efficiency in transactions among jewelers.

The market AGMS served can be divided into two major submarkets: diamonds and colored stones. The system for rating diamonds had been created by the Gemologists Institute of America (GIA), an organization that dominated the industry. Dealers typically reviewed the merchandise in person when buying stones. A dealer who was interested in a stone another dealer held could request that the stone be sent to him "on memo" using a delivery service like Federal Express. Some dealers retained representatives in foreign countries to gather inventory and ship samples to the United States on memo. But the vast majority of all stones (approximately ninety percent) were sold in person.

INNOVATIVE ONLINE SERVICE

AGMS instituted several innovations in an attempt to change jewelers' buying behavior and create a more efficient system of exchange. It maintained a list of available stones online and offered a means for trading them. A dealer wishing to sell a gem could dial into the system, describe the stone, and add it to the AGMS database. A buyer could then dial into the system to review the available stones, which were indexed by weight, shape, color grade, clarity, grading lab, price per carat, dimensions, and user ID. With a few keystrokes, a jeweler could order a diamond on memo, buy the stone, or haggle on price using the telephone, e-mail, or fax.

In 1987, seventeen thousand transactions occurred on the network, a figure that was artificially low, since AGMS could not track sales that were not closed at list price—an estimated ten percent of the trades done on the system. AGMS used information gleaned from list-price transactions on the network to create price databases, called Average Trade Prices (ATP), which reflected at least five transactions done over a reporting period of no longer than one month. The average ATP was based on twenty-nine transactions. For grades and stones that were rarely traded, prices were extrapolated from a small sample.

To facilitate the trading process, AGMS took advantage of the standard grading criteria for diamonds, defined by the GIA. Each diamond in the database was rated according to these standards. For colored stones, management created an exclusive grading system based on a measurement device they called "ColorMaster," which yielded precise measurements of the color quality of colored stones. AGMS also established a lab for grading gemstones. Its certificates of appraisal were available for $40.00 to $115.00 per stone.

REASONS FOR FAILURE

Despite the significant number of transactions on AGMS, the service never succeeded in becoming economically viable. In late 1987, the vast majority of stones continued to be sold in person rather than online. Adoption of the AGMS ColorMaster peaked at about one-and-a-half percent of the potential market for the system. The company folded in the early 1990s.

Why did this innovative service fail? Creating trust in the process of remote buying was a challenge. The GIA's diamond-rating system was not entirely reliable. Because the GIA was a cooperative association, founded and funded by members, jewelers were allowed considerable latitude in rating their diamonds, a practice that diminished the reliability of the ratings. Furthermore, some nonrated characteristics, principally the cut, were vital in determining a stone's value. Depending on how they had been cut, two stones of the same color, clarity, and carat (weight) might differ markedly in value.

Moreover, the fit between the dealer's customary buying process and the process available online was not good. For the new system to work, dealers would have had to simultaneously adopt a new rating system and change their buying behavior. Even in an emerging industry, the creation of a new rating standard is challenging. In an established industry, it is even more problematic. Time, capital, and much selling effort are required to create trust in a new content standard. When a multitude of local variations complicates the application of the existing standard, the task may be insurmountable.

AUCNET: A Successful Electronic Market

AUCNET, a highly successful electronic market for used cars, facilitates the trading of vehicles among auto dealers in Japan. The process begins with a call or message to the system by a dealer hoping to sell a car. An AUCNET inspector first visits the car to inspect and photograph it. Noting any mechanical problems or cosmetic blemishes, the inspector fills out a rating sheet, grading the car on a scale from one to ten (poor to excellent). To give prospective buyers a "feel" for the vehicle and its condition, the inspector takes one interior and one exterior photo. His ratings and photographs appear with the vehicle listing during the auction.

Throughout the week, AUCNET gathers listings. On Saturday and Sunday, dealers throughout Japan sit at specially designed and dedicated AUCNET terminals to participate in the largest auto auction in the nation. As of July 1995, some three thousand dealers were involved in AUCNET.[13]

ENGAGING INTERFACE

The system is fast and easy to use. Masataka Fujisaki, founder of AUCNET, designed an interface with the flow and engaging quality of a video arcade game.

> It is important to provide realism and excitement in the auction. The video image we provide . . . is not really necessary for the dealers to buy and sell cars—they rely almost entirely on the inspector's report—but it draws them into the auction process. The beep each participant hears when someone else enters a bid is for the same purpose. When a car is sold, we display the name of the successful buyer, so other dealers will think, "My competitor just bought a car; I had better get into the bidding as well."[14]

Like a sophisticated video game, the screen is packed with information for both buyer and seller. During the auction, the buyer sees a screen showing nine vital pieces of information. In the upper left-hand corner is the car's overall rating. To the right is the number of dealers participating in the auction; in the upper right-hand corner, the price. In the lower left-hand corner appears information about the number of dealers who are bidding for the car. To the right is more specific information about the car, including details from the inspection report. Photographs of the car occupy the middle of the screen.

The comprehensive information about the car, and the exciting manner in which it is presented, makes remote trading efficient and effective. The inspector's report and photographs help to build trust in the system. The fact that the entire fleet of cars in Japan is relatively young means that vehicles are likely to be in good condition mechanically. The fact that AUCNET adjudicates any disputes and rapidly resolves them reinforces dealers' confidence in the system.

REAL-TIME AUCTION

In creating a real-time electronic auction, AUCNET faced the difficult challenge of representing market activity onscreen. In a physical auction, the seller can see at a glance how many buyers are interested in the product. This information is very important to both the seller and the auctioneer. To show market activity online, AUCNET created an electronic grid which the auctioneer at AUCNET headquarters can see at all times (Figure 10-6). Squares on the grid represent various geographic locations: circles within the square represent bidding activity in that part of the market. The seller sees a screen similar to the auctioneer's. Buyers, however, cannot see the market activity on the seller's screen.

This engaging system has an extremely fast response time. During an auction, bids are registered onscreen in less than .2 seconds.

To achieve this lightning-fast response time, Fujisaki had to lease and assemble his own telecommunications infrastructure; the public networks proved too slow and unpredictable. By maintaining their own network, AUCNET managers have also obtained a reasonable amount of protection against tampering.

Virtual Markets Are Good Business

AUCNET's electronic market system has significant operating leverage. From 1986 to 1992, prices dropped from 7.6 percent of turnover to 4.7 percent of turnover. During the same period, profit as a percentage of sales revenue increased from 4.45 percent to 22.2 percent. Table 10-1

FIGURE 10-6   **Screen Showing Online Bidding Activity**

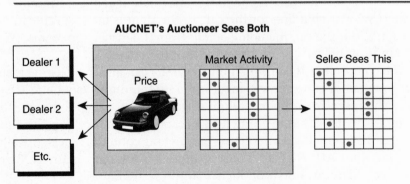

TABLE 10-1 **AUCNET Sales Revenue and Operating Profit**

Year	Turnover Value of Cars Traded	AUCNET Revenue	Operating Profit	Profit as % of Sales	Revenue as % of Turnover
1986	13,232	1,005	44	4.4%	7.6%
1987	19,848	1,159	101	8.7%	5.8%
1988	31,747	1,835	344	18.7%	5.8%
1989	38,800	2,063	335	16.2%	5.3%
1990	58,500	3,095	604	19.5%	5.3%
1991	68,000	3,679	732	19.9%	5.4%
1992	86,900	4,100	912	22.2%	4.7%

illustrates the system's increasing operating leverage and decreasing price over this period.

Note that as the revenue decreased from 7.6 percent to 4.7 percent as a percent of turnover (a thirty-eight percent drop in price to the end customer), profit increased from 4.4 percent of sales to 22.2 percent (a four hundred and four percent increase). These "increasing returns to scale" makes sense. In an electronic market, incremental volume is unlikely to increase variable cost significantly. Moreover, network externalities (e.g., the value each new participant garners from joining the network) should be significant. The price and profit figures for AUCNET support this idea.

Both Edmund's and AUCNET's performance is consistent with economies of scale in their businesses. For each, the marginal cost of additional customers is very low—in Edmund's case, near zero. Thus, marginal revenue is almost all profit. Network externalities work to the advantage of the first mover, and may be difficult for competitors to overcome.

Both these companies are niche competitors; they serve a small market share. The scalability of electronic markets and electronic intermediaries is not yet clear and will not be for some time. But those who have been successful in launching such businesses with sufficient scale, performance, and trust have realized handsome profits.

The Emerging Managerial Issues

Predicting the future of marketspace markets and market facilitators is a challenging task. Following the logic of Oliver Williamson,[15] Yates, Malone and Benjamin[16] have suggested that the increasing availability of information technology will reduce coordination costs, moving more and more transactions from the hierarchical coordination that exists inside firms to market coordination. Thus, we can expect to see increasing use of market mechanisms. As coordination costs fall, electronic markets and market facilitators may become important institutions. There are many examples on the Internet already of this increasing orientation toward market mechanisms, two of which are discussed later in this chapter.

Internet Liquidators, Inc. (ILI)

An Internet-based Dutch auction company, ILI was founded toward the end of 1995 and began conducting business in the Spring of 1996.[17] Dutch farmers conceptualized this auction style during the late nineteenth century as a way to increase profits for their popular flowers and undermine the machinations of frugal buyers who played sellers off one another. In a Dutch auction, the price of a product drops until the supply is exhausted, thus playing buyers against one another and giving sellers better prices. If a buyer waits too long before deciding on a price, there may not be any inventory left to purchase. ILI takes this concept and substitutes consumer electronics for flowers and marketspace for the marketplace. Consumers can access the site and review descriptions and photos of products such as stereo equipment or cellular phones. Information for the items on the block is updated by three counters: the unit counter, the time clock, and the price display. These counters keep the consumer posted on the number of units remaining, the amount of time left in the auction, and the current price level of competing bidders.

This firm is rapidly becoming a "standard" auction exchange for different businesses. Their largest customer is America Online, which is using the ILI technology to provide live auctions that contain hundred, thousands, even hundreds of thousands of bidders in one auction.

ONSALE Dealer Exchange

ONSALE Dealer Exchange is another Dutch auction company that has a web site on the Internet.[18] It operates in the same manner as ILI and subsets products into categories and lists of "hot deals." Their products consist of computer components and peripherals as well as high fidelity audio and home appliances. Images of the items are featured as well as information on the list price, minimum bid, quantity available, and current bidders.

INCREASING PRICE PRESSURE

With this increasing number of new market-based intermediaries, we can expect to see increasing price pressure throughout most industries. Prices and their components will become more visible throughout the value network. Edmund's electronic service is much more accessible to end customers than its books, helping to spread the information even faster. Interviews with auto dealers confirm that the electronic buyer is more price-oriented than the traditional buyer. We do not yet know whether the price-sensitive buyer gravitates to Edmund's, or Edmund's data make buyers more price oriented. In either case, the consumer now has a valuable and powerful information resource. ONSALE provides an environment where inventory can be liquidated, as does Internet Liquidators.

THE GEOGRAPHIC SCOPE OF MARKETS

Another issue for the executive is that it will be much easier for a distant competitor to operate in your local market. In AUCNET, the cars and dealer competition were no longer local, but nationwide. Many markets that are local or regional now may go national or global as technology streamlines the channel structures of various industries. Existing intermediaries will not be put out of business, but new services that the individual intermediary cannot provide will become available. If they are well managed, their cost structure should become less asset-intensive, enabling more aggressive but still profitable pricing. On the web, we already see some of the market facilitators starting to make this distant competition come closer to home.

China Business Net Pages

China Business Net Pages is a resource, available on the web[19] that provides information on businesses. Core to the site is the China Business Center (CBC), which aids companies in marketing their products in China. This company provides its clients with services that help analyze their competitors by gathering data on the market share and price of existing products, as well as market size and growth rate. In addition, companies can have the CBC recruit local distributors for their products and develop an exhibition and advertising campaign for them.

This site also has a host of other areas that can be reviewed by prospective companies. These areas supply data on a variety of areas such as weekly business briefs, investment projects, stock and exchange data, and products and companies currently interacting with China.

GE Trading Process Network (TPN)

The GE TPN is a collection of web-based products and services developed to increase productivity and create new markets and business opportunities.[20] This site allows buyers and sellers to conduct business electronically and simplify tasks associated with purchasing, sales and marketing. The purchasing process benefits from TPN's combination of software and service that assists buyers in locating suppliers worldwide thus reducing their cycle times. Sales costs are reduced through the automation of sales, bidding, and ordering procedures. Also, product information and specifications can be submitted electronically to interested customers. In addition, the buyers and sellers who use the TPN to trade goods and services are able to market their companies to customers from around the world.

THE EMERGENCE OF NEW INSTITUTIONS

At least one implication of the increasing trend toward market making and the new scope of markets will be the creation of new institutions that take advantage of these two capabilities. These new institutions will enjoy economies of scale and scope. To date, much of what has been written about the "virtual organization"[21] has argued either implicitly or explicitly for a decrease in the economic scale of the business enterprise. We argue here that though virtual markets may be less asset-intensive than their forerunners, it does not mean that they will be smaller. Consumers benefit from strong brands. Significant benefits will accrue to organizations that sense the customer's needs and meet them at a profitable price through vertical or virtual integration.

Finally, the rise of new electronic markets and intermediaries may lead to important new economic institutions with significant economies of scale and scope. Will there be a "global clearinghouse" for automobiles? For used parts? As markets become more important, the institutional power of existing organizations may wane. New markets and market facilitators may gain significant scale and scope, rendering themselves more or less impervious to competition by new entrants. The challenge for the manager is to begin to assess where and how these new institutions might arise. In order to begin to see the outline of an answer to that question, it is necessary to understand how the Internet and the web are changing the fundamental nature of exchange. The above examples imply a larger, more universal set of issues explored below.

Markets as Technological and Social Inventions

With the advent of the Internet and the WWW, we now have the beginnings of standard parts of knowledge work. This has profound implications for the conduct of business because the rules, method, and median of exchange can be established by companies, not just governments.[22] At a very elemental level, the advent of the Internet and its web created a platform that enabled standardization of documents, file transfer, and e-mail addressing.

Technology as Transaction Engine and Social Artifact

In order to understand the potential of different organizations to act as market makers, we use a model of technology which has two fundamental parts: a technical component and a social component. The bias that technology is solely a tangible construct is the first and primary assumption that must be challenged. In many discussions of technology, a clear definition is not offered. In the research realm, traditional models of technology often implicitly assume that technology was well known and its uses clear (Figure 10-7).

FIGURE 10-7 Traditional Model of Technology

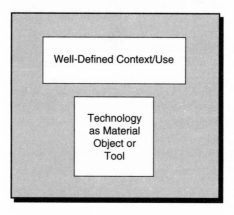

However, the traditional model does not adequately describe the social components of technology. Tools and methods involve social context in their development and use. For example, the shaving razor's design incorporates cultural changes in personal grooming. Using it to peel potatoes would seem ridiculous. The design of the razor embeds notions of how, when, where, and by whom it will be used. Informed investigations[23-25] consider the social context as well. The revisionist model acknowledges that at the core of the concept of technology lies some business or scientific knowledge applied to yield some method or tool. In turn, these artifacts sit within a social context interpreted at individual and organizational levels (Figure 10-8).

Grasping the social components of technology is crucial to the discussion of electronic markets. Electronic markets often take methods that are specific to one form or to one standard-setting body and codify them into tools. As the WWW becomes more pervasive, it will embody and share more of these electronic exchange tools. Thus the technical

FIGURE 10-8   **Revisionist Model of Technology**

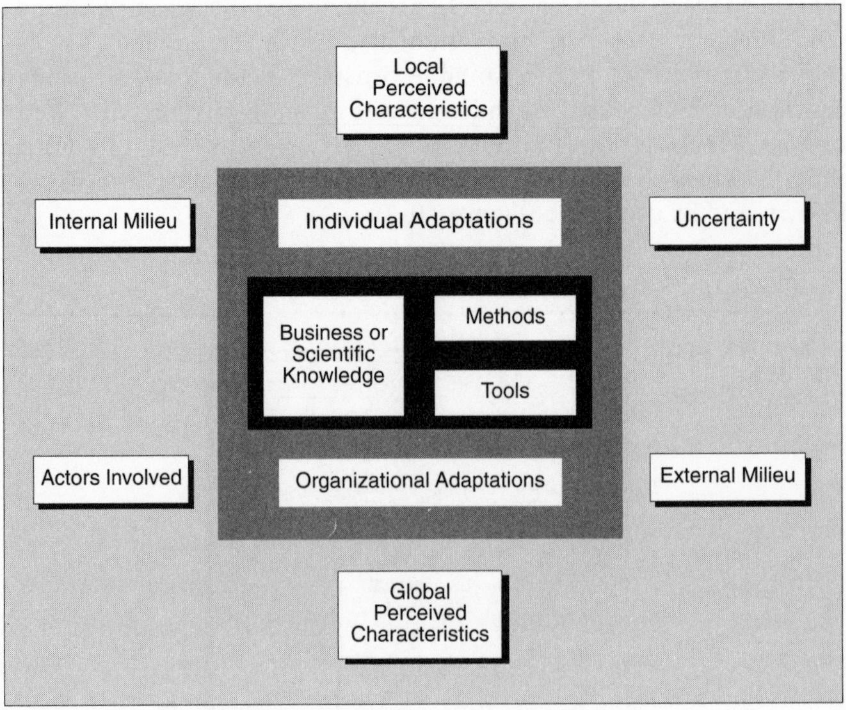

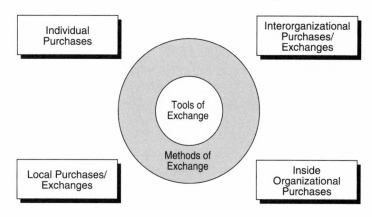

Figure 10-9 **Model of Technology-in-Context**

core is embedded in a related constellation of social contexts. Figure 10-9 shows a focused model of technology-in-context.

The technical components of some technologies are almost completely tool-oriented. For example, an umbrella is a tool that has a very thin band of method wrapped around it. This is the technical core of the umbrella technology. Other technologies, such as getting a medical physical examination (if one is healthy), rely on a very heavy dose of method and utilize very little tool.

The analytic usefulness of this model is that it highlights a core aspect of information technology: the constraint aim of information technology is to take methods and embed them in tools (e.g., software/hardware).

Social context can range from the individual domain to the global domain. For example, individuals using personal computers often use highly-personalized tools and methods. Airline reservation systems use a very standardized set of tools and methods across the industry. They became the electronic market of choice in that industry. Often, the progress of information technologies moves across an increasingly expansive social context (e.g., counterclockwise around the grid), as if pursuing a trend toward stability and conformity.

The social side includes the myriad local, organizational, and/or global adjustments and routines developed to make the tools and methods useful in context. This definition of technology purposely puts people and social context in front of creating, defining, and using technology in these new markets.

Management and Technology Transfer

Creating new markets is one aspect of creating change. The process of market making can be viewed as transferring relevant tools and methods from one environment to another. Moving an individual's productivity tool across the organization is one form of technology transfer. Moving a technology out of the global context and into an organization is another type of transfer. In this chapter, we have seen that in order to effectively manage a transaction often at the inter-organizational level, a mass of trusted content is one strong, patented enabler of such a market. There will be others as organizations begin to share their core "purchasing" technology with broader and broader environments.

The interesting challenge for management is that as they employ the WWW, to create a set of standard tools for the handling of files, documents, and communication, they are laying the groundwork for an open, worldwide, market-making infrastructure that is the same, desktop to desktop, around the globe. That is a profound change in markets and transaction environments.

Conclusion

In the shift from marketplace to marketspace, a fundamental economic change has begun to occur. Electronic intermediaries or markets that can create the content, context, and infrastructure consumers want have the chance to develop a successful new business model. Trusted content, a viable economic scale, and compatibility with the consumer's buying habits are critical to this business model.

With the advent of the Information Age, the nature of the value proposition is changing for products as well as services. To maximize their firms' competitive position, managers should be mindful of developing trends in their industries, especially toward new marketspace intermediaries that can tap the power of a well-managed virtual value chain. Executives need to understand that these new standard parts for knowledge work will provide the platform for the evolution and sustenance of many, many new forms of transactions. New economies of scale and scope are available to innovators; second movers may suffer the consequences of inaction.

Endnotes

1. J. Rayport and J. Sviokla, "Managing in the Marketspace," *Harvard Business Review* (November–December 1994). Reprint, 141–150.

2. A. Armstrong and J Hagel, III, "Real Value of On-Line Communities," *Harvard Business Review* (May–June 1996). Reprint 96301.
3. We are indebted to Benn Konsynski, Emory Business School, Emory University, for this distinction between electronic markets and electronic market facilitators.
4. McKinsey & Company was one of the first proponents of the value chain concept, as was Joe Bower of the Harvard Business School. Michael Porter, in his book *Competitive Advantage*, has performed the most complete explication of the value chain concept
5. J. Sviokla and W. Schiano, "Pacific Pride Services, Inc.," *Harvard Business School Publishing* (July 1993). Reprint 194–007.
6. B. Konsynski, A. Warbelow, and J. Kokuryo, "AUCNET: TV Auction Network System," *Harvard Business School Publishing* (July 1989). Reprint 190–001.
7. See Pacific Pride's Web Site http://www.pacificprideusa.com/
8. J. Rayport and J. Sviokla, "Exploiting the Virtual Value Chain," *Harvard Business Review* (November–December 1995). Reprint 95610, 75–85.
9. B. Arthur, "Positive Feedbacks in the Economy," *Scientific American* (November 26, 1989).
10. See Edmund's Publishing Web Site http://www.edmunds.com/
11. This distinction draws on a conversation I had with Jeffrey Rayport in January 1996.
12. A. Warbelow and B. Konsynski, "American Gem Market System," *Harvard Business School Publishing*. No. 189-088.
13. AUCNET: The Story Continues, *Harvard Business School Publishing* (January 1995). No. 195–122.
14. B. Konsynski, A. Warbelow, and J. Kokuryo, "AUCNET: TV Auction Network System," *Harvard Business School Publishing* (July 1989). Reprint 190–001, 2.
15. O. E. Williamson, *Markets and Hierarchies, Analysis and Antitrust Implications: A Study in the Economics of Internal Organization* (New York: Free Press, 1975).
16. J. Yates, T. Malone, and B. Benjamin, "Logic of Electronic Markets," *Harvard Business Review* (May–June 1989).
17. See ILI's Web Site http://www.internetliquidators.com/
18. See ONSALE Dealer Exchange's Web Site http://www.onsale.com
19. See China Business Net Page's Web Site http://www.business-china.com/
20. See GE Trading Process Network's Web Site http://www.ge.com/
21. J. Sviokla, "Making Money with Information: Marketspace and the Engines of Profit" (working paper, Boston: Harvard Business School Division of Research, 1997).
22. D. Spar and J. Bussgang, "Ruling the Net," *Harvard Business Review* (May–June 1996). Reprint 96309.
23. C. H. Pava, *Managing New Office Technology* (New York: Free Press, 1983).
24. R. E. Walton, *Up and Running: Integrating Information Technology and the Organization* (Boston: Harvard Business School Press, 1989).
25. S. Zuboff, *In the Age of the Smart Machine: The Future of Power and Work* (New York: Basic Books, Inc., 1988).

11 *Real Shopping in a Virtual Store*

Raymond R. Burke

"RETAILING WILL NEVER BE THE SAME"—so proclaimed the cover of the July 26, 1993, issue of *Business Week*. The article inside described how home shopping using interactive television would revolutionize retailing. Through fiber optic cable, digital image compression, video servers, and powerful set-top boxes, five hundred or more TV channels would bring engaging new applications like home shopping, banking, and video-on-demand to consumers' homes. Major agreements had been made among cable, telephone, computer, and entertainment companies to develop and deploy the new interactive services. Jupiter Communications was forecasting that interactive TV sales would approach $10 billion by 2002, involving 17.6 percent of U.S. households. R. Fulton Macdonald, president of International Business Development Corp., went even further, predicting that home shopping would grow to $250 billion in ten years.

Unfortunately, the industry agreements collapsed and the new services never materialized. Today, similar claims are being made about the Internet. Business publications, consultants, academics, and high-tech companies—all trumpet the news that the Internet will change forever the way we work, play, shop, bank, communicate, and learn. But business history suggests we should be pessimistic. Will our lives never be the same? And if they will be different, how will the relationships among consumers, manufacturers, and retailers change?

Why Shop in a Virtual Store?

Electronic shopping has been available for several years through various online services, including America Online (AOL), CompuServe, and Prodigy, as well as on the Internet and on television channels like QVC and HSN. Sales results to date have been unimpressive. Of the $2.2 trillion in annual U.S. retail sales, only about $70 billion is made through nonstore formats, including catalogs, television, and mail order. Television and other electronic sales account for just $4 billion, or 0.2 percent of total annual retail sales—and forty percent of that amount is for jewelry! Sales through the Internet and online services amounted to only about $520 million in 1996—less than 0.03 percent of the total.

Despite this poor performance, electronic shopping may yet become a significant force in retailing. Consumer acceptance of nonstore retailing is higher than the sales figures suggest. Each year about fifty-five percent of U.S. households purchase products from catalogs, and about seven percent from television. Sales are limited in part because few products are available through these channels. Once most consumers are able to purchase high-volume items like groceries and drugs through the Internet, electronic sales may increase dramatically.

Another reason for optimism is the recent rapid growth in home computing and the communications infrastructure. American homes now hold over forty million PCs, most of which have advanced communications and multimedia capabilities. Connections to online services have been growing steadily. Nielsen Media Research reported that between August 1995 and March 1996, the number of people in the United States and Canada with Internet access jumped by fifty percent, to an estimated twenty-four percent penetration level. An ongoing survey by INTECO Corporation indicated that between May and September 1996, the number of adult Internet users in the United States rose from twenty-eight million to thirty-three million. By April 1997, the number had mushroomed to forty-eight million; with nineteen million people accessing the Internet from home, seventeen million from work or school, and twelve million from both home and work or school.

The Virtual Store in Historical Context

Consumers will shop electronically only if the experience provides significant advantages over conventional shopping. While this fact may seem obvious, few of the firms that are developing interactive shopping applications have conducted research on consumers' needs and desires for such services. Instead, they have been focusing on what is technically possible.

In the past, two major consumer benefits have driven the emergence of new retail formats: convenience and economy. The first gave us convenience stores, which offer consumers a limited selection of products at convenient locations, with extended hours of operation and short waiting lines. The benefit of convenience also drove the development of huge supercenters that sell groceries, prepared foods, general merchandise, soft goods, and a variety of other items, all under one roof. Consumers have responded positively to the convenience of one-stop shopping. They now buy more nonprescription drug products and flowers from supermarkets than from drug stores and florists.

The second major benefit, lower prices, drove the development of warehouse clubs (Sam's, Costco, BJ's) and mass merchandise outlets like Wal*Mart. These channels are designed to maximize operational efficiency. Through bulk purchasing, centralized inventory, inexpensive store locations and fixtures, and continuous replenishment, they cut costs and pass the savings on to consumers.

The virtual store has the potential to deliver both convenience and economy. In conventional retailing, the physical store handles all the distribution functions, including the provision of product information, taking of orders, delivery of merchandise, and handling of post-sales customer service. In this setting there is a natural tension between the need to offer high levels of convenience, customer service, and product variety and the need to minimize costs. Such a conflict does not exist in the virtual store, which splits apart the distribution functions, providing product information and taking orders electronically and then delivering merchandise to the consumer's home from a centralized fulfillment center. By eliminating the expense of maintaining conventional retail stores, and handling deliveries from a dedicated warehouse, virtual retailers can cut distribution costs by twenty-five to thirty percent, while simultaneously offering a larger product assortment and reducing the problems of being out-of-stock on certain items.

The Virtual Grocery Store

Groceries are an important part of both the U.S. and global economies. In 1996, U.S. grocery sales were about $400 billion, or one-fifth of total retail sales. Half the world's population is involved in the production, distribution, or sale of food products.

Even in industrialized nations, shopping for food takes a considerable amount of time. Each week, consumers in the United States spend an average of about 1.5 hours grocery shopping, making 2.5 trips to the store. Their method of shopping is incredibly inefficient. Shoppers purchase the same products week after week, walking up and down the aisles each time. An analysis of the average customer's shopping basket reveals that about eighty-five percent of the items are replenishment purchases—milk, bread, meat, produce, deli, paper products, and soft drinks.

Not surprisingly, most people don't like grocery shopping. A 1990 University of Michigan study asked respondents to rank twenty-two daily activities by how much they enjoyed doing them. Food shopping ranked next to last, just above housekeeping.

The virtual store provides a potential solution to the inefficiency of conventional shopping. To measure consumers' reactions to the concept, researchers conducted six focus groups in the eastern, midwestern, and western regions of the United States. Each group included eight to ten people, screened to exclude those who were not the principal grocery shoppers in the home. Participants shopped for groceries and over-the-counter drugs using a three-dimensional (3D) shopping simulation developed by the author (Figure 11-1).[1] Inside the virtual store, shoppers could remove a product from the shelf, rotate it to examine its packaging, and purchase it by dropping it into a shopping cart. Afterward, participants were asked to discuss their reactions to the system.

Though most people liked virtual shopping, reactions varied by consumer segment. Those who reacted most positively—consumers from dual-income households or single-parent families, and the disabled—had significant time or mobility constraints. They perceived grocery shopping as an unpleasant but necessary task and complained of long checkout lines and poor service. Those who reacted less positively had

FIGURE 11-1   Picking Up and Examining a Product in the 3D Virtual Store

ample time available and saw shopping as a chance to get out of the house and socialize with others. For stay-at-home mothers, grocery shopping was an excuse to get away from the children. For retirees, it was entertainment and a chance to make social contacts.

Convenience proved an important feature of the new system. Shoppers appreciated the ability to visit the virtual store at any hour, and to perform other activities, like exercise, cooking, and child care, while shopping. They could shop even when transportation was unavailable and avoid crowded parking lots or bad weather. The simulation eliminated drive time and checkout time, and allowed shoppers access to distant stores. The weight and bulk of packages no longer constrained the size of their orders. Shoppers were concerned about the timing and handling of deliveries. They worried that delivery times might be inconvenient—especially for products they needed immediately, like milk and bread—and that perishable items might spoil or melt in transit.

Shoppers commented on the differences in the quantity and quality of information provided in the real and virtual shopping environments. The virtual shopping simulation did not allow them to make contact with the merchandise, so they could not touch, smell, or taste products. Because shoppers made their selections at the product type or shopkeeping unit level, they could not pick the ripest fruit or the dairy products with the latest expiration dates. On the other hand, they could often make better and faster decisions in the virtual store and could construct their shopping lists at home as the need arose, with input from family members.

Once shoppers entered the virtual store, the computer would display only relevant and desired product categories and brands (deleting, for example, the pet food aisle for non-pet-owners, and high-salt and -cholesterol products for consumers with dietary restrictions). The computer also facilitated comparison shopping by providing additional product information and highlighting new products and store specials. Because consumers did not need to compress their shopping into a single weekly trip, they had more time to shop. And because displays were not constrained by floor space, shoppers expected to find a greater selection of products in the virtual store.

Participants noted several economic costs and benefits of virtual shopping. Though catalog shopping had required them to pay shipping and handling fees, some virtual shoppers objected to paying delivery charges for groceries. They compared groceries with fast food, which was delivered without extra charges. Other virtual shoppers said they would be willing to pay a fixed charge for grocery delivery and would amortize the cost by making larger orders less frequently. Consumers expected that delivery charges would eventually be eliminated as competition between retailers increased, employees became more efficient at selecting, packing, and transporting groceries, and stores were closed, reducing overhead. Many also expected to shop more efficiently in a virtual store, clipping and redeeming coupons electronically and monitoring the cost of the products they purchased continuously. Some consumers mentioned other advantages, including the safety and entertainment of shopping from home and the ecological benefit of eliminating short driving trips. Respondents were split on the social implications of the technology. Some felt that electronic shopping would isolate consumers from the real world, removing the sensory stimulation of the store displays, contact with other shoppers, and the exercise of walking the aisles. Others argued that virtual shopping would allow more time for more fulfilling activities with family and friends.

Delivering the Goods

Creating customer value though information technology is just one of the key requirements for success in electronic retailing. Another is delivering that value to consumers through the physical fulfillment process. While the cost of information technology declines exponentially,

logistics costs fall at a much more gradual rate. And because food products are low margin, bulky, and perishable, efficient logistics are critical to the profitability of a virtual grocery shopping business.

What is the best way to deliver grocery products to consumers?
Home shopping services in the United States have, for the most part,
taken one of three approaches to product fulfillment. The first and most
common approach is the store-to-door model. When a customer places
an order, the list of items (sorted by aisle) is transmitted to an existing
retail store, where store personnel pick and pack the order. A courier
then loads the merchandise onto a delivery van and drives it to the
customer's home at the specified time. This approach was pioneered by
Shoppers Express, Inc., of Bethesda, Maryland, one of the oldest and
largest grocery shopping and delivery services in the United States.
Founded in 1987, Shoppers Express has expanded to ten major U.S.
markets in as many years. A similar fulfillment approach was taken by
Shopping Alternatives, Inc., a firm started in 1994 by three former
Shoppers Express executives. Peapod L.P., an Evanston, Illinois-based
home shopping company, followed a similar procedure but used its
own employees to pick and pack the merchandise and deliver it to customers' homes. Peapod was launched in Chicago, Illinois, in 1990, and
had expanded to seven major U.S. markets by the Spring of 1997.[2]

This approach minimizes the initial capital investment required to
offer a home shopping service because it uses existing retail space and
delivery services. However, it has the highest operating cost, ranging
from $10 to $20 per order. The largest part of this expense is the courier
service, which is in greatest demand during the evening, when most
people are at home. None of the store overhead cost is eliminated. Not
surprisingly, the high cost of this service severely limits its appeal; most
customers are unwilling to spend more than $10 for home delivery.

A second approach is the warehouse-to-pantry model, which was
introduced in 1995 by Streamline of Westwood, Massachusetts. For a
$30 monthly fee, Streamline handled a variety of routine tasks in ad-
dition to grocery shopping, including dry cleaning and video rentals. In
this approach, the home shopping company provides each household
with a storage receptacle ("pantry") with three separate temperature
zones: room temperature, refrigerated, and frozen. The pantry is located at the customer's home—in the garage, on the porch, or in some
other secure but easily accessed place. Although the customer can place
an order at any time, orders are filled on a regular schedule. They are
picked and packed at an automated warehouse, loaded onto a truck
several orders at a time, and delivered to the customers' pantries. Because deliveries are scheduled in advance and are made throughout the

day, whether or not the customer is at home, trucks can be routed and operated more efficiently.

As noted earlier, the dedicated warehouse has lower costs for real estate, inventory, fixtures, lighting, and personnel than the conventional store. With sufficient volume, these savings can offset delivery costs, so that merchandise can be sold to consumers at prices the same as, or lower than, conventional store prices. Whether or not most people will be willing to allow service providers to install and access the pantries remains to be seen. If consumer acceptance is high, a powerful barrier to competitive entry may arise, since customers are unlikely to install more than one pantry in their homes.

A third approach to product fulfillment, pioneered by Groceries To Go of Medford, Massachusetts, is the depot-to-car model. When a customer places an order, the list of desired items is transmitted to a drive-through depot. Service operators pick and pack the order and store it in three bundles: room temperature, refrigerated, and frozen. Because each bundle is stored at the proper temperature, orders can be held for an extended period. When the customer arrives at the depot to pick up the order, operators pull the three bundles of merchandise together and load them into the customer's car. At some facilities, shoppers can leave their cars to select fresh produce, flowers, prepared meals, and other value-added products.

The depot-to-car model eliminates the single biggest cost of most home shopping services: home delivery. In consumer focus groups, a significant percentage of shoppers stated that they would prefer driving to a depot for an order than waiting for it at home, especially if doing their own driving would reduce the cost of the service. While the real-estate costs for depots are lower than those for conventional supermarkets, these facilities must still be located in high-traffic areas, to allow convenient customer access.

Each of these three fulfillment models has unique advantages and disadvantages, some or all of which may appeal to different consumer segments. No single approach is likely to prevail in the near future. Instead, as home shopping companies test and refine their systems, various hybrid models will emerge.

Designing the Customer Interface

As we move from the physical to the virtual store, manufacturers and retailers are faced with many options concerning the design of the customer interface. Is it better to use a text-based catalog shopping system or a 3D model of the physical store? How much product information should be available? Should we allow comparison shopping? Do we need to provide online customer service representatives? These are important decisions, because the design of the customer interface can have a dramatic impact on consumers' purchase behavior as well as affect the costs to set up and administer the home shopping system. The interface can influence the system's ease of use and speed of operation, it can encourage or discourage planned purchasing, make product information more or less accessible, and facilitate or inhibit the purchase of certain brands.

TEXT-BASED VERSUS GRAPHICAL SYSTEMS

A basic choice in the design of a home shopping system is whether to use a text-based or graphical system. Until recently, the limited processing capacity of home computers and the narrow bandwidth of the Internet made it impractical to offer systems that used extensive graphics. However, these technological constraints are rapidly disappearing.

To explore this issue, the author and several colleagues at the Wharton School of the University of Pennsylvania recruited a panel of consumers from a suburban community in the northeastern United States. Participants were asked to keep a written record of and receipts for all grocery purchases they made during a seven-month period.[3] At the end of the period, they were brought to a laboratory and asked to try two types of home shopping systems. The first, a text-based system, displayed alphabetical lists of brands and the associated size, price, and promotional information for each product category. Shoppers highlighted their preferences and typed in purchase quantities; they were free to delete items they did not want from the list. The second system, a graphical one, displayed realistic images of product packages, shelf displays, and shelf tags, arranged as in a conventional store (Figure 11-2). Respondents selected items from the shelves using a trackball.

For both systems, product category sales were fifty to one hundred percent higher than sales levels observed in physical stores. These results were consistent with those of commercial home-shopping companies. They may be a consequence of the freedom from the constraints of available cash and carrying capacity that consumers experience in in-store shopping. (A similar increase in order size was observed in 1936, when Sylvan Goldman introduced the shopping cart to replace the hand-held basket.) Another explanation might be that shoppers were placing larger orders less frequently to amortize the fixed delivery fees.

FIGURE 11-2   **A Customer Shops with the Graphical System**

While order size was larger, the distribution of preferences across brands was similar to that of in-store shopping Correlations between estimated brand shares in the two environments ranged from 0.70 to 0.96 across product categories. The electronic shopping systems did not bias consumer preferences in favor of national or private-label brands.

Across shopping trips there was significantly less brand switching in the two virtual stores than in physical stores. The computer simulations minimized extraneous events that might disrupt habitual purchasing, such as out-of-stock conditions, manufacturers' coupons, promotions, and the activities of other shoppers. If participants had been given the option to recall their last shopping trip and place the same order again, the inertia in brand preference would likely have been even greater.

On a number of dimensions, the text-based and graphical systems produced different patterns in consumer behavior. First, shoppers took significantly longer to make their purchases in the text-based system, particularly during their first few shopping trips, in which brand selection often took several minutes per category. Because the text-based system did not provide familiar visual cues like package location, shape, and color, shoppers were forced to recall and search for the names of their preferred brands in the alphabetical lists. Second, shoppers were significantly more price sensitive in the text-based simulation than in either the graphical simulation or in-store shopping. While the graphical system displayed price tags in correct proportion to the shelves and packages, the text-based system gave prices the same prominence as the package size information and brand names. Third, consumers tended to buy the same size packages in the graphical system as they did in the real store, but not in the text-based system. This result suggests that shoppers use a package's appearance rather than its weight as a purchase cue, and become confused if they must rely exclusively on the latter.

In summary, because the text-based shopping interface was a greater departure from the physical store than the graphical system, it took longer for consumers to learn its operation and produced more significant changes in customers' purchase behavior.

THE HUMAN SIDE OF VIRTUAL SHOPPING

Another choice in designing a home shopping system is whether to provide customers with the option of communicating with a salesperson or customer service representative. Most existing computer shopping systems are designed to reduce costs by replacing expensive human labor with computerized shopping assistance. However, some people have expressed concern that this will reduce human contact, social interaction, and personal service. This trend may not be a problem in retailing environments that have traditionally been self-service, such as grocery and mass merchandise stores. Consumers are generally familiar with the product categories and brands in these stores, and the computer can effectively supplement their knowledge with keyword search engines, product descriptions, and photographs. And because most of the products sold in these stores are relatively inexpensive, the economic risk of making a poor decision is low.

In other shopping environments, however, human interaction can play a critical role in a transaction. When consumers with widely varying levels of existing knowledge must select among several complex products, providing one shopping interface that addresses everyone's needs is difficult. Examples include financial services, insurance policies, medical products, and complex durable goods. In these cases, shoppers may not be willing to make online purchases with information that is incomplete, conflicting, or hard to understand. Marketers of such products and services might benefit from developing interfaces that provide real-time interaction with customer service personnel, including voice and video-conferencing. In the short term, consumers are unlikely to have video cameras in their homes. However, the image of the customer service representative (CSR) can still be displayed on the consumer's monitor using one-way video-conferencing. The quality of the interaction is somewhat lower in the one-way system, since the CSR cannot tailor the presentation based on the facial reactions and body language of the customer. However, some customers are relieved that they are not "on camera" and do not need to be concerned about their appearance.

To explore the issue of audio- and video-enhanced electronic shopping systems, the author and a Harvard graduate student, Teymour Farman-Farmaian, conducted two studies. In the first, we worked with a Boston-area bank to create a Virtual Financial Center. In the second, we created a Virtual Bookstore, based on a chain store's electronic catalog system. Both systems provided textual product descriptions through a "point and click" interface.

In our study of the Virtual Financial Center, we found that customers made purchases faster and with greater satisfaction when they moved from using a computer system with audio alone to one-way video-conferencing, and then to two-way video-conferencing. Yet we did not observe the same effect in the Virtual Bookstore. Asked about their reactions to the Virtual Bookstore and Financial Center, customers were enthusiastic about the speed and convenience of both services and appreciated the access they provided to customer service representatives. However, bookstore shoppers did not feel that the video-conferencing element added value and complained that they could not browse the store's aisles.[4] In contrast, people liked making visual contact with the bank staff, and were more likely to switch banks to gain that feature.

We also found that the appeal of the technology varied by customer segment. Heavy users of automated teller machines (ATMs) gave the Virtual Financial Center a higher overall rating than non-ATM customers. However, the latter group responded more positively to the addition of video-conferencing (see Figure 11-3). These "branch wed" customers appeared to require a greater sense of human contact in their electronic banking transactions. Thus video-conferencing may be a valuable tool for increasing the use of electronic shopping systems by customers who have been slow to adopt information technology.

ENHANCED INTERFACES

The systems tested by researchers provided only the most basic levels of functionality. One can speculate about the results that enhancements of the interface might produce. For example, a grocery shopping

FIGURE 11-3 **Electronic Banking Using Video Conferencing**

interface that is designed to allow shoppers to recall shopping lists, access product categories directly rather than in a fixed sequence, and access and apply coupons electronically would likely result in more planned and fewer impulse purchases. A computer that allows shoppers to sort brands based on price per ounce, nutritional content, and performance dimensions might commoditize product categories, shifting consumer preferences to high-value products and reducing interest in premium-priced branded merchandise. As it becomes easier to comparison shop, markets may become more efficient, and retailers' gross margins might drop.

In seeking to increase their shopping efficiency through enhanced systems, consumers may reallocate their time across categories, reducing the time they spend shopping for household and other functional products (perhaps by automating those purchases) and increasing the time they spend shopping for food, health and beauty aids, travel, and entertainment products—categories in which variety is highly valued.

As a consequence, high-value brands in functional categories may achieve high loyalty (inertia), whereas specialized niche products in the food, personal care, and other sensory-based categories may gain increased purchases. With direct access to categories and brands through their home shopping systems, consumers will be able to find the products they want more easily. John Kaula, president of the Point of Purchase Advertising Institute, indicates that this benefit alone may increase retail sales by an average of 6.7 percent.

Many of these issues are currently being investigated at Indiana University's Customer Interface Lab, which studies the impact of new technologies on the way customers shop. Researchers there use advanced 3D graphics, multimedia, and communications technologies to rapidly establish prototypes and test new physical and virtual shopping environments. While the equipment in the lab is more sophisticated than the computers consumers have in their homes today, these new capabilities are likely to become commonplace within the next few years.

The Future of Virtual Shopping

As retailing has moved from the country store to the superstore, and branded merchandise has proliferated, consumers have become comfortable buying products without physically handling them. This change in behavior, along with the development of interactive media, has created the opportunity for the emergence of virtual stores. Consumers are attracted to the potential benefits of convenience, economy, and improved decision making. Yet they continue to hold reservations about buying some products, like perishables and soft goods, without handling them. Over the short term, interactive retailers can address these concerns by building consumer trust through familiar store names, branded merchandise, conventional prices, delivery checking, and product guarantees.

Another barrier to virtual shopping is the reluctance of many people to try new technologies. In the past, users have had to learn a complex set of commands to shop electronically—a surmountable barrier for the experienced computer user, but an impossible obstacle for the novice. Keep in mind that seventy-one percent of the adult U.S. population does not have a college education, and that about half of all adults do not know how to program their VCRs! People have also been reluctant to buy products sight unseen from text-based shopping interfaces. For electronic commerce to become a mass-market phenomenon, interactive shopping systems must be made psychologically as well as physically accessible to customers through intuitive and familiar graphical representations of stores and their products. Consumers must be able to move easily between the physical world and the virtual world of retailing, seeing and interacting with products in the same way in both.

Over the long term, virtual stores can be seen as a natural extension of the food industry's Efficient Consumer Response initiative, an effort to streamline the logistics of moving products from manufacturers to consumers. As one participant in the study noted:

> You know what I expect? You'll have warehouses and then you'll have 7-Elevens and that would be it. . . . All the major stuff would come out of these central locations. . . . You're interested in the cheapest cost for the product that you want. Then you go to the convenience stores for the last minute things that you need.

While traditional stores are unlikely to disappear, even a small shift in purchases from physical to virtual stores would have dramatic implications for manufacturers and retailers. The customers who are most likely to shop electronically are those with high income and educational levels, whose purchases represent a disproportionate percentage of retailers' profits. As the online market develops, new forms of competition for their business will undoubtedly emerge. For example, grocery stores may compete with fast food restaurants to deliver prepared foods and beverages to upscale consumers. It has been estimated that retail vacancy rates may rise from the current thirteen percent to as high as thirty-three percent, shifting channel power from the conventional retailers and distributors back to manufacturers.

Whatever the outcome, customers should be better served as a result of the new technologies. Unlike conventional stores, the virtual store can carry an unlimited variety of products, styles, flavors, and sizes. New products can be stocked in response to customer requests, and stores can be tailored to the preferences and purchasing habits of individual shoppers. Products can be shown in entertaining and informative contexts, perhaps a model of the consumer's home. Thus the virtual store becomes a channel for direct, personal, and intelligent communication with the customer.

Endnotes

1. For additional information on the virtual store, see Raymond R. Burke, "Virtual Shopping: Breakthrough in Marketing Research," *Harvard Business Review* (March–April 1996).

2. For additional information, see the Harvard Business School case, "Shopping Alternatives, Inc.: Home Shopping in the Information Revolution," case #9-796-132.
3. Raymond R. Burke, Bari A. Harlam, Barbara E. Kahn, and Leonard M. Lodish, "Comparing Dynamic Consumer Choice in Real and Computer-simulated Environments," *Journal of Consumer Research* 19 (1992) 71–82.
4. The enormous success of Amazon.com in selling books over the Internet suggests that this type of easy to understand product is ideal for virtual shopping.

PART FOUR

Transforming
the Organization

12 | Inventing the Organizations of the Twenty-first Century: Control, Empowerment, and Information Technology

Thomas W. Malone

ARE CONTEMPORARY MANAGERS stifling innovation and creativity by trying to micromanage their organizations? Or are they managing their organizations like so many autonomous fiefdoms, failing to reap the benefits of one big company? Is empowering employees just a fad—or is it the only way to succeed in the future?

When and how to exercise control is one of the oldest and most difficult problems in management, and one of the central tasks of managers in the next century will be finding the right balance between top-down control and bottom-up empowerment.[1] These issues will not go away, because for the foreseeable future, the changing economics of communication and information technology will guarantee that the right answers keep changing. Just when one thinks one has found the right balance, some new way of sharing information and making deci-

Note: Reprinted from "Is 'Empowerment' Just a Fad? Control, Decision-Making and Information Technology" by T. W. Malone *Sloan Management Review*, 38 (1997), pp. 23–35, by permission of publisher. Copyright 1997 by Sloan Management Review Association. All rights reserved.

sions becomes feasible, and one is thrust into a race with the rest of the industry to figure out how to exploit it.

In fact, the very notion of decentralization needs revising. When most people talk about empowerment, they are thinking about relatively small shifts of power within a conventional hierarchical structure. To fully exploit the possibilities of the new information technologies, however, we may need to expand the concept to include radically decentralized organizations, like the Internet, free markets of all kinds, and scientific communities—all models for new ways of organizing work in the twenty-first century.

The Effect of Information Technology on Organizational Structures

Though the issues are complex,[2] research suggests that a simple pattern underlies many of the changes that will take place. As improvements in technology reduce the costs of communication and coordination, decision-making structures move through three stages. In the first stage, when communication costs are high, decisions tend to be made by *independent decentralized* decision makers. For most of human history, most economic decisions have been made this way, in largely independent tribes, villages, and towns around the world.

As the costs of communication fall, it becomes desirable to concentrate decision making in one place, where *centralized* decision makers can take a more global perspective than isolated local decision makers. The economic history of the twentieth century has been, in large part, a story of the centralization of economic decision making in large global corporations. In fact, for many kinds of decisions, the substantial benefits of centralization are yet to be exploited.

As communication costs fall even further, however, there comes a point at which *connected decentralized* decision makers can be even more effective than centralized ones. Sharing information with each other, these decentralized decision makers can combine the best information available anywhere in the world with their own knowledge, energy, and creativity. As the world's economy becomes increasingly dependent on creative innovation and "knowledge work," and as new technologies make possible the connection of decentralized decision makers on a scale never before possible, exploiting such opportunities for local empowerment may well become one of the most important themes in economic history of the next century.

Of course, many other factors affect the distribution of decision making in organizations. For example, competitive dynamics, government regulation, managerial egos, and national culture all influence where and how decisions are made. But as relentless technological improvements continue to reduce the cost of communication, shifts toward centralized control in some areas, and toward local empowerment in many others, will be a continuing fact of organizational life.

TWENTIETH-CENTURY TRENDS

This simple logic explains some of the most salient aspects of twentieth-century economic history. The dramatic rise of large organizations over the last hundred years was motivated in part by the economic benefits of centralized decision making, rendered feasible by advances in various information technologies. Centralized decision makers can efficiently integrate diverse information and thus can often make better decisions than independent local decision makers.[3] For much of this century, centralization was the "main game in town." As recent mega-mergers illustrate, many managers believe significant benefits are still to be gained from it, at least in certain situations.

In the latter part of the century, however, a different trend has become increasingly apparent. It began with decentralizing many decisions to divisions, strategic business units, or matrix managers. More recently, it has become much more extreme with companies "flattening" their organizations by removing some middle managers and increasing the spans of control of others. In many cases, managers who are supervising significantly more people than their predecessors are being forced to delegate important decisions to their subordinates. The managers' role, then, becomes one of coaching their employees—helping them to solve problems—rather than making decisions, giving orders, and monitoring companies. One sign of all these changes is the fact that "empowerment" has become such a popular buzzword.

In addition, more work is being coordinated outside the boundaries of traditional hierarchical organizations. Large companies are outsourcing more and more of their noncore activities. Small companies are playing an increasingly important role in many industries. Virtual corporations, networked organizations, and other shifting alliances of people and organizations are performing more and more of the work that once was done inside large corporations.

What explains this reversal of direction? Making decisions closer to the point where they are actually carried out—"closer to the customer"—can have many advantages. People are likely to be more energetic and creative if they have more say in how they work and what they do. Local decision makers may also have access to information critical to good decisions, for example, the customer's unstated preferences, which are difficult to communicate to the central office. These, then, are economic motivations for the decentralization of decision making.

But for decentralized decision makers to make intelligent decisions, they may also need to take into account the diverse kinds of information that help centralized decision makers make better decisions in the first place. Fortunately, information technology now makes possible the communication of such information to large groups of decision makers, at a cost and on a scale never before possible. Logic suggests, therefore, that the recent trend toward decentralization is not just a fad, but a dynamic that is likely to become even more important in the twenty-first century. The recent evolution to retailing, especially in small towns in the United States, will illustrate.

A CASE IN POINT: RETAILING

For much of the twentieth century, small-town retail stores were owned and operated largely at the local or regional level. Mom-and-pop stores were common, not only in the grocery and restaurant businesses, but in clothing, hardware, toys, and many other products. In these stores, decision making was necessarily local. Individual store owners made the decisions on pricing, promotion, and product selection. For the most part, they made their decisions without much knowledge of what was happening in stores outside the local area.

Into this seemingly placid scene came the late Sam Walton, founder of Wal*Mart. By centralizing pricing, buying, and promotion at the national level, Walton delivered higher quality products for lower prices than most of his competitors. Today, small towns across the nation hold the empty hulls of local retail stores driven out of business by Wal*Mart. Though other factors were involved, Wal*Mart's centralized decision making was made feasible by its state-of-the-art electronic ordering and inventory control systems.

According to the theory just described, we should expect that as the retailing industry continues to evolve, some decisions will eventually return to local store managers. This time, however, local managers will have access to national sales data. In fact, Wal*Mart is already moving in that direction: its store managers have considerable autonomy in allocating their space and ordering stock. Though most pricing is done centrally, Wal*Mart allows store managers to set prices for five to six hundred price-sensitive items depending on local competitors' prices.[4] In other words, we may be seeing the first signs of the next wave in retailing: local managers making decentralized decisions using global information. As the CIO of Wal*Mart puts it, "I think the challenge . . . is to enable a chain as big as Wal*Mart to act like a hometown store, even while it maintains its economies of scale."[5]

An even more decentralized form of retailing is now beginning to emerge on the Internet. Almost anyone can set up a retail sales operation on the Internet and gain immediate access to customers the world over. Consider PicturePhone Direct, a mail-order reseller of desktop videoconferencing equipment. According to founder Jerry Goldstein, "When we started our business, we thought we would concentrate on the northeastern United States. But when we put our catalog on the Internet, we got orders from Israel, Portugal, and Germany. All of a sudden, we were a global company." Another example is the International Underground Music Association (IUMA), an Internet site that provides music samples and information on hundreds of bands, and expects soon to sell compact disks online. Part of the IUMA's rationale is to provide a distribution channel for unknown musicians, whose work would not be sold in mainstream music stores. In all these cases, local retailers make their own decisions, without supervision by national chains or a need to appeal to mass markets. But because these small local retailers have access to global markets, they have the potential for rapid and dramatic expansion.

Three Types of Decision Making

To get a better idea why the historical pattern just described should occur, one needs an overview of how decisions can be made. There are three basic ways to make decisions, each suited to a different set of circumstances. Figure 12-1 shows simplified representations of three basic types of decision makers; independent decentralized decision makers, centralized decision makers, and connected decentralized decision makers—"Cowboys," "Commanders," and "Cyber-Cowboys," respectively.

INDEPENDENT DECENTRALIZED DECISION MAKING ("COWBOYS")

By definition, independent decision makers have a relatively low need for communication. Alone on a horse, a cowboy can see and hear only his immediate environment. Similarly, when local store managers set prices using only locally available information, they do not require na-

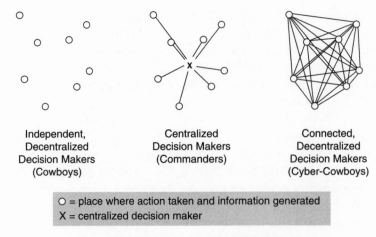

Independent,	Centralized	Connected,
Decentralized	Decision Makers	Decentralized
Decision Makers	(Commanders)	Decision Makers
(Cowboys)		(Cyber-Cowboys)

O = place where action taken and information generated
X = centralized decision maker

FIGURE 12-1   **Three Alternatives for Decision Making**

tionwide information systems or long-distance telephone service. In the same way, independent local banks making their own loan decisions need not confer with national headquarters before approving a loan, and individual farmers making their own planting decisions need not communicate much with anyone else.

The price these independent decision makers pay for the simplicity of their decision making process is that their decisions are relatively uninformed. They don't know what is happening elsewhere, cannot learn from the experiences of those outside the local area, and cannot easily pool resources or take advantage of economies of scale.

CENTRALIZED DECISION MAKING ("COMMANDERS")

Centralized decision makers are likely to have significantly greater communication needs than independent decision makers. To make informed decisions, Commanders need information from diverse sources. If Wal*Mart sets prices at a national level, the people who make those decisions should at least have sales histories for the products they are pricing. Much more detailed information about consumer tastes could be quite helpful. Similarly, if loan policies or advertising strategies at local banks are decided on a national level, then significant communication between local branches and national headquarters is needed.

One advantage of centralized decision making, of course, is that in taking more information into account, better decisions can be made. Pricing and promotion experiments can be run in a few stores and the results used in others. The best suppliers can be identified and economies of scale captured. Finally, best practices can be shared among stores. For example, Wal*Mart's regional managers share stories every week. As Sam Walton described it, "If they've been to that Panama City Beach store and seen a suntan cream display that's blowing the stuff out the door, they can share that with the other regionals for their beach stores."[6]

In some cases, new technologies even allow individualized local decisions to be made at the national level. Until a few years ago, Mervyn's grouped its local stores into categories based on sales volume, then distributed inventory based on category averages.[7] The problem was that individual stores varied greatly in the sizes and colors they sold. Some stores could sell lots of black jeans, while others needed traditional blue. To cope with these problems, Mervyn's recently implemented a highly successful new central system that distributes to each store a mix of products, sizes, and colors matched precisely to local sales.

CONNECTED DECENTRALIZED DECISION MAKING ("CYBER-COWBOYS")

Connected decision makers generally require even more communication than centralized ones. I call them "Cyber-Cowboys," because they combine the autonomous local decision making of the Cowboys with the global connectivity of computer networks (sometimes called "cyberspace"). Sometimes these decentralized decision makers cooperate with each other, at other times they compete. In both cases, relevant information needs to be brought not just to one central point, but to all decentralized decision makers. For instance, at Edward D. Jones & Co., a retail brokerage firm based in St. Louis, all thirty-one hundred sales representatives report directly to the national sales manager. This extremely flat organization makes heavy use of information technology. Sales representatives update their files and download new product information from central computers in St. Louis, making frequent calls to headquarters about client problems and questions. They also benefit from the company's television network, a primary channel for new product information, training, and motivation.[8]

An important element of this decision-making structure is the highly motivated people involved. "The kind of people we attract are self-starters, entrepreneurial type 'A' personalities, the type who might otherwise be running their own businesses," says Doug Hill, who provides product training and support to the sales force.[9] What about quotas? "I don't have any quotas," says one sales representative. "I have a profitability responsibility for this territory." In other words, at Edward D. Jones, information technology has allowed the decentralization of decision making while retaining the benefits of global information-sharing.

Even more extreme examples of decentralized decision making can be seen in the interaction among buyers and sellers. Whenever a company chooses to buy a product or service from an outside supplier rather than make it internally, it is using the decentralized structure of the marketplace (rather than the hierarchical structure of the firm) to coordinate production. In many cases market-based structures are cheaper, faster, and more flexible than internal production. For example, consider how two entrepreneurs compared Silicon Valley's vendor network with the larger, more vertically integrated firms common near Boston's Route 128:

> "One of the things that Silicon Valley lets you do is minimize the costs associated with getting from idea to product. Vendors here can handle everything. If you specify something—or, as is often the case, if the vendor helps you specify it—you can get hardware back so fast that your time-to-market is incredibly short. . ."[10]

> "There is a huge supply of contract labor—far more than on Route 128. If you want to design your own chips, there are a whole lot of people around who just do contract chip layout and design. You want mechanical design? It's here, too. There's just about anything you want in this infrastructure."[11]

By expanding markets and increasing their efficiency, information technology can greatly increase the desirability of buying rather than making.[12] For instance, in the 1980s, computerized airline reservations systems enabled the airlines to outsource much of their sales function to independent travel agents. Now there are online markets for all kinds of products, from electronic parts to insurance. These markets in turn allow autonomous decision makers access to knowledge and customers all over the world.

Factors That Determine How Decisions Are Made

Three key factors are especially important in determining the economics of various modes of decision making: decision information, trust, and motivation.

DECISION INFORMATION

Making good decisions requires good information. And as has just been illustrated, different decision-making structures have different information needs. By reducing the costs of communication, information technology makes feasible decision-making structures that require heavy communication, in situations in which they would otherwise be impossible.

Information technology also reduces the importance of distance in decision making. Now as never before, information technology can be used to bring information to decision makers wherever they are. That does not mean, however, that any decision can be made anywhere with equal effectiveness. Some people are better at making certain decisions than others, and some kinds of information are inherently easier to communicate than others. It is relatively easy for a field representative to communicate her dollar volume for the month; much harder to communicate her sense, based on years of experience, of the new products customers want. Likewise, it is easy to communicate the temperature of a container in a chemical refinery, but harder to communicate the reason why a specific temperature is necessary.

In general, information is easier to communicate if it is already explicit—already written down or expressed in quantitative form. It is harder to communicate, or "sticky," if it is based on long experience or implicit, qualitative impressions.[13]

One implication of this fact is that technology should be used to bring decisions to the places where sticky information is located. That is, information technology should be used to bring easily communicable information (such as financial data, news reports, and so forth) to people who have either knowledge or capabilities that are hard to communicate (such as customer understanding, technical competence, or interpersonal skills).

TRUST

Trust is fundamental. If one person doesn't trust another, he will not want that other person to make decisions on his behalf. In a centralized system, that means decision makers will avoid delegating decisions to local managers they don't trust. If they must delegate, they will try to control and monitor local decision makers as much as possible.[14]

Information technology can be used to foster trust (or deal with the lack of it) in several ways:

1. *Information technology can help remote decision makers to be more effective.* For example, Mrs. Fields' Cookies is able to hire very young and inexperienced employees in part because its stores are run using centrally developed software that manages operations at a detailed level. The software helps to determine quantities of ingredients and baking schedules based on seasonal and locally adjusted sales projections. It even suggests when store managers should go out to the sidewalk to entice customers with free samples.[15]

2. *Information technology can help to control and monitor remote decision makers more effectively.* Several years ago the Otis Elevator Company replaced its decentralized service system with a centralized one in which calls bypassed field service offices. Top executives were then able to spot numerous examples of chronically malfunctioning elevators, the poor records of which had been buried in files at field offices for years.[16]

3. *Information technology can help to develop loyalty among remote decision makers.* One use of the television network at Edward D. Jones is to indicate a feeling of corporate identity and team spirit. By making it easier to maintain personal contacts over great distances, electronic communication technologies (for telephones to e-mail and videoconferencing) can also help to maintain a spirit of community and a sense of loyalty in geographically dispersed organizations.[17]

Of course, not all these uses of technology are desirable in all situations, but they illustrate how technology can help to increase trust or deal with the lack of it. In a centralized system, technology can help decision makers to trust local managers to faithfully implement decisions made centrally, or to make more important decisions themselves. Thus technology helps centralized systems to become more decentralized. On the other hand, if a system is so decentralized that major decisions are already made by local decision makers (as they are in a market, for instance), technology can help local decision makers to trust central decision makers, like centralized suppliers. But in most cases, technology should lead to mixed systems, in which some important decisions are made by central decision makers and others by local decision makers.

MOTIVATION

The amount of energy and creativity people bring to their work often depends on who decides what they do and how they do it. In certain kinds of work, such as highly routine or purely physical work, people may work harder when others tell them what to do. That seems to be the rationale behind coaches' pushing athletes or drill sergeants' driving raw recruits beyond the physical limits they thought they had. But in general, one thing that makes a job more enjoyable is having some degree of autonomy. When people make their own decisions about how to do their work and allocate their time, they tend to enjoy their jobs more and put more energy, effort, and creativity into them. An important part of entrepreneurial motivation, for instance, is not just getting to keep the rewards of one's own work, but making one's own decisions.

One advantage, then, of empowering local decision makers is to increase their motivation and thus the quality and creativity of their decisions. This factor is likely to become increasingly important as more and more work becomes "knowledge work" and innovation becomes more critical to business success.

Because information technology can be used either to centralize decision making or to decentralize it, technology sometimes increases the motivation of decision makers and sometimes decreases it. Table 12-1 summarizes the conditions under which centralization and decentralization are desirable.

Costs and Benefits of the Three Types of Decision Making

No single factor determines what kind of decision making is best in a specific situation. Each type has its pros and cons. Table 12-2 summarizes the relative costs and benefits of the three different types of decision making already described. The costs and benefits of communication are clearest. Cowboys have the lowest communication costs, because they do the least communicating, followed by Commanders and Cyber-Cowboys. Both Commanders and Cyber-Cowboys benefit from considering information the Cowboys ignore.

The costs and benefits of the other two factors, trust and motivation, are more ambiguous. The cost of a lack of trust does not depend primarily on decision-making structure, but on the extent to which important decisions are delegated. Similarly, the cost of a lack of motivation, initiative, or creativity depends on the kind of work being done.

TABLE 12-1   **Summary of Circumstances Under Which Centralization and Decentralization Are Desirable**

Factor	Centralization *is desirable when . . .*	Decentralization *is desirable when . . .*
Information	Remote information is valuable in decision making, and can be communicated to central decision makers at moderate cost	Local decision makers have access to important information that cannot be easily communicated to central decision makers *OR* Remote information is not valuable in local decision making ("Cowboys") *OR* Remote information is valuable in decision making and inexpensive to communicate ("Cyber-Cowboys")
Trust	Central decision makers do not want to (or cannot) trust local decision makers to make important decisions	Local decision makers do not want to (or cannot) trust central decision makers to make important decisions
Motivation	Local decision makers work harder or better when told what to do by someone else	Local decision makers work harder or better when they make decision for themselves

TABLE 12-2   **Costs and Benefits of the Three Decision-making Structures**

Decision-making Structure	Costs and Benefits		
	Costs of Communicating Remote Decision Information	Benefits of Considering Remote Decision Information	Other Costs (trust, motivation, etc.)
Independent decentralized ("Cowboys")	Low	Low	?
Centralized ("Commanders")	Medium	High	?
Connected decentralized ("Cyber-Cowboys")	High	High	?

Because these costs are somewhat unclear, they are included under "all other costs" in the table. Other costs might also include the cost of making decisions (e.g., the cost of salaries for decision makers) and the cost of economies of scale (or the lack thereof) realized by a particular decision-making structure.

How should these different costs be weighed? To answer this question, consider the two about which there is the least ambiguity: (1) the value of remote information (i.e., the cost of not considering it), and (2) the *costs* of communicating it. Different decisions differ on these two dimensions. Imagine plotting the average value of remote information and the average costs of communicating it on a graph along with the most desirable type of decision making in each case. Figure 12-2 shows the results. Of course, the exact shape and location of the three regions depend on the nature of the various costs of decision making. But the shapes and relative positions of the regions shown in Figure 12-2 follow mathematically from the assumptions in Table 12-2, and one additional assumption: that Cyber-Cowboys' other costs are lower than those of Commanders'.[18]

This last assumption would be true of any situation in which the motivational advantages of autonomous decisions by local decision makers are important. Motivational factors are important in manage-

Figure **12-2**   **Desirable Decision-making Structures for Different Kinds of Decisions**

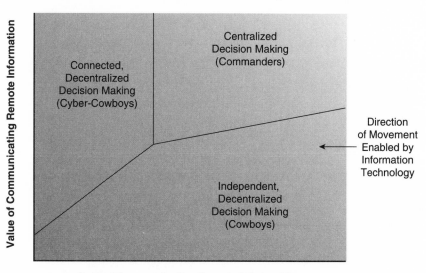

ment of all kinds, and in most "knowledge work"—sales, marketing, finance, product development, and consulting. They are even important in many physical jobs, such as assembly-line work, when creativity and innovation are valuable. The last assumption is also applicable whenever local decision makers have important but hard-to-communicate knowledge, such as what customers really want, or subtle but critical aspects of new technologies. If the assumption is not true, then Cyber-Cowboys are never desirable, and the Commanders' region extends all the way to the vertical axis. For instance, if local decision makers are highly unskilled, like the young workers in Mrs. Fields' stores, then decentralization may never be desirable.

Consider where two different kinds of decisions would fall in Figure 12-2. Decisions in which remote information is expensive to communicate relative to its value would fall toward the right-hand side of the figure. As the figure shows, such decisions should generally be made by the Cowboys, who already have the information. Even in national retail chains, for instance, local store managers usually make the decisions about whom to hire as clerks. On the other hand, if remote information is valuable enough, the decision would fall near the top of the figure. In that case, paying the significant communications cost to transmit it somewhere else may be worthwhile. For instance, basic accounting information from each store in a chain has significant value in many business decisions and is nearly always communicated elsewhere, whether for centralized decision making (Commanders) or decentralized decision making (Cyber-Cowboys).

The Decentralizing Effect of Information Technology

A key insight that follows from Figure 12-2 is the realization that an important contribution of information technology is to reduce the costs of communicating many kinds of information. In general, as the unit cost of communicating information drops, decision making can be expected to move gradually leftward in the figure. The figure therefore summarizes the logical basis for the evolutionary pattern just described. When communication costs are extremely high, the Cowboys' structure is most desirable. But as information technology reduces communication costs, many decisions will pass through a Commander's stage before eventually moving to that of the Cyber-Cowboys.

Sometimes this entire progression will not occur. In situations in which remote information is only moderately valuable (and other costs of centralized control are high), decision making might go directly from

Cowboys to Cyber-Cowboys. For example, Caterpillar, the manufacturer of truck engines, chose recently, instead of creating a chain of local repair shops, to develop a PC-based service that allows independent repair shops to use Caterpillar's national database of repair histories.[19] In situations in which remote information is even less valuable (and the costs of connected decision making relatively high), Cowboys may be the most desirable operatives, even if communication costs drop to zero. On the other hand, if the other costs which Cyber-Cowboys bear are higher than those of Commanders', then Cyber-Cowboys would not even appear on the graph.

In sum, decreasing communication costs should lead to movement along the path just described when:

- local decisions can be improved significantly by considering remote information, and *either or both* of the following conditions holds true:

  - local decisions can be improved significantly by taking into account "sticky" (hard-to-communicate) information, *and/or*

  - local decision makers are significantly more enthusiastic, committed and creative when they can work autonomously.

Though these conditions are not true for all decisions, they certainly appear to be true for many important decisions. Therefore, one should expect a significant long-term migration along the path just described.

Radically Decentralized Organizations

Today, when people talk about empowerment, they usually mean delegating decisions to a lower level. But what if power didn't get delegated to lower levels, but instead originated there? How much energy and creativity could be unlocked if everyone in an organization felt "in control"?

In a free market, for instance, no one "on top" delegates decisions about what to buy and sell to different players in the market. Instead, a buyer and seller can exchange almost anything on which they mutually agree (subject to their abilities and financial constraints). The marvel of overall coherence emerging from these countless paired decisions is what Adam Smith called the "invisible hand" of the market.

This approach is increasingly viewed as a desirable basis for political organizations (witness the current trend toward returning federal functions to the states) and business organizations.[20] In essence, it turns the whole notion of delegation upside down. Instead of all legitimate power coming from the top of an organization and being delegated downward, it originates at the bottom and is delegated upward only when there are benefits from doing so.

THE DECENTRALIZATION CONTINUUM

Consider two questions: Who makes the most important decisions, and who can overrule decisions made by others? As Figure 12-3 shows, these two questions can be used to place organizations on a continuum, ranging from highly centralized systems to highly decentralized systems. Even though it is logically possible to have other combinations of the two factors, most real-world companies fall somewhere on this continuum.

In highly centralized systems, for example, central decision makers make most important decisions and can overrule most decisions they delegate to local decision makers. Military organizations embody an extreme form of centralized control, in which high-ranking officers make all important decisions and can overrule even the most trivial decision of subordinates.[21] In highly decentralized systems, on the other hand, local decision makers make most of the important decisions and can overrule most decisions they delegate to central decision makers. For instance, Internet users can communicate in any way they want with other users, as long as their computers follow standard protocols (interconnection procedures) approved by the Internet's governing boards. If a subgroup of Internet users wants to create a new protocol, it is free to do so.

Between these two extremes lie mixed systems in which both central and local decision makers make some important decisions and certain decisions made by each cannot be overruled by the other. For instance, the U.S. Constitution spells out a mixed system of relationships between federal and state governments, in which each has certain powers the other cannot override.

One of the most important implications of this figure is that *almost all discussions of empowerment stop halfway, at the middle of the continuum.* By definition, one cannot empower someone unless one has the ultimate right to make or overrule the decisions one is delegating. Thus, *radical* decentralization is not something people at the top do for people at the bottom. Rather, radical decentralization *starts* at the bottom.

What would it mean for ultimate power to come from the bottom up rather than the top down? One way to create such a structure is to have the users of a service be its owners, such as occurs in Visa International.

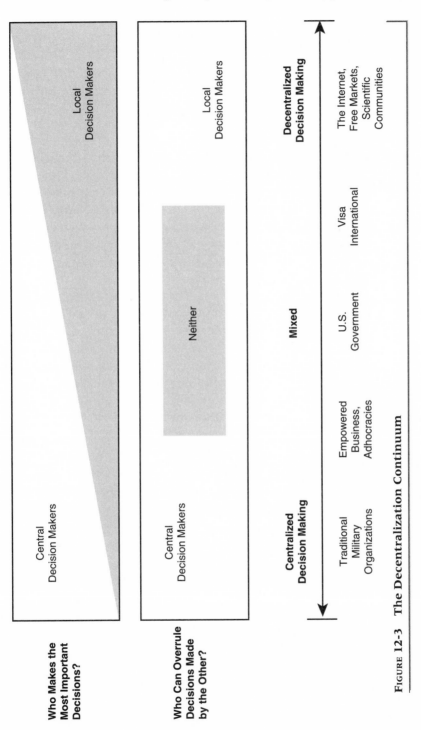

FIGURE 12-3   **The Decentralization Continuum**

VISA INTERNATIONAL

Visa International is what its founder, Dee Hock, calls an "inverted holding company." Visa is owned by the banks and other institutions that issue Visa cards. They are simultaneously Visa's owners and customers; in many cases they are also its suppliers.

Designed as a federal system, the Visa organization includes a series of regional, national, and international suborganizations, each with its own members and board of directors.[22] Each level of the organization receives its power from the levels below it, decisions are made by vote of the various boards, typically on a sixty- to ninety-day cycle. For instance, Visa members have voted to pay a service charge for all transactions, as well as processing fees for certain services. Member organizations are free to take or leave any Visa product, to leave the organization if they choose, and to offer competing products. In fact, most banks do also offer the primary competing product, Mastercard.

Though inefficient for some purposes, this highly decentralized structure has been extremely successful. In the two decades since its founding, Visa has become a global organization with over twenty-three thousand member institutions, three hundred million customers, and sales of $650 billion annually. Perhaps more important, this decentralized structure has been able to provide centralized services, such as a global transaction clearinghouse and global brand management, for members who are in many cases direct competitors. From this fundamentally decentralized structure has emerged a very successful global organization.

THE INTERNET

Decentralized structures can also be created without ownership. Though one doesn't usually think of the Internet as an organization, it is one of the most striking examples of a decentralized organization in the world today. The Internet has been doubling in size every year since 1988; it now has over thirty million users. Used for everything from ordering flowers and checking weather conditions to participating in discussion groups on topics from soap operas to particle physics, the Internet and communication networks like it will have a profound effect on how business is conducted in the twenty-first century.

In addition to being a technological enabler of other organizations, the Internet is also an organizational model itself. Both the technical architecture and the governance structure of the Internet provide models for highly decentralized organizations. In a very real sense, no one is in charge of the Internet. No one can unilaterally shut it down or deny access to a particular person or organization. Instead, anyone who follows the agreed-upon rules for communicating can connect to any other node, and thus to the entire worldwide network. Furthermore, anyone who is connected to the network can be a service provider or a service user. In the rare cases in which Internet protocols need to be altered, changes are approved by a combination of elected and volunteer boards. Users who want to experiment with new protocols are free to do so. In fact, new protocols are generally accepted only after they have been widely and successfully used on an experimental basis.

In a sense, then, no one controls the Internet and everyone controls the Internet. The role of the "center," that is, the standards boards, is simply to establish the framework through which members interact, not to tell members what to do. Out of this highly decentralized structure has come amazing growth and innovation.

It is easy to imagine the Internet's principles being used in other kinds of organizations. For instance, even though global consulting firms like McKinsey are mixed organizations, they have a structure based on similar principles. The firm establishes a strong organizational culture, including norms about how employees are hired and promoted and how they are expected to work with others in the firm. But management does not tell partners what kind of work to do, which clients to work for, or which employees to select for their teams. Instead, partners make largely autonomous decisions about what to do and how to do it. When it works well, this highly decentralized effort—within the overall interaction framework provided by the firm—produces an extremely flexible global organization.

Conclusion

Empowerment is one of the most popular buzzwords in business today. Talk about distributing power and decentralizing decision making is hard to avoid. But as this chapter shows, decentralization is not just a fad. Rather, it is a response to fundamental changes in the economics of decision making enabled by new information technologies. In some organizations, of course, decentralization may never occur; in others, increased centralization may precede decentralization. But in the emerging knowledge-based economy, globally connected decentralized decision makers will play an increasingly important role. Learning how to design such decision-making systems and mange the continually shifting balance of power will not be easy. But it will help to determine which organizations will succeed in the twenty-first century and which will not.

Endnotes

1. See, for example, B. Johansen, A. Saveri, and G. Schmid, *21st Century Organizations: Reconciling Control and Empowerment* (Menlo Park, CA: Institute for the Future, 1995).
2. For summaries of previous research see, for example, P. Attewell and J. Rule, "Computing and Organizations: "What We Know and What We Don't Know," *Communications of the ACM* 17 (December 1984) 1184–1192; and J. F. George and J. L. King, "Examining the Computing and Centralization Debate," *Communications of the ACM* 34 (July 1991) 63–72.
3. See, for example, A. D. Chandler, *The Visible Hand: The Managerial Revolution in American Business* (Cambridge, MA: Belknap Press of Harvard University Press, 1977).
4. M. Stevenson, "The Store to End All Stores," *Canadian Business Review* (May 1994). See also K. S. Anand and H. Mendelson, "Information and Organization for Horizontal Multimarket Coordination," Research Paper #1359, Stanford: Stanford University, Graduate School of Business (January 1995).
5. B. Fox, "Staying on Top at Wal-Mart," *Chain Store Age Executive* 70 (April 1994) 47.
6. S. Walton with J. Huey, *Sam Walton: Made in America* (New York: Bantam Books, 1993).
7. R. Dvorak, D. Dean, and M. Singer, "Accelerating IT Innovation," *McKinsey Quarterly* 4 (1994) 123–135.
8. W. Keenan, Jr., "Death of the Sales Manager," *Sales and Marketing Management* 146 (October 1994) 66 ff.
9. Ibid.
10. L. Denend, "3Com Corp.," in A. Saxenian (ed.), *Regional Advantage: Culture and Competition in Silicon Valley and Route 128* (Cambridge, MA: Harvard University Press, 1994) 114.
11. Jeffrey Kalb, founder of MasPar Computer Corp., in A. Saxenian, op. cit., p. x.
12. See T. W. Malone, J. Yates, and R. I. Benjamin, "Electronic Markets and Electronic Hierarchies," *Communications of the ACM* 30 (1987) 484–497.
13. E. von Hipel, "'Sticky Information' and the Locus of Problem Solving: Implications for Innovation," *Management Science* 40 (1994) 429–439.
14. For useful discussions of these issues, see, for example, M.C. Jensen and W.H. Meckling, "Theory of the Firm: Managerial Behavior, Agency Costs and Ownership Structure," *Journal of Financial Economics* 3 (October 1973) 305–360; and V. Gurbaxani and S. Whang, "The Impact of Information Systems on Organizations and Markets," *Communications of the ACM* 34 (January 1991) 59–73.
15. T. Richman, "Mrs. Fields' Secret Ingredient," *INC Magazine* (October 1987) 65–72.
16. F. W. McFarlan and D. B. Stoddard, "OTISLINE (A)" Case 186-304, Harvard Business School (1986). See also W. J. Bruns and F. W. McFarlan, "Information Technology Puts Power in Control Systems," *Harvard Business Review* (September–October 1987) 89–94.
17. W. Keenan, Jr., op. cit.

18. The mathematical proof of this result is given in G. M. Wyner and T. W. Malone, "Cowboys or Commanders: Does Information Technology Lead to Decentralization?", Proceedings of the International Conference on Information Systems (ICIS 96), Cleveland, OH, December 15–18, 1996.

19. D. Sullivan, "On the Road Again," *CIO Magazine* (January 15, 1995) 50–52.

20. See, for example, C. Handy, "Balancing Corporate Power: A New Federalist Paper," *Harvard Business Review* (November–December 1992) 59–73.

21. Interestingly, even military organizations are now moving away from this extreme form of centralization. See, for example, L. Smith, "New Ideas From the Army (Really)," *Fortune* (September 19, 1994) 203–212.

22. See E. Breuner, "Complexity and Organizational Structure: Internet and Visa International as Prototypes for the Corporation of the Future" (unpublished M.S. thesis, Cambridge: MIT, Sloan School of Management, 1995); and J. Nocera, *A Piece of the Action* (New York: Simon & Schuster, 1994).

$\underline{13}$ Virtual Teams: Using Communications Technology to Manage Geographically Dispersed Development Groups

Dorothy A. Leonard, Paul A. Brands,
Amy Edmondson, and Justine Fenwick

Businesses have been producing and marketing new goods and services around the world for centuries. Within the last couple of decades, however, globalization has entered a new phase. Competitive pressures to deliver highly customized products and services to customers' doorsteps—and sometimes within their facilities—have stimulated the need to coordinate development activities across geographic boundaries. Moreover, the market for talent is increasingly global. Fortunately, communication technologies have matured into a strong, diversified, and reasonably reliable network, connecting distant nodes and enabling a degree of long-distance coordination and innovation that was once inconceivable.

Pros and Cons of Dispersed Development

Geographically dispersed development projects offer some special advantages. They potentially tap into sources of expertise at least as varied as that of co-located groups—often *more* so. Skilled people who might refuse employment if required to leave their chosen countries or cities of residence can be identified, hired, and linked to the parent company using electronic umbilical cords. For instance, Black Sun Interactive, a company that produces software tools used to create virtual worlds in cyberspace, bases its software development both in San Francisco and in Munich, in part because talented programmers are more readily available and less expensive in Germany than in the Silicon Valley. Moreover, operations that take advantage of the earth's rotation can run around the clock. VeriFone, a credit card transaction business, employs software programmers in Bangalore, India, and runs its quality testing in Dallas, Texas. Work schedules for the two groups of engineers are almost exactly complementary.

There are some extra costs to operating such virtual teams, however. While business is being transacted across ever-expanding distances, much of it still requires the high degree of interaction traditionally offered by face-to-face transactions. Distance and time zone differences between team members exacerbate the challenges of development, rendering difficult the coordination of even simple tasks. Complex problem solving or brainstorming seems nearly impossible at long distance.[1]

Technology is an incomplete panacea for these problems. Paradoxically, the very pace of technological progress often leaves management lagging in both equipment and an understanding of its uses. Unfortunately, research on information technology has focused on the use of same-time, same-place software for decision making by co-located groups,[2] and on the use of electronic mail for the routine distribution of information.[3] We know much less about managing multiple technologies (from faxes to video conferencing) for development purposes—especially across geographic boundaries—than we do about single technologies used in a single setting.

We therefore undertook a study of the use of technology in geographically dispersed development teams. We chose a company in which the management of such virtual teams is absolutely critical to its success, even survival: American Management Systems.

Dispersed Development at American Management Systems

American Management Systems (AMS) is an approximately $800 million international consulting firm that specializes in customized software and systems integration. With forty-seven offices, including ten in Europe, and seven thousand employees in those offices and at client sites around the world, AMS typifies the modern global firm. The company has four divisions, each serving a different vertical market: the U.S. federal government (fifteen percent); state and local governments and educational institutions (seventeen percent); financial services (twenty-three percent); and telecommunications (thirty-nine percent). An additional six percent of sales derives from various corporate clients.

Repeat business is extremely important to AMS. The company fits the characteristics of firms Treacy and Wiersema[4] have termed "Customer-Intimate." That is, they grow through intensive long-term relationships with targeted clients. The firm's viability depends on the ability of project teams (not individuals) to deliver such high-quality systems and business process re-engineering services that clients will return for follow-up work. Moreover, these services cannot be delivered remotely from a central location or even from local offices scattered throughout the world. Although the software systems of firms within a given market segment (and sometimes across segments) may address similar needs, the necessity of hooking into existing client software systems, of customizing their new computer systems, and of re-engineering business processes requires extensive on-site collaboration.

AMS also develops leading-edge software for customers who want to participate in technological innovation. Such partnering requires coordination among dispersed sites. Technical advances are driven by AMS's Virginia-based Center for Advanced Technology and other corporate centers of innovation, but they are shaped by user needs as identified in the client's business setting. Whether an AMS development team is working on well-understood systems or totally new ones, then, managers are confronted with the need to coordinate the delivery of product and service through "virtual" teams.

To understand the challenges such teams face, we interviewed twenty AMS project managers and four senior managers. Based on those interviews, we constructed an extensive questionnaire which was administered to over two hundred team members, as well as a shorter questionnaire for project managers. The observations offered in this chapter are based on an analysis of those questionnaires as well as on data gathered in the interviews.[5] The analysis explored the relationship between descriptor variables and three evaluations of team performance—two offered by the team members (perception of team success and overall performance) and one by the project manager.

DEGREE OF TEAM DISPERSION

One of our first observations was the wide variation in the degree of dispersion of "virtual" development teams at AMS. Some team members telecommuted from home several days a week, but they could drop by a local office with relative ease if they wished. Other teams were split between a distant client site and an AMS office. For instance, a group based in Sarasota, Florida, was developing an advanced consumer lending system for banks in St. Louis, Missouri, and Hartford, Connecticut. Another group was developing telecommunications systems in Boston and New York supported by a technical team that was split between Fairfax, Virginia, and Redwood City, California. The team that was coping with the most severe time-zone gaps had developers in Fairfax, Virginia, and business analysts at client sites in Sweden, Switzerland, and the Netherlands.

Members of such teams often spent a large part of their work lives away from the office; many worked longer hours at client sites than within their own organizations. On average, the teams we studied spent forty-three percent of their time away from the home office. One team spent no time at all at AMS; another team spent ninety-eight percent of its time at AMS.

When team members are separated that often, one might ask whether they can truly be considered a team. Management researchers have identified three essential characteristics of work teams. First, a work team must be an actual group—an intact, bounded social system whose members are interdependent. Second, a work team must have collective responsibility for the group's product. Finally, a work team must share responsibility for managing its own work. The virtual teams at AMS fit all three criteria. Not surprisingly, however, they scored lower on traditional measures of team integrity than co-located teams. That is, they were somewhat less interdependent than teams whose members are stationed together.[6]

Significantly, the physical dispersion of team members at AMS did not translate into lower performance on the projects studied. That is, dispersed teams were no more likely to suffer performance problems, as judged by their managers, than were teams whose members had more opportunity to interact face-to-face.[7] From the perspective of AMS, physical dispersion *per se* is not a threat to team performance. Or if it is, skillful management mitigates its negative effects, as our evidence led us to believe.

TEAM VERSUS CLIENT AFFILIATION

One concern managers have about virtual teams is the possibility that off-site members will become divorced from the parent organization. In customer-intimate businesses, a certain amount of "going native" is necessary if developers are to build a deep understanding of clients' needs and nurture the personal relationships that will bring more business. Yet the fear exists that the team will become so strongly affiliated with the client that they will identify more with the client's organization than their own. In fact, senior managers reported that *extreme* affiliation with the client did lead to problems such as an inability to manage project scope. That is, analysts who were too closely identified with the client occasionally promised deliverables that exceeded project bounds.

AMS managers were sensitive to the need to enlarge and maintain relationships with their clients. Yet they also worked to ensure that employees would remain loyal to the parent company that hired them. One manager noted that though getting employees close to the customer was important, he found he needed to provide a "separate home" for team members who were "beginning to feel like client employees." Such management attention to this issue may explain why we found that the more that AMS employees reported feeling closer to clients than to the parent organization, the more highly they evaluated their own team's performance. However, that relationship disappeared when other influences on team effectiveness were taken into consideration.

TEAM LEARNING SKILLS

Interestingly, teams that scored high on a learning scale were high performers. That is, teams whose members reported discussing ways to improve group processes, discussing and correcting errors, and communicating frequently with other groups at AMS tended to be more highly rated by managers and by themselves as a team. Their learning was also somewhat related to the amount of face-to-face interaction among team members, suggesting that the ability to interact facilitates team learning, or that teams' with learning objectives strive for more personal interaction.

Moreover, team members who reported learning behaviors also communicated more frequently with the highest-ranking person on the team. The type of communication with these managers most strongly associated with learning behaviors was face-to-face consultation about work, personal, or career issues. Thus, managers of dispersed teams play a critical role in establishing a culture in which learning opportunities are seized and used, even when members do not see each other frequently.

AMS managers varied in the depth of their experience, but many were quite sophisticated in their understanding of their role as team builders and norm setters. One manager, who described his role as "coach-manager," felt it was his duty to stay in touch with key members of his team through daily voice mail, encouraging them to express doubts and concerns as soon as they occurred. He stressed that they should think of themselves not as all-knowing experts, but as problem solvers in need of resources. "At AMS," he said, "we want you to be successful and will offer our expertise to help in that effort. Don't ever be afraid to ask for help."

COMMUNICATION WITH TEAM LEADERS

Overall, communication with the top-ranking individual in the work group was related to individual perceptions of project success, but not to perceptions of overall team performance or to managers' ratings of team performance. The relationship between project success and level of upward communication was a negative one. That is, increases in communication with the top ranked person were associated with a lower perceived success rate. One plausible interpretation for this result was that as projects began to falter in the eyes of a team, members tended to communicate more with managers to ask for assistance or warn of potential problems. Interestingly, there was no relationship between the amount of upward communication and managers' ratings of project success. One could speculate that unlike team members, managers took a holistic and experienced view of project outcomes—one that was less sensitive to the often temporary ups and downs of the projects. In any case, these results suggest that upward communication was not integral to project success.

Two types of communication were positively related to self-reported team performance: face-to-face consultation with managers about personal, work, or career issues and sharing a meal or going to a social event. These results suggest that in-person meetings with managers—including informal access—is important to how team members feel a project is going. Or one could say that projects that are believed to be going well are also the ones in which team leaders have paid close attention to team members.

Interestingly, the only type of communication specifically related to team members' perceptions of project success was video or telephone conferencing—and that relationship was negative. This finding could be interpreted in several ways. One could speculate that team members believe that communicating with managers through video or telephone conferencing rather than in person lowers the likelihood of success.

However, it is more likely true that team members believe projects that are in trouble are more likely to require frequent (albeit distant) communication with managers than projects that are going well.

ORGANIZATIONAL SUPPORT FOR TEAMS

When a number of key influences, such as team integrity, task design, learning behaviors, and affiliation, were tested simultaneously in a regression analysis, the best predictor of project performance (as rated by managers) was the degree of organizational support reported by the team.[8] Organizational support refers to the availability of information, training, and other resources the team needed to perform its work.[9] One likely interpretation of this statistical relationship is that managerial sensitivity to a team's resource needs paid off in better performance. Managers of virtual teams reported having to pay a great deal of attention to the infrastructure, training, and moral support needs of their teams—including the need for communication technology.

Uses of Communications Technology in Managing Virtual Teams

One objective of this study was to better understand the role of communication technologies in managing virtual teams. The teams we studied had a wide variety of communication media available to them, including e-mail, voice mail, fax, Lotus Notes, and video conferencing.[10] They could choose which of these media to use for particular tasks.

We asked three questions about preferences for and use of media by virtual teams. First, was there a relationship between the type of task and the degree of media richness preferred by team members? That is, would team members match technology with task? Second, would team members be able to use the medium they preferred for a given task, or would infrastructure and group norms dictate the media actually used? As a number of scholars have pointed out, preferences for media are often constrained by social and organizational factors, which shape perceptions and influence behavior.[11] Third, would such constraints have noticeable effects on the morale or performance of the group?

Academic research provided some concepts to use in our exploration of team behavior. The "Media Richness" theory posits a continuum of communication technologies, arrayed according to the following characteristics: (1) number of channels (audio, visual, tactile); (2) capacity for feedback (nonexistent to continuous); (3) ability to be personalized (nonexistent to infinite); and (4) language variety.[12] According to this theory, effective communication results from matching the character- istics of the medium to the requirements of the task.[13] In other words, complex and ambiguous tasks such as conflict resolution and brain- storming, require "richer" media than simple assignments such as rou- tine information distribution. Too little media richness may result in miscommunication; too much could be wasteful and costly.

Tests of this theory, which were developed before video conferencing and sophisticated multimedia applications were commonly used, have focused mostly on the "leanness" of e-mail versus the "richness" of face-to-face interaction. In our study, we arrayed the communications media available to respondents along a continuum, from faxes at the low end to video conferencing at the high end. Face-to-face communi- cation was treated as the very richest medium because it provides mul- tiple channels, takes place in real time, enables immediate feedback, and allows messages to be personalized. Faxes, in contrast, are re- stricted to a single text-band channel, eliminate any social presence, and constrain communicators to respond to entire messages.

In general, respondents preferred and used richer media for more com- plex tasks. When a task required only one-way communication, team members preferred and used less rich media. When a task required signifi- cant interaction among team members (e.g., brainstorming or decision making), participation by multiple sources (e.g., advice and consensus seeking), or resolution of discord (e.g., personal or intellectual conflict), team members used richer media. Even so, team members *always* would have liked to use a richer medium than the one they did. It is therefore likely that at least some team members experienced frustration over the necessity to communicate through leaner-than-desired media.

Shortcomings of Communications Technology

Some managers believed that the less rich media caused disagreements that would not have occurred had team members been able to commu- nicate in more detail, using a greater number of channels. A manager in Birmingham, Alabama, recalled: "Sometimes e-mail discussions can get to a flash point. Once in our project we reached a design impasse; the Birmingham developers wanted to use one [system architecture] and the Fairfax group had a more traditional viewpoint on how to re- solve this design issue. The next thing you know developers were hav- ing a disagreement at thirty-thousand feet! The Fairfax manager and I had to intervene to move the discussion from a 'religious argument' to a pragmatic discussion of 'how this capability can be coded'!"

Client preferences also caused some teams to use media less rich than they would have liked. One manager who dealt with an extremely complex European project pointed out, "We at AMS live and die by voice mail and e-mail. In Europe there is a cultural difference. . . [clients] generally won't use e-mail or voice mail systems. They live and die by fax machines. Managers don't sit at personal computers. Typing information into a computer is something their secretaries do."

Moreover, many managers insisted that some tasks necessitate face-to-face communication. Even video conferencing, at least at its present state of maturity, does not transmit subtle and important body language. For instance, viewers could see a head nod or shake, but were unlikely to pick up on a slight rolling of the eyes or a general body stiffening in response to a suggestion. Video conferencing participants cannot see the whole room, and therefore who else might be hearing the discussion; nor can they govern who might walk in.

Furthermore, video conferencing technology is still lacking in resolution, speed, and reliability. For example, a delay in transmission causes the contributions of distant parties (those "in the box") to disrupt the flow of the meeting, since everyone has to stop and listen very attentively, when they speak. In addition, our informants believed that comments by those "in the box" tended to be accorded more weight than comments made by people in the room. This phenomenon could be a halo effect of television—the person "in the box" appears to be "speaking from on high"—as well as the result of an abnormal amount of concentration on the individual's speech necessitated by the transmission delay.

What is more, there is no set etiquette yet for video conferencing, with the result that people don't know when or how to interrupt each other or take turns. Side conversations, which are acceptable in face-to-face discussions, seem very rude in video conferences. As one manager indicated, "Currently we lack protocols for how to interact on all these different modes of technology. We need to have rules for how to behave during a video conference." Finally, video conferencing generally has to be scheduled quite a bit ahead, and at least at AMS, sites tend to be overbooked.

Recommendations for Managing Virtual Teams

Socialization and communication norms that occur naturally in co-located groups have to be consciously created when team members are physically dispersed. The managers we interviewed clearly believed that working with virtual teams involved re-thinking their managerial roles in order to face newly created challenges. They made a number of recommendations for anyone directing virtual teams.

BUILD THE TEAM BEFORE DISPERSING IT

Managers recognized the critical need to build a sense of teamwork *before* members tried to work together from scattered geographical locations. Several team leaders described paying a huge amount of attention to project kickoff meetings. For example, one manager whose client site was in Birmingham, Alabama, and who worked with a group of developers from the Fairfax headquarters, said that having a full-day face-to-face meeting with all members involved in the project was essential. This meeting served two purposes: it formalized the commitment of developers to work for the client site and allowed developers to see the client environment, have extended conversations with users, and develop credibility informally. "Those kind of conversations," she remarked, "can't be scripted in a meeting."

Another manager agreed vigorously. "You need to have meetings with all members of the team to build a common vision, state what their individual responsibilities are, and design a work plan." She sees these meetings as opportunities for open sharing of information and preferred work styles. Enlisting the guidance of a meeting facilitator is a good idea when team members and their managers have just begun their relationship. "Building a team," she emphasized, "could take weeks and several meetings, but it is an absolutely necessary activity. You either pay now or pay later."

Other managers planned the agenda for these kickoff sessions differently. One manager thought that process was the key: "The first interactions should be face-to-face and they should be process-oriented. Plan on getting something done and do it collaboratively. It doesn't matter what you do; the point is to demonstrate collaboration." Another manager believed that adding stress produced the best results: "It is a good exercise to present a common issue that team members can work on with an aggressive deadline, so that they will be forced to drop their good behavior. I mean, it's like the difference between going to your in-laws for dinner and spending a month aboard a boat with them." This manager has asked her team to write a mission statement, define their deliverables, and get executive sign-off in two days. She claims that by putting team members under stress together, they "form bonds more quickly."

PROVIDE NEEDED RESOURCES

As noted above, of all the team characteristics we studied, the one that most strongly predicted team performance as reported by managers was the presence of organizational support. That is, the presence or absence of needed information, training, and other resources most clearly distinguished high-performance teams from low-performing teams. Indeed, a number of the most experienced AMS managers mentioned the importance of providing such support, stating that it was even more critical for virtual teams than for co-located teams and that, in particular, setting up a communications infrastructure at the very beginning of a project was essential.

Providing adequate communications systems did not always mean using information technology. A manager on the West Coast instituted a buddy system to keep all team members well-informed. A buddy's role was to keep his or her traveling counterpart up-to-date on all formal and informal communication regarding a project. For example, if a team member could not attend a meeting, her buddy would send her a voice mail or e-mail summary of the meeting. The manager summarized, "It is very difficult to keep everyone informed when you have a big group to manage, but this buddy system works very well."

Information technology clearly played a critical role in supportive teamwork, however. For example, a manager whose project with a telecommunications company broke down into thirteen subprojects observed, "You need to spend a lot of time up front thinking about your methods of communication. This should not be left to an office manager. This is more than just a technical issue of deciding which software you should use. Rather, it is a real management issue that determines how people will interact with one another. Once these communication protocols are in place, they take on a life of their own. It is better to plan them out early on; otherwise you pay a huge price in integrating the various pieces different individuals have developed. For instance, think about what would happen if you allowed two hundred people to experiment with Lotus Notes. You would have two hundred different styles. Once you have spent the time up front thinking about your communication needs, the implementation is simple."

MANAGE BY FLYING AROUND

Asked whether there were times when they just had to get on an airplane for a face-to-face meeting, six managers topped their list of such occasions with the instance of client discontent. "If a client isn't happy, I had better be there." Others mentioned building the relationship with a client. For instance, one project manager said he took his client to a baseball game. While they munched popcorn, the client said, "Things seem fine, but I'm not sure." The manager was able to explore this comment in a casual setting, which allowed him to forestall potential problems. Other tasks that required face-to-face communication included delivering performance reviews and collaborating on creative work.

Conclusion

The most significant predictor of project success at our study site was the degree to which team members were conscious of strong organizational support for their work. To maintain the desired "comfort level" with dispersed teams, managers need to attend to a number of factors involving group psychology. First, they need to be aware of the communication gaps that can occur when work teams are not located in the same physical space. Communication technologies can aid in maintaining a team dynamic, but significant thought should be given to how those technologies are managed. There is a temptation to think that technologies such as fax, e-mail, and voice mail can substitute for high-touch management. As this case suggests, successful managers cannot rely on technology alone, but must *use* it to pay enormous attention to the individual needs of team members. Some managers recommended carefully developing communication strategies prior to project implementation.

Another important contributor to the coordination of virtual teams was the bonding of individuals into a team with a common purpose. When team members are co-located, individual and group interaction—both formal and informal—occurs naturally and helps to facilitate a project's progress. For dispersed work groups these kinds of activities must be created artificially.

The need for distributed work that must be highly coordinated is increasing, and rapid technological change is meeting the need with sophisticated methods of collaboration. The development of three-dimensional "virtual" worlds, in which people can meet as if in person, is one example. While development projects that require dispersed work environments have created new challenges for managers, the manager's role has not changed significantly. In fact, the need for leadership to enhance the ability of a team to produce high-quality work in a reasonable time frame has never been greater.

Endnotes

1. G. Thill and D. Leonard-Barton, "Hewlett-Packard: Singapore (A)," Case No. 694-035; "Hewlett-Packard: Singapore (B)," Case No. 694-036; and "Hewlett-Packard (C)," Case No. 694-037 (Boston: Harvard Business School, 1993).

2. D. Schreibman and D. Leonard-Barton, "Group Decision Support Systems," (note prepared for Managing Innovation course, Boston, MA: Harvard University Graduate School of Business Administration, 1995).

3. R. E. Rice and B. M. Johnson, *Managing Organization Innovation: The Evolution from Word Processing to Office Information Systems* (New York: Columbia University Press, 1987).

4. M. Treacy and F. Wiersema, *The Discipline of Market Leaders* (New York: Addison-Wesley Publishing Co., 1995).

5. Of 377 questionnaires sent, 232 were returned, for a response rate of 62%. The eighteen development teams (twelve serving external clients and six supporting internal AMS clients) were selected because members made some use of video conferencing and therefore met two criteria important to the study: (1) they had one or more members who were geographically distant from others in the group; and (2) they had access to the full range of technologies that could be used to coordinate team interactions. (Video conferencing was the only communication technology not uniformly available to all.)

6. The mean team integrity of these virtual teams was 3.72 on a seven-point scale, with a low of 2.45 and a high of 4.66. In contrast, measures of the mean integrity of co-located work teams previously studied by one of the authors using a similar questionnaire were substantially higher—including product development teams working on new medical technology (5.65), product development teams working on office equipment (5.35), nursing teams in hospitals (4.79), and manufacturing teams (4.85). See also Amy Edmondson, "Learning from Mistakes is Easier Said than Done: Group and Organizational Influences on the Detection and Correction of Human Error," *Journal of Applied Behavioral Sciences* 32 (1996a) 5–32; and Amy Edmondson, *Trust Cognitions and Learning Behaviors: Group and Organization Influences on Team Learning* (Harvard University, unpublished Ph.D. dissertation, 1996b).

7. In this study, we defined degree of dispersion according to the extent to which team members interacted with each other in person. We developed a measure of relative use of face-to-face communication ("facetime") from the sum of the number of times in which "face-to-face" was selected by team members as the "most used" communication medium in a series of questionnaire items asking about specific team objectives and activities. For these eighteen teams, the range for this measure, which is a scale from zero to nine, was 0.75 to 5.55, with a mean of 2.95. As intended, selected teams in fact varied in degrees of dispersion; four teams rarely or never interacted face-to-face; nine teams reported moderate use of face-to-face interaction; and five teams frequently relied upon face-to-face communication to plan and conduct their work.

8. We controlled the regression analysis for two potentially confounding variables: the novelty of a project (the degree to which the type of software system being built was familiar to AMS), and length of time that a project had been under way (because managers tended to rate more novel and more recent projects lower, reflecting their uncertainty about project outcomes).

9. Hackman, J. R. (ed.), *Groups That Work and Those That Don't* (San Francisco, CA: Jossey-Bass, 1990).

10. The Internet was not included in the study, because its use among many companies was not as prevalent as it is today. However, AMS project teams had extensive e-mail facilities, enabling linkages across continents as well as hallways.

11. M. L. Markus, "Electronic Mail as the Medium of Managerial Choice," *Organization Science* 5 (1994) 502–527; J. Fulk, C. W. Steinfeld, J. Schmitz, and J.

G. Power, "A Social Information Processing Model of Media Use in Organizations," *Communications Research* 14 (1987) 529–552.

12. L. K. Trevino, R. L. Daft, and R. H. Lengel, "Media Symbolism, Media Richness, and Media Choice in Organizations," *Organization Research* 14 (1987) 176–197.

13. R. L. Daft and R. H. Lengel, "Information Richness: A New Approach to Managerial Behavior and Organization Design," in B. M. Staw and L. L. Cummings (eds.), *Research in Organizational Behavior* (Greenwich, CT: JAI Press, 1984).

References

C. P. Aldefer, "An Intergroup Perspective on Organizational Behavior," in J. W. Lorsch (ed.), *Handbook of Organizational Behavior*. (Englewood Cliffs, NJ: Prentice-Hall, 1987).

R. L. Daft and R. H. Lengel, "Information Richness: A New Approach to Managerial Behavior and Organization Design," in B. M. Staw and L. L. Cummings (eds.), *Research in Organizational Behavior* (Greenwich, CT: JAI Press, 1984).

Amy Edmondson, "Learning from Mistakes is Easier Said than Done: Group and Organizational Influences on the Detection and Correction of Human Error," *Journal of Applied Behavioral Sciences* 32: 5(1996a) 32.

——, *Trust Cognitions and Learning Behaviors: Group and Organization Influences on Team Learning* (unpublished Ph.D. dissertation, Boston, MA: Harvard University, 1996b).

J. Fulk, C. W. Steinfeld, J. Schmitz, and J. G. Power, "A Social Information Processing Model of Media Use in Organizations," *Communications Research* 14 (1987) 529–552.

R. C. Ginnett, "Airline Cockpit Crews," J. R. Hackman (ed.), In *Groups That Work and Those That Don't* (San Francisco, CA: Jossey-Bass, 1990).

D. L. Gladstein, "Groups in Context: A Model of Task Group Effectiveness," *Administrative Science Quarterly* 29 (1984) 499–517.

J. R. Hackman (ed.), *Groups That Work and Those That Don't* (San Francisco, CA: Jossey-Bass, 1990).

M. L. Markus, "Electronic Mail as the Medium of Managerial Choice," *Organization Science* 5 (1994) 502–527.

R. E. Rice and B. M. Johnson, *Managing Organization Innovation: The Evolution from Word Processing to Office Information Systems* (New York: Columbia University Press, 1987).

D. Schreibman and D. Leonard-Barton, "Group Decision Support Systems," (note prepared for Managing Innovation course, Boston, MA: Harvard University Graduate School of Business Administration, 1995).

G. Thill and D. Leonard-Barton, "Hewlett-Packard: Singapore (A)," Case No. 694-035; "Hewlett-Packard: Singapore (B)," Case No. 694-036; and "Hewlett-Packard (C)," Case No. 694-037 (Boston: Harvard Business School, 1993).

M. Treacy and F. Wiersema, *The Discipline of Market Leaders* (New York: Addison-Wesley Publishing Co., 1995).

L. K. Trevino, R. L. Daft, and R. H. Lengel, "Media Symbolism, Media Richness, and Media Choice in Organizations," *Organization Research* 14 (1987) 176–197.

14 Virtual Offices: Redefining Organizational Boundaries

Richard L. Nolan and Hossam Galal

TRADITIONAL MAKE AND SELL organizations used physical boundaries to create control-oriented cultures, which facilitated the execution and coordination of the numerous small tasks required to produce complex products or services. In these organizations, workers' roles and responsibilities were highly stratified.

One of the authors worked for the Boeing Airplane Company in the late 1960s. Upon employment, he was given a color-coded badge, which signified he was a white-collar rather than a blue-collar worker. This badge gave him entry into Boeing's physical plant, where he did not have to "punch the clock" after entering through the guard gate. It defined where he could park his car, where he could go inside the plant, and where he was allowed to eat lunch. All 60,000 workers who entered the Boeing plant had assigned tasks, grouped by departments and monitored by engineers and middle managers. The result was remarkable: every few days, several extremely sophisticated jet aircraft emerged from the assembly line onto Boeing Field.

Boeing's physical plant, delineated by the chain link fence and guard gate, bounded and defined the organization. When a worker entered through the gate, he or she assumed the Boeing culture and carried out highly defined tasks and roles. One group of workers defined the way work was to be done, monitored and controlled it—the white-collar workers. The other group executed tasks as designed, and did not question the authority of middle managers who controlled the quality and coordination of the work as it moved from one workstation to another. Within the organization, workers' time was the company's; after the shift, once past the guard gate, workers' time was once again their own, and they could do with it what they wanted.

Boeing, in the late 1960s, typified the large multi-unit business enterprise that replaced turn of the century single-unit business enterprises. These single-unit enterprises, operated by an individual or small group of owners, carried out a single economic function in limited product lines, and within one geographical area.[1] When administrative coordination enabled by information and communication technologies, such as the telegraph and telephone, began emerging, larger multi-unit organizations permitted greater productivity, lower costs, and higher profits than those single-unit enterprises, largely coordinated by market mechanisms. As Malone describes in Chapter 12 of this book, the continued decreased cost of information technologies (the modern digital computer) now results in a new economics for business coordination and, in turn, is spawning new organizational forms.[2]

We characterize their ability to sense and respond.[3] Enabled by information technology, sense and respond organizations extend beyond the physical boundaries of the plant or office to carry out their activities where the customers are. Their physical boundaries are no longer so clear, nor are the traditional boundaries as useful for defining the organization. Much of the reengineering initiatives of the 1990s, directed at combining simple tasks into complex tasks through Information Technology, had this effect.

Commensurate with these more complex tasks, which are carried out by front-line workers, are simplified business functions—commonly called business processes.

Traditional business functions are generally quite complex, requiring a large complement of middle managers to coordinate the workflow. Because sense and respond organizations get a lot of the work done at the customer interface, they reduce this administrative burden. Consequently, when a traditional organization becomes a sense and respond organization, the resulting downsizing of the workforce not only reduces the number of middle managers (and offices), it permits a redeployment of office workers in the field.

The term "virtual," as in "virtual office," or "virtual organization," refers to ways of organizing that adhere to the phenomenon described above.

In this chapter, we develop a framework for describing organizational boundaries, through which to describe the changes apparent in the transition from traditional industrial to sense and respond organizations. We first consider the concept and functions of traditional organizational boundaries. We then present three cases—IBM, Chiat/Day, and VeriFone—with "virtual" type organizations to illustrate how boundaries are being transformed by sense and respond IT-enabled strategies.

The Concept and Function of Organizational Boundaries

In an industrial economy, the concept of boundaries is essentially an administrative one. The traditional or Industrial Era organization made the concept of boundaries explicit through detailed rules and principles that govern all aspects of organizational membership. These rules and principles were based on perceived notions of legitimate authority. Four fundamental types of boundaries may be identified: social, political, economic, and legal (Table 14-1).

Combined choices in the different boundaries may be referred to as a *boundary condition*. Describing how each of the boundaries is implemented for an organization allows us to understand changes in structure and compare these over time and across companies. The *boundary condition* is also helpful in studying the relationship between different types of boundaries—for example, to assess whether social and economic boundaries are aligned for a company.

The Industrial Era organization emerged in the late 1800s with the use of steam engine technology in manufacturing.[4] This organization, which revolved around the factory, adopted a hierarchical management

TABLE 14-1   A Typology of Organizational Boundaries

Boundary Type	Definition	Delimiter	Primary Role	Managerial Levers
Legal	The legal boundary of an organization is defined by assets and resources owned, obligations for which the organization is liable, and regulation of its activities.	Assets	Legitimacy	Legal contracts
Political	The political boundary of an organization is defined by assets and resources over which the organization has influence but does not directly own.	Resources	Predictability	Contractual arrangement; interlocking boards
Economic	The economic boundary of an organization is defined by the activities the organization chooses to undertake directly or indirectly related to the production of products or services.	Activities	Efficiency	Task specification; job specification
Social	The social boundary of an organization is defined by the membership of the organization.	Members	Norm setting	Organizational structure; formal rules; superordinate goals

approach. In addition to the benefits of coordination achieved through a centralized command and control system, these organizations realized tremendous gains in productivity through division of labor.

Societal conditions, in particular, the abundance of "free-floating" labor that resulted from the mechanization of farming, further contributed to the spread of the industrial organization.[5] These new labor resources were formed predominantly from rural migrants and poor immigrants, who had little education and few skills. Rational methods had to be developed to predict and manage their behavior.[6] Especially important was the need to change their attitudes toward work and the way it was to be done. Although preindustrial workers made no distinction between work and life, Industrial Era workers had to acknowledge a difference. Within the organization they were governed by supervisory hierarchies, assigned roles based on technical competence, standardized operating procedures, and clearly specified responsibilities. An organization's boundaries were considered to extend as far as these formal standards applied.[7]

Industrial Era managers were aware of the potential for role conflict that arose from the existence of informal groups and affiliations based on ethnic, religious, or class origins. Their solution was to disacknowledge membership in groups outside the organization and to reinforce the organization's social boundary through intricate procedures and supervisory layers. Initially, organizational boundaries were marked through physical symbols and objects, such as uniforms, factory walls, guarded gates, company logos, and security badges.[8]

These formal physical boundaries facilitated the development of more sophisticated internal organizations leading up to the multidivisional corporate form. This maturation of organizational structure in turn allowed boundaries to be implemented through less "physical" means. At the departmental level, formal planning and budgeting soon became very sophisticated. Quotas, monthly goals for expenditures, and variance analyses of actual versus planned figures became a means for controlling behavior and achieving high performance. Performance review systems such as the Hay Point System and their associated rewards were based on workers' budgetary responsibilities and their positions in the organization.

The resultant organization was adapted to react to predictable situations in a preprogrammed manner. Each individual knew his or her function well but had little understanding of how the process as a whole worked. Jobs were simple and integrated through complex routines executed by administrators and technical specialists. As a company grew larger, the hierarchy was divided into smaller subhierarchies based on criteria such as line of business, function, and geography. The hierarchy's centralized communication system reduced the problem of information overload by managing information flows on a "top-down need-to-know" basis.[9] Although these organizational characteristics are now considered to be negative, they worked well for most of the twentieth century, allowing the refinement and aggressive implementation of the multidivisional form in major organizations around the world.

Our discussion thus far suggests that while Industrial Era managers and theorists viewed organizations as tools designed to achieve predefined goals, they deliberately ignored or attempted to minimize perturbations or opportunities resulting from links to the broader environment. This perspective assumes that goals are known, tasks are repetitive, output of the production process somehow disappears, and resources in uniform qualities are available.[10] Within this context, management is able to structure an organization through specializations, departmentalizations, and controls.

Beginning in the late 1950s and continuing to the present, there has been an effort to view decisions in structuring organizations as partly resultant from external or environmental stimuli. Whereas on one extreme there existed the highly formalized, centralized organizations with clearly specified goals, on the other extreme, there were less formalized organizations dependent on the initiative of participants and with less clearly defined goals.[11] These two extremes can be viewed as distinct forms of organization rather than different aspects of the same organization. Furthermore, each form emerges depending on the type of environment to which a company must relate. In homogenous, stable environments, formalized and hierarchical forms are more appropriate whereas in more diverse environments with continuously changing requirements and goals, less formalized and less rigid organizations are appropriate.[12]

We propose that as organizational requirements vary, boundaries take on various roles, demarcating property, differentiating among groups, distinguishing between the organization and its environment, and defining appropriate behavior. The concept of boundaries, however, remains an essential management tool for organizing people and resources. The task of mapping a typology of boundaries to sense and respond organizations is difficult—not only because there is no unified view of what constitutes such organizations, but also because traditional notions and theories of organization are themselves currently being reviewed and challenged. For instance, physical boundaries are now less meaningful, a fact that raises a number of important questions. Are there some boundaries that take precedence over others? How does the business environment, specifically changing customer demands and increased competition, affect an organization's boundaries? What is the effect of information technology on how boundaries are conceived and defined?

In the following sections, we analyze the sense and respond structures in three very different organizations to see how boundaries are implemented and used.

IBM: Changing an Organization's Structure

In the late 1980s, IBM was still a model of the industrial organization. Its formal organizational structure, steep, rigid hierarchies, and intricate reporting systems gave it an inflexible and inward focus. Although these characteristics had served the company well for most of the twentieth century, they placed it in dire straits at the close of the 1980s.

CONVERSION TO A VIRTUAL OFFICE

In the spring of 1993, still reeling from massive layoffs and facing huge competitive pressures in a rapidly evolving industry, IBM initiated a "virtual office" work model. The purpose of its program was two-fold: first, to "stop the bleeding," and second, to reach out to customers. Like other corporations, IBM had discovered it did not need the large amount of office space it owned. The discovery was particularly true in the case of IBM's 13,000 sales-related employees. All sales, marketing, technology, and administrative staff members were issued portable computers, printers, and fax/modems.

Two pioneers in the telecommuting program were IBM's Midwest division and its Cranford, New Jersey sales operation. The Midwest division was able to reduce its office space by fifty-five percent and to raise the ratio of workers to workstations from four to one to ten to one. IBM's Denver operation, for example, was able to decrease its use of office space from nine floors to four, for a projected savings of $6 million over the next few years. Similarly, IBM's New Jersey office achieved a seventy-five percent reduction in space by consolidating five different locations. Space requirements fell from four hundred thousand to one hundred thousand square feet, consolidated on one floor. As a consequence, facilities and overhead costs shrank by $70 million. New Jersey employees were asked not to come to the office except for major presentations, to pick up mail, or to break the monotony of working at home. When they did come to the office, the company used a "hoteling" system to assign them resources. The program worked better than IBM had expected. Initially, the company set up cubicles to be shared by four people. Administrators were surprised to discover that up to six people could use a single workspace. To support virtual offices, the structure of the specialized sales function must change. Instead of dedicated technical experts, a pool of technical experts is required to support account teams, accessed mainly through interlinked computers. These successful telecommuting programs appear to be more than isolated events as companies not only transition their sales forces into virtual offices, but also begin moving their senior executives to virtual office arrangements as well.

CHALLENGES OF THE VIRTUAL OFFICE

The shift toward a mobile work force has not come without challenges for IBM. Until recently, IBM promised lifetime employment to workers in return for loyalty and satisfactory output; that ended with the lay-offs. The biggest hurdles, however, were related to employee identity and status. Managers, particularly those who had worked for many years, found shifting from private offices to common work pods diffi-cult. Shared work areas have also meant that family pictures and other personal trappings have had to disappear. The other major issue was that of employee isolation. Peers, in particular, feared they would be separated from one another.

IBM has dealt with these problems by providing training and educa-tion, to help employees adapt to the new environment. The company distributed booklets covering topics ranging from time management to family issues. It also instituted voluntary outings to events like the In-dianapolis 500 as a means of mitigating fears of isolation from other workers. A survey of the mobile work force in its Midwest division sug-gested that eighty-three percent were accepting the new working ar-rangements and would not want to return to the old environment.[13] In fact, contrary to their concerns prior to implementation of the program, peers were communicating more effectively and more broadly through the use of information technology.

CHANGES IN ORGANIZATIONAL BOUNDARIES

IBM's virtual office initiative has radically altered the company's boundaries. Traditionally, IBM has had a strong culture that emphasizes inward control of employees. That control included not only what was expected of a worker in terms of behavior, but of appearance as well— for instance, all managers were expected to wear white shirts. In fact, the social boundary appeared to supersede the economic one. Defined by rules, procedures, and social norms, it seemed to take precedence over economic efficiency and the long-term viability of the company. This boundary was managed conservatively according to an outdated perception of the external environment that stressed efficiency and internal control of low-skilled workers. Thus, even though the economic boundary had changed, the social boundary had not.

Misalignment of this boundary condition—a bias toward an inward versus an outward market orientation—may have contributed in the late 1970s to IBM's underestimation of the potential of the personal computer market. By the 1990s, Microsoft rather than IBM had become the most dominant force in the computing industry. The first at IBM to recognize the new reality were groups with tentacles outside the organization—namely, the direct marketing and sales functions. These were the first groups to be targeted for change in the company's virtual initiative, an initiative aimed at allowing the sales functions to change their boundary condition. Today, IBM is closer to its customers through strategic use of technology, and the company's social boundaries support rather than supersede its economic boundaries. Instead of focusing the attention of employees internally, social boundaries now provide only the necessary cohesion for peer-to-peer and manager-to-peer relationships.

Significantly, the adjustment has been made by relying less on budget-based performance systems and co-location of managers and workers. The new team performance measurement criteria reflect customer satisfaction and stockholder value. The company's *economic* boundary is defined by activities that increase these measures, and its *social* boundary supports the *economic* one. Thus, the organization is prepared for any change in the external environment, whether new competition or fickle consumers.

IBM's external orientation has altered its *political* boundary as well. In the 1960s and 1970s, IBM provided large amounts of service to its mainframe clients, at a high cost. With little competition, the company could afford to do so. But in the 1990s, as companies migrated to PC-based solutions, IBM had to build a much more interdependent relationship with customers. *By changing the role of its specialized sales personnel, the company was able to move from "making and selling" to "sensing" customer needs precisely and providing targeted "responses" to those needs.*

In sum, although the initial motivation for IBM's virtual initiative may have been to change the company's cost structure, the more important long-term benefit has been not decreasing costs, but rather a new way for employees to manage their work and reach customers. Interestingly, IBM, like other large organizations, overestimated the difficulty of adjusting to the change.

Chiat/Day: Implementing a New Concept of Work

Chiat/Day undertook its virtual office initiative primarily to achieve a high level of innovation. Firms in the advertising industry are highly dependent on innovation *for* survival. Since its founding in 1968, California-based Chiat/Day has intentionally gone against the tide to establish a market position that often bordered on eccentricity. The firm is known for its ability to set new standards in advertising. Chiat/Day developed the Energizer bunny campaign, engendering the ubiquitous phrase "It keeps on going and going and going." During the 1984 Super Bowl, Chiat/Day broke from advertising tradition by airing an Apple Macintosh commercial that did not show the product or describe its characteristics, but instead positioned Apple as different from its main competitor. By extension, the advertisement implied that Apple's competitor was a rigid, traditional company.

PULLING DOWN THE WALLS

Chiat/Day's philosophy of continuous innovation extends beyond the advertising it produces to the heart of the organization. As early as 1978, the company's president was experimenting with new organizational designs. By the late 1970s the company had done away with walled offices in an effort to promote teamwork and creativity. The new work arrangement did more than define the company's cutting-edge image. Chiat/Day believed that bringing down the physical boundaries in an office would also break down mental barriers to cooperation, raising productivity.

By the 1990s, Chiat/Day was pushing the envelope once again in embracing the concept of the virtual office. Ironically, this time the goal was to keep employees away from the office rather than together in one large space. The idea was that if employees did not come to the office, they could spend more time with clients. Indeed, the objective was not only to better sense clients' needs, but also to respond by working closely with clients at their sites. In the short term, this set-up did not necessarily reduce costs. While expenditures on office space certainly went down, expenditures on the latest in portable computer hardware and training skyrocketed. But when employees did come in to the office, a very different workplace awaited them.

Chiat/Day moved into new headquarters in Venice, California. The building's non-traditional architecture, with the entrance marked by a pair of hundred-foot high black binoculars, is meant to suggest a departure from the past. Inside the building, there are no offices. Because employees are organized into temporary teams whose membership changes with each new project, permanent offices are not necessary. Instead, work spaces are assigned on an as-needed basis. Rooms can be "checked out" by teams for the duration of a project. Competitor and other intelligence is maintained in these rooms, where clients are invited to work side-by-side with Chiat/Day employees. Workers store their personal belongings in lockers, and receive telephones and computers from a concierge when they check in. A computer routes calls, facsimiles, and e-mail to the assigned extension.

These changes have been accompanied by changes in the rules of engagement between workers and managers. Traditional titles have been eliminated; there are no vice-presidents or executives at Chiat/Day. Instead, managers are referred to by their functions: "copy writer," "art director," or "managing partner." In terms of performance measurement, workers are judged on the final product rather than their physical presence at the office. Chiat/Day's goal is ultimately "to change the way people work by making the atmosphere more energetic, more creative, and more useful."

ADAPTING TO THE NEW ENVIRONMENT

The transition to Chiat/Day's virtual office was not smooth. Some employees adapted, but others found coping with the changes difficult.[14] Although one might expect older employees to be the hardest hit by the changes, Chiat/Day claims the younger employees actually had the greatest difficulty. What would their career paths be now that they could not move from cubicle to corner office? Would they be noticed if they were not in the same place every day? "When you take away corner offices, photos of the family, and all the other ego perks, you have to replace them with something else," says the company president. Chiat/Day has tried to compensate by providing a "clubhouse" for employees—a lounge with TV sets, a pool table, and punching bags bearing the images of managing partners.

The company has managed to establish an energetic and creative atmosphere. The effect on the bottom line is unclear, as is the long-term impact of the changes. Shortly after the changes, the agency lost two major accounts. Although these problems may not be tied to organizational structure, we know that over the short term, going "virtual" involves some inevitable disruptions in work arrangements.

Continuously Changing Boundaries

Chiat/Day's boundary condition is difficult to describe, partly because it is continuously changing and partly because some of its boundaries, particularly its social boundaries, are not well-defined. The company's symbols from its binocular facade to the futuristic multicolored lockers employees use radiate the message: *We are different, we are leading edge.* While the economic boundary is clearly defined by creative activities, the social boundary is freeform and dictated by the required output.

VeriFone: Exploiting Global Opportunities

VeriFone views itself not as a virtual office, but as a virtual organization. Founded in 1981 by William Melton, an entrepreneur with a habitual distaste for structure and bureaucracy, VeriFone produces low-cost electronic terminals for validating credit cards and authorizing checks.

Managing a Virtual Organization

By the mid-1980s, VeriFone had yet to make a profit, and it was clear that the company's innovative products could not alone guarantee its success. In 1986 Hatim Tyabji, a high-ranking executive at Sperry Corporation, took over as head of the badly ailing firm. Tyabji fitted the organization's decentralized structure with relevant control systems to better extract the benefit of its novel products. By 1988, the company was growing at an average rate of twenty-five percent per year, and profits were growing even faster. Through the mid-1990s, VeriFone was able to capture sixty-five percent of the global market in transaction authorization systems. The future looked promising.

The question of whether their company is "virtual" or not does not seem to be an issue for VeriFoners. When questioned about his company's way of doing business, Tyabji answered, "Organizationally as in business, we are going to create and lead. If what we are doing coincides with what the rest of the world is preaching, that's fine. Otherwise, we are more than willing to march to our own drummer. Hopefully, some day people will say that the VeriFone method is the right method." For VeriFone, the right method means being as close to the customer as possible, providing products of the highest reliability, and leveraging the firm's global resources to outperform the competition.

Toward this objective, VeriFone emphasizes close physical proximity to customers and emerging markets—a concept it refers to as "forward deployment." To take advantage of local expertise more efficiently, the company locates itself near "centers of excellence," or areas known for their intellectual or capital resources. The company does systems engineering in India, engineering and manufacturing in Taiwan, and research on transactions security in France. Roughly one-third of all employees are on the road more than half the time, at a cost of over $5 million per year in airfare and hotels. Tyabji himself is comfortable working anywhere he can connect to a phone line. This man to whom the term "Corporate Headquarters" is taboo, logs over four hundred thousand air miles per year.

Using Information Technology

Information technology plays an integral role in this virtual organization. At VeriFone, it serves three main purposes: (1) to provide shared objectives, (2) to identify and report areas of weakness, and (3) to provide real-time feedback at all levels in order to help employees to accomplish their tasks. "Ours is a company which does not sleep," proclaims CIO Will Pape. "The network is the heartbeat of our company, and because of our geographical dispersion, work is being acted upon and results are being reported twenty-four hours a day." At VeriFone, employees send out company-wide "distress messages" on business problems, knowing that they will return to work the following day to find at least half a dozen responses.[15]

While VeriFone may be one of the most virtual of organizations, the technology employees use is much less sophisticated than might be expected. The company philosophy is that you do not need a Ferrari to drive to the supermarket; a Ford Fairlane or Chevy Impala will do. Similarly, an organization does not need the latest wireless device to enter the information age; today's technology will serve just as well.

VeriFone's "forward deployed," information-intense strategy has allowed the company to maximize its interaction with customers. This achievement has come at the expense of internal interaction among employees, however. The company's primary challenge now is to maintain the sense of cohesion and unity that has been so important to its historical success.

Aligning and Strengthening Boundaries

VeriFone started out with a boundary condition similar to Chiat/Day's. As an entrepreneurial organization, its boundaries were not well defined or aligned: work was done in a free-form structure, and there were few controls. The result was an unprofitable performance despite the production of high-quality products for an accepting market. In 1986, when Tyabji took over and instituted tight controls and strict accountability, he changed the company's boundary condition in a way that allowed VeriFone to capture the benefits of its distributed organization. The company's new goal was to capture core competencies without having to bring them together in central locations—the reason being that in the long run, tapping these competencies remotely would be much less costly and more efficient than centralizing them. The result was that the company's social and economic boundaries became better aligned.

The key to the success of this strategy was a high level of communication. Historically, VeriFone has been very effective at enabling both personal and electronic communication. Intensive communication serves two major purposes: to support the alignment between different boundaries and to strengthen particular boundaries. VeriFone also likes to think of itself as having a highly focused business strategy. Its economic boundary, although flexible, is precisely defined. Tyabji maintains that the company "will stay away from what it knows that it doesn't know and nothing will shake it from its core competencies." The result is that the company outsources all activities it considers noncritical to maintain its competitive edge.

For an entrepreneurial company, VeriFone has a strong and well-defined social boundary. Employee behavior is remarkably consistent with the prescribed set of norms preached by the company's managers who take an almost evangelical approach to instilling values to everything from customer relations to environmental responsibility. The company's Bible is a manual titled *VeriFone Philosophy*, which has been translated into all the languages spoken by company employees. In addition to clarifying the social boundary, the manual helps to define the legal boundary of the organization—in particular, how the company views its obligations to its employees and its expectations of them. Rather than creating detailed contractual agreements with employees, VeriFone relies more on the persuasion of social norms to get the best from its employees.

The company's political boundary can be understood in terms of its view of the competition. VeriFoners like to consider competitors not as adversaries but as potential clients. First, competition increases the size of the overall market through the introduction of new products to new customers. Second, VeriFone believes that because of its focused business strategy, it can always produce equipment that is cheaper and better than competing products and still push further ahead in terms of innovative new products. This attitude has resulted in the company agreeing to create components for competitors, such as NEC.

In sum, VeriFone has been able to merge two polar cultures: an original entrepreneurial culture that stressed informality, creativity, and value to the customer, and the more traditional culture of accountability stressed by Sperry veteran Tyabji. VeriFone has become an outstanding performer, the top provider of transaction automation systems in the world, in less than a decade. The company owes its success in large part to its innovative organizational structure and its choice of the appropriate boundary condition for its environment. For an organization that claims to have no headquarters, and whose employee base is growing at twelve percent per year, the only question that remains is how long it will be able to maintain its success.

Toward Sense and Respond Organizations

We have proposed that each of the boundaries in the typology presented in this chapter plays a particular role in industrial or traditional organizations. Specifically, legal, political, economic, and social boundaries afford legitimacy, predictability, efficiency, and norm-setting, respectively. While these functions are still necessary for sense and respond organizational forms such as Chiat/Day and VeriFone, the means by which the boundaries are implemented are different and so, too, are their characteristics. From these cases, we can set forth some preliminary predictions for how these boundaries are changing in this regard.

Economic Boundaries: From Efficiency to Added Value

Economic boundaries are defined by the activities an organization chooses to undertake. In Industrial Era organizations, the focus was on efficient production through a make and sell approach that implied large volumes of cheap but standardized goods. Adhering to this philosophy, companies could not achieve both high product differentiation and low prices simultaneously.

Modern sense and respond companies pursue low-cost customized production. They have achieved this goal by using information technology to get close to customers, understand their requirements, and respond with products and services tailored to customers' needs. This strategic reorientation has impacted their economic boundaries in two ways:

1. *Their definition of the economic boundary is more sophisticated than that of traditional organizations.* The organizations examined were ruthless in terms of focusing on their core competencies. They define the set of activities they choose to undertake precisely in terms of how they add value to customers.

2. *They redefine their economic boundary more rapidly than traditional organizations.* Just because a company focuses its choice of activities, that does not mean that its activities are static. Rather, its boundaries are continuously being redefined as a result of the rapid transfer of knowledge facilitated by global information networks.

SOCIAL BOUNDARIES: FROM RULES TO NORMS

The role of the social boundary in the Industrial Era organization was to control behavior within the organization. Productive work was achieved by imposing rules, procedures, and control checks on the workforce.

In virtual organizations, there is much less focus on formal coordination of work. Rules and supervisory hierarchies tend to be secondary to the emphasis on creating output that is relevant to the customer. What is most surprising is that while we would expect to observe *less* conformity in conjunction with less structure, what we observed was, in fact, *more* conformity. In the virtual organization, social conformity is achieved by instilling core values and principles in employees. Norms of conduct take precedence over formal rules.

The following observations can be made about the social boundary in sense and respond organizations.

1. *Work methods are more output-oriented than input-oriented.* Job specifications are becoming less explicit with respect to how individuals undertake their work. Intellectual flexibility, innovation, and a process orientation are fostered by specifying the required output rather than the required method of producing the output.

2. *Membership in the company is transient.* Lifetime employment and long-term tenure are not feasible. Employer-employee relationships are based on what the two parties can offer each other in terms of adding value to the customer. Continuous restructurings, temporary project groups, and other temporary work arrangements are the norm.

3. *Specification is loose with respect to time and space, tight with respect to commitment and loyalty.* To be recognized as part of an organization, employees need not reside in physical proximity to each other, or work in the same time horizon (say, 9 AM to 5 PM). Rather, their membership in the organization is defined by the output they produce and their fit with the strategy, values, and culture of the organization.

LEGAL BOUNDARIES: FROM INTERNAL TO EXTERNAL LABOR MARKETS

An organization's legal boundary is defined in broad terms based on the assets it owns and its obligations to different constituencies.[16] The legal boundary was a much more useful and operational boundary when most of a firm's productive assets were physical in nature, and its relationship with employees long-term and contractual. As the creation of economic value has become more dependent on intangible assets like information and intellectual property, the legal boundary has begun to blur. For example, with the advent of the Internet, intellectual property in the form of software has become extremely hard to protect. The ability of patent and copyright law to protect intellectual property rights has substantially broken down.

People create intellectual assets, and thus the organization's relationship with its employees and other workers feels this impact. The Industrial Era organization's authority arose from the employee contract. While the tasks or functions required of the employee were often elaborately described, the output, duration, and quality of the work were not. Employees were motivated by job ladders, pay scales, and long-term career paths.[17] This type of arrangement, in which the formal contract is not complete, is sometimes known as an "internal" or "soft" labor market.

In contrast, in external labor markets parties negotiate complete ("hard") contracts. Virtual organizations engage in a far greater degree of hard contracting. For instance, the move away from formal organizational titles and corner offices at Chiat/Day and IBM was followed by a new pay-for-performance incentive system. That is not to say that soft contracting is not used. VeriFone, for example, seems to prefer a soft contracting to purely pay-for-performance systems, perhaps as a result of its rapid growth and the need to fill new managerial positions quickly. Since in this case the contract is not explicit, it requires a much higher degree of investment and trust on the part of both VeriFone and its employees.

In regard to the legal boundary of virtual organizations, we can make the following observations:

1. *The legal boundary is becoming more explicit and more complex.* Hard contracting is on the increase and pay-for-performance compensation systems have become the norm. This development raises difficult issues, such as who should bear the cost of training—management or the worker?

2. *More negotiation is required to set legal boundaries.* With soft contracting, the industrial organization had implicit control over employees. It could unilaterally assign duties to employees in return for promised long-term career rewards. Hard contracting between employer and employee requires bilateral bargaining between two independent contractors.

POLITICAL BOUNDARIES: FROM INDEPENDENCE TO INTERDEPENDENCE

Political boundaries are closely tied to economic boundaries. To focus on core competencies, companies must accept a new concept of organizational sovereignty based on increased interdependence with customers and suppliers. That is the only way they can hope to fulfill the requirements of the widest range of customers, while building on existing process capabilities, experience, and knowledge.[18]

Regarding the political boundary of virtual organizations, we can make the following observations:

1. *Political boundaries are moving toward mutually negotiated limits.* That is, companies are showing a greater willingness to give up control and a greater tendency toward interdependence. Today's highly competitive and complex environment suggests cooperation and flexibility in response to changing markets. Although mutual trust is required for healthy cooperation, the rapid access to distributed information, available through technology, allows mutual monitoring as a means of building confidence in new business relationships.

2. *Political boundaries are contracting.* Economic liberalization and free trade mean that companies can more effectively explore economic niches in global markets. Standardization of products will occur more rapidly through the negotiated transfer of technology, thus reducing dependence on a few parties.

Conclusion

Management theorists continue to emphasize changes in coordination structure as a basis for understanding how organizations are evolving in the 1990s. In this chapter, we have attempted to rely on the notion of multiple boundaries as a means for describing organizations and how they are changing to better sense and respond to their environment. While at times this approach may appear overly eclectic, it provides a perspective by which organizations can be compared irrespective of differences in labor organization or coordination systems employed.

The recognition that activities can be undertaken remotely seems to have guided the emergence of virtual organizations. We have focused on these types of companies as exemplars of sense and respond organizations. The driving tenets of these companies—namely, proximity to customers and reactiveness to customer requirements—has radically altered the conception of boundaries as understood for industrial organizations. Accordingly, questions regarding who constitutes a member of an organization and which activities a company chooses to undertake and how it undertakes them should necessarily be reconsidered. This implies revisiting employee incentive systems, product value added to customers, customer service, and company to company relationships.

There has been much skepticism about whether the virtual organization would move beyond rhetoric and the handful of nonmainstream organizations that have implemented it to become a practical replacement for the traditional organization.[19] The three cases we described are by no means isolated ones. AT&T, Travelers Corporation, Apple Computer, Corning, McDonald's, Whirlpool, and Toyota, to mention just a few, are among the firms exploring and investing in virtual offices.[20] However, the caselets are of particular interest in demonstrating how traditional companies like IBM are abandoning old concepts of organization, and companies like VeriFone and Chiat/Day can propel themselves to leadership positions in their respective industries.

The types of organizations we have described are particularly suitable for certain business functions. Sales-related activities are good candidates because they are distributed by nature, and performance is easily measured. Computer programming and customer support are also good candidates for the same reasons. On the other hand, managerial activities may be more difficult to conduct in a virtual office because of their centralized and inherently personal nature. Companies like VeriFone certainly show that they can be carried out from a distance. Arguments that manufacturing activities cannot follow similar arrangements, because of physical manipulation of materials, are quickly eroding with information systems that can be integrated independent of location. VeriFone, for example, shows that component manufacturing can be carried out across the globe, as can system development. Ultimately, it can all come together at one site—and we see no reason why that one site could not be the customer's site as well as the company's.

Endnotes

1. See description by Alfred D. Chandler, Jr., *The Visible Hand* (Cambridge, MA: The Belknap Press of Harvard University Press, 1977) 307.
2. Indeed, we address new organization structures emerging from information technologies with some trepidation. James Beniger in his 1986 book, *The Control Revolution* includes a table with over seventy major works on new organizational forms, beginning in 1950 with David Reisman's *Lonely Crowd.*
3. "Sense and Respond" as an IT-enabled strategy is described by Stephan Haeckel and Richard L. Nolan in "Managing by Wire," *Harvard Business Review* (September–October 1993).
4. Cf. Rosenberg (1982).
5. Eisenstadt (1958); Scott (1992)
6. The earliest contributors to these methods included Taylor and Gantt (scientific management) and Fayol (modern operational theory). Later, work in what would become known as the behavioral sciences drew on not only the results of these fathers of modern management, but also on concepts from economics, psychology, and political theory. Refer to *The History of Management Thought* by Claude George (Englewood Cliffs, NJ: Prentice-Hall, 1972) for a detailed source on early contributors to management theory.
7. Cf. Weber (1947), Barnard (1938), and Badaracco (1991).
8. In *Corporate Identity*, Olins (1989) suggests that this type of "visualization" provided social cohesion in the view of both insiders and outsiders.
9. Cf. Arrow (1974).
10. Thompson (1967).
11. Lawrence and Lorsch (1967).
12. Scott (1992).
13. Cf. Greengard (1994).
14. Contrary to press clippings (cf. Garland 1994), company managers maintain that turnover has decreased slightly since implementation of the virtual office.
15. See "VeriFone: The Transaction Automation Company" by Galal, Stoddard, Nolan (1994).
16. Refer to Galal and Nolan (1995) for an in-depth discussion on "legal" boundaries of organizations.
17. See Williamson and Ouchi (1981); Scott (1992).
18. Cf. Boynton and Victor (1991); Gomes-Casseras (1994).
19. Cf. Nohria and Berkley (1994).
20. Indeed, the percentage of U.S. companies that have telecommuting programs has more than doubled in half a decade. Almost eight million employees in the United States now work through telecommuting arrangements, a number that is expected to grow by at least 20 percent a year. This figure does not include "mobile workers"—those who use their cars, client's offices, hotels,

and satellite work areas to get their work done. Cf. Sussman (1995) and Greengard (1994).

References

K. Arrow, *The Limits of Organization* (New York: W.W. Norton, 1974).

J. L. Badarraco, *The Knowledge Link: How Firms Compete Through Strategic Alliances* (Boston, MA: Harvard Business School Press, 1991a).

—— "The Boundaries of the Firm," in A. Etzioni and P. R. Lawrence (eds.), *Socio-Economics: Toward a New Synthesis* (New York: M. E. Sharpe, Inc., 1991b) 293–328.

C. I. Barnard, *The Functions of the Executive* (2nd ed.). (Cambridge, MA: Harvard University Press, 1968 [1938]).

A. C. Boynton and B. Victor, "Beyond Flexibility: Building and Managing the Dynamically Stable Organization," *California Management Review*, Fall (1991) 54ff.

J. Champy and M. Hammer, *Reengineering the Corporation* (New York: Harper Collins, 1993).

A. D. Chandler, *Strategy and Structure* (Cambridge, MA: MIT Press, 1962).

R. H. Coase, "The Nature of the Firm," in O. E. Williamson and S. G. Winter (eds.), *The Nature of the Firm* (Oxford, UK: Oxford University Press, 1993 [1937]).

R. Crain, "IBM's Mobile Work Force Virtual Success Year Later." *Crain's New York Business*, February 13 (1995a) 11.

—— Virtual Reality: Touring IBM's Office of the Future. *Crain's Chicago Business*, February 27 (1995b) 13.

S. N. Eisenstadt, "Bureaucracy and Bureaucratization: A Trend Report and Bibliography." *Current Sociology*, 7 (1958) 99–164.

H. Galal, and R. L. Nolan, "Toward an Understanding of Organizational Boundaries" (working paper, Boston, MA: Harvard Business School 95-057, 1995).

—— R. Nolan, and D. Stoddard, "VeriFone: The Transaction Automation Company," Harvard Business School Publishing, Case 195-245, 1994.

E. Garland, "Entering the Virtual Office," *Marketing Computers*, February 1994, 6ff.

B. Gomes-Casseres, "Group Versus Group: How Alliance Networks Compete," *Harvard Business Review*, 72 (1994) 62–74.

S. Greengard, "Making the Virtual Office a Reality," *Personnel Journal*, 73 (1994) 66–70ff.

P. Lawrence and J. Lorsch, *Organizations & Environment* (2nd ed.). (Boston, MA: Harvard Business School Press, 1967).

H. C. Lucas and J. Baroudi, "The Role of Information Technology in Organization Design," *Journal of Management Information Systems*, 10 (1994) 9–23.

N. Nohria and J.D. Berkley, "The Virtual Organization: Bureaucracy, Technology and the Implosion of Control," In C. Heckscher and A. Donnellon (eds.), *The Post-Bureaucratic Organization: New Perspectives on Organizational Change* (Newbury Park, CA: Sage Publications, Inc., 1994).

R. C. Nolan and D. C. Croson, *Creative Destruction: A Six Stage Process for Transforming the Organization* (Boston, MA: Harvard Business School Press, 1995).

H. Ogilvie, "This Old Office," *Journal of Business Strategy*, 15 (1994) 26–34.

W. Olin, *Corporate Identity* (Boston, MA: Harvard Business School Press, 1989).

S. Perez, "Enter the 'Virtual Office'," *Santa Cruz Sentinel*, April 14, 1995, 5.

B. J. Pine, *Mass Customization: The New Frontier in Business Competition* (Boston, MA: Harvard Business School Press, 1993).

N. Rosenberg, *Inside the Black Box: Technology and Economics* (New York: Cambridge University Press, 1982).

R. Scott, *Organizations: Rational, Natural, and Open Systems* (Englewood Cliffs, NJ: Prentice-Hall, 1992).

D. Sussman, "Firms 'Virtually' Opt for Future," *Minneapolis-St. Paul CityBusiness*, May 5, 1995, 17.

J. D. Thompson, *Organizations in Action* (New York: McGraw-Hill, 1967).

M. Weber, "Legitimate Authority and Bureaucracy," in *The Theory of Social and Economic Organisation* (Glencoe, IL: Free Press, 1947a), 328–340.

—— *The Theory of Social and Economic Organization*, translated by A. H. Henderson and Talcott Parsons (Glencoe, IL: Free Press, 1947).

O. E. Williamson, *Hierarchies and Markets: Analysis and Antitrust Implications* (New York: Free Press, 1975).

—— and W. G. Ouchi, "The Markets and Hierarchies and Visible Hand Perspectives," in A. H. Van de Ven and W. E. Joyce (eds.), *Perspectives on Organization Design and Behavior* (New York: John Wiley, 1981) 347–370.

Index

About the Contributors

P. William Bane is a Director and Group Head of Mercer Management Consulting, Inc., where he focuses on identifying and exploiting profitable growth strategies in the converging industries of communications, content, and computing. Prior to joining Mercer, Mr. Bane was a Vice President and Director of The Boston Consulting Group, and was Founder, Chairman, and Chief Executive of ManageWare, a venture-capital-funded PC software developer and marketer. Compete!, ManageWare's spreadsheet product, received *PC Magazine's* Best Software of 1990 award. Mr. Bane received his undergraduate degree in engineering from Tulane University, where he graduated first in his class and with Honors. He was awarded an M.B.A. with Distinction from the Harvard Business School.

Kathy Biro is President of the Strategic Interactive Group, a Bronner Slosberg Humphrey Company, which assists clients in developing and executing Interactive Media strategy. Ms. Biro has more than 17 years' experience in marketing and new business development, with particular expertise in all forms of direct response and alternative electronic delivery, including catalog marketing and interactive online information services. Prior to joining BSH, Kathy was Senior Vice President at Bankers Trust, where she was in charge of international product management and marketing for the Global Operating and Information Services division. Before Bankers Trust, she was a partner in a consulting firm. Her start-up experiences include the launching of Shearson Lehman Hutton's credit business and development of the first premium credit cards for Citicorp and Chase Manhattan. Ms. Biro was a pioneer in the early days of Videotex and online services, and was responsible for the development and introduction of Chase Manhattan Bank's interactive home information service in 1984. She holds an M.B.A. in marketing and finance from Columbia University's Graduate School of Business.

Stephen P. Bradley is William Ziegler Professor of Business Administration and Chairman of the Competition and Strategy area at the Harvard Business School, where he currently teaches "Competing in the Information Age," and "Business and the Internet: Strategy, Policy, and the Law," in the M.B.A. Program. Professor Bradley's research interests center on the impact of technology on industry structure and the competitive strategies of firms. He has written numerous articles and five books on operations research and competitive strategy, including *Future Competition in Telecommunications* (with Jerry A. Hausman) and *Globalization, Technology, and Competition* (with Jerry A. Hausman and Richard L. Nolan). Professor Bradley received his B.E. in electrical engineering from Yale University, where he was elected to Tau Beta Pi, and his M.S. and Ph.D. in operations research from the University of California, Berkeley. He is a member of the Board of Directors of Xcellenet, Inc. and the Controlled Risk Insurance Company, Ltd.

Paul A. Brands is Chief Executive Officer of American Management Systems, Inc. (AMS), where he has been involved in systems and consulting for the Federal civilian and defense agencies since 1977. In 1992, Mr. Brands' responsibilities were expanded to include state and local government groups and private-sector consulting, and he was appointed Vice Chairman and a member of AMS's Board of Directors. Mr. Brands served in the Office of the Assistant Secretary of Defense for Systems Analysis from 1967 to 1973, and held the office of Deputy Assistant Administrator for Planning and Evaluation at the U.S. Environmental Protection Agency from 1974 to 1977. He holds a degree in economics from Wesleyan University and an M.B.A. from the University of Rochester's Simon Graduate School of Business Administration.

Raymond R. Burke is the E. W. Kelley Professor of Business Administration at Indiana University and Director of the school's Customer Interface Laboratory. He teaches "Applied Marketing Research" in the M.B.A. program, as well as classes in the executive and Ph.D. programs. Prior to this, Dr. Burke was an Associate Professor of Business Administration at the Harvard Business School and an Assistant Professor of Marketing at the University of Pennsylvania's Wharton School. Dr. Burke's research focuses on the influence of point-of-purchase factors on consumer shopping behavior, and the market impact of the introduction of electronic home shopping services. He has served as a research consultant to a number of leading companies in consumer packaged goods, durable goods, and service industries, and his virtual shopping technology is used by research firms throughout the world. Professor Burke is also co-author of the book, *ADSTRAT: An Advertising Decision Support System.* His articles have appeared in various journals, including the *Harvard Business Review, Journal of Consumer Research, Journal of Marketing, International Journal of Research in Marketing,* and *Marketing Science.*

Eric K. Clemons is Professor of Operations and Information Management at The Wharton School of the University of Pennsylvania, where he is a senior fellow of the Wharton Financial Institutions Center. He is also Project Director for the Reginald H. Jones Center's Sponsored Research Project on *Information Industry Structure and Competitive Strategy.* Professor Clemons' research and teaching interests include strategic information systems, information economics, and the impact of information technology on procurement and outsourcing. He specializes in assessing the competitive implications of information technology and managing risk in large-scale implementation efforts. Professor Clemons holds an S.B. in physics from MIT and an M.S. and Ph.D. in operations research from Cornell University.

David J. Collis is an Associate Professor in the Business, Government, and Competition area at the Harvard Business School. Professor Collis' research interests center on corporate strategy and global competition. He is the co-author (with Cynthia Montgomery) of the book *Corporate Strategy.* His work has appeared in various journals including the *Harvard Business Review, Strategic Management Journal,* and *European Management Journal,* and in the books *Managing the Multibusiness Company, International Competitiveness,* and *Beyond Free Trade.* Professor Collis received his M.A. from Cambridge University, his M.B.A. from the Harvard Business School, and his Ph.D. in business economics from Harvard University.

Jack Dangermond is President of Environmental Systems Research Institute, which he founded with his wife, Laura, in 1969. ESRI is now the world's leading supplier of geographic information systems (GIS). Mr. Dangermond is a leading figure in GIS, the author of hundreds of publications, a frequent keynote speaker, and recipient of many awards. He holds degrees from California Polytechnic University, the University of Minnesota, and Harvard University.

Mark W. Darling is Director of Strategic Planning at American Isuzu Motors, Inc., where his responsibilities include oversight of product planning, market research, sales and market analysis, and corporate brand and product and marketing strategy development. Mr. Darling began his Isuzu career as regional sales manager in the Southeast Region. Prior to joining Isuzu, he held a variety of positions with American Honda Corporation and Volkswagen of America. Mr. Darling holds a Bachelor of Science in finance from The Ohio State University, and has completed the New Marketing Concept and Leveraging Core Competencies programs at Dartmouth's Amos Tuck School of Business.

Amy Edmondson is an Assistant Professor of Business Administration at Harvard Business School, where she teaches the first-year M.B.A. course in Technology and Operations Management. Ms. Edmondson's research examines organizational and team learning in a variety of industries. Her most recent publications include articles in the *Journal of Applied Behavioral Science, Human Relations*, and *Management Learning*. She is also co-editor of *Organizational Learning and Competitive Advantage,* an anthology of papers on the role of learning in the achievement of strategic advantage. From 1987 through 1990, Edmondson was Director of Research for Pecos River Learning Centers, Inc., where she developed and implemented organizational change programs for a variety of companies. Prior to that, she worked as Chief Engineer for Buckminster Fuller, an experience that became the basis for her book about the late architect-inventor's work, *A Fuller Explanation: The Synergetic Geometry of R. Buckminster Fuller.* Edmondson received her Ph.D. in organizational behavior from Harvard University and received her A.B. from Harvard College where she studied engineering sciences and visual and environmental studies.

Justine Fenwick is a doctoral candidate in organizational behavior at the Harvard Business School where she studies "knowledge nomads" or highly skilled hi-tech contract workers. Ms. Fenwick is currently working with Netscape on assimilating new hires and newly acquired companies. Prior to arriving at Harvard, she worked in software design at IBM and Hewlett Packard.

Hossam Galal recently received his Ph.D. in business administration from the Harvard Business School. His research interests include technology management, company restructuring, and corporate strategy. Mr. Galal has written Harvard Business School case studies and working papers and is active in presenting his research at academic and professional conferences. Before joining HBS, he held professional and managerial positions at AT&T and the United Nations. His background is in computer science.

Jerry A. Hausman is the John and Jennie S. MacDonald Professor of Economics at Massachusetts Institute of Technology where he currently teaches a course, "Competition in Telecommunications," to graduate students in economics and business. He is the Director of the MIT Telecommunications Economics Research Program. Professor Hausman received the John Bates Clark Award from the American Economics Association in 1985 for the most outstanding contributions to economics by an economist under forty years of age. He also received the Frisch Medal from the Econometric Society. Professor Hausman has worked in the areas of demand for voice and data services, central office switches and PBXs, mobile telecommunications, broadcast TV, DBS services, radio, satellite service providers, the Internet, and information services. He is the author of numerous articles and two books, *Future Competition in Telecommunications* (with Stephen P. Bradley) and *Globalization, Technology, and Competition* (with Stephen P. Bradley and Richard L. Nolan).

Marco Iansiti is an Associate Professor in the Technology and Operations Management area at the Harvard Business School. He has taught several courses at Harvard University and Harvard Business School, including "Technology and Operations Management" and "Managing Product Development." He is the Faculty Chairman of "Leading Product Development," a summer executive program. Professor Iansiti's research focuses on the management of technology and product development; his area of technical expertise is in microelectronics, with emphasis on the development, fabrication, and testing of very small electronic circuits. Professor Iansiti's work has appeared in the *Harvard Business Review, California Management Review, Research Polity, Industrial and Corporate Change, Production and Operations Management,* and *IEEE Transactions on Engineering Management.* His most recent book, *Technology Integration: Making Critical Choices in a Turbulent World,* was published by Harvard Business School Press. Professor Iansiti received his A.B. and Ph.D. degrees in physics from Harvard University.

Dorothy A. Leonard (formerly Leonard-Barton), William J. Abernathy Professor of Business Administration, joined the faculty of Harvard University in 1983 after teaching for three years at the Sloan School of Management at the Massachusetts Institute of Technology. Professor Leonard has conducted executive courses on a wide range of innovation-related topics at Harvard, MIT, and Stanford and at corporations like Kodak, AT&T, and Johnson & Johnson. She is the author of *Wellsprings of Knowledge: Building and Sustaining the Sources of Innova-*

tion (1995). Her research interests and consulting expertise include technology strategy, commercialization, and the identification and management of knowledge assets in knowledge-intensive companies. Leonard has consulted for the governments of Sweden, Jamaica, and Indonesia and for major corporations like IBM and Digital Equipment Corporation. She serves on the Board of Directors of American Management Systems, an industry leader in custom software development. Her writing appears in academic journals like the *Strategic Management Journal*, practitioner journals like the *Harvard Business Review*, and in books on technology management such as *The Perpetual Enterprise Machine*. Her Ph.D. is from Stanford University.

Alan MacCormack is a doctoral candidate in Technology and Operations Management at the Harvard Business School. His research explores the management of technology and product development in rapidly changing environments, such as the Internet software and computer workstation industries. Mr. MacCormack's work has appeared in a number of journals, including the *Harvard Business Review* and the *Sloan Management Review*. Before arriving at Harvard, he worked as a management consultant for Booz•Allen & Hamilton, where he focused on the automotive and aerospace industries. Mr. MacCormack holds a master's degree in management from MIT's Sloan School of Management.

Thomas W. Malone is Patrick J. McGovern Professor of Information Systems at MIT's Sloan School of Management, where he is the founder-director of the Center for Coordination Science and a founding co-director of a new research initiative on organizations of the twenty-first century. Professor Malone's research focuses on the ways in which computers and communications technology change how people work together in groups and organizations. Long before their advent, Professor Malone predicted the trends toward smaller firms, electronic buying and selling, and "outsourcing" of firms' noncore functions. He has published over fifty research papers and book chapters, and is frequently quoted in publications like *Fortune, Scientific American*, and *The Wall Street Journal*. Before joining MIT, Professor Malone was a research scientist at the Xerox Palo Alto Research Center (PARC), where he designed educational software and office information systems. His background includes a Ph.D. from Stanford University as well as degrees in applied mathematics, engineering, and psychology.

Andrew P. McAfee is a doctoral candidate at the Harvard Business School in the Technology and Operations Management area. His research interests include the impact of new internetworked information technologies on trade and production. Mr. McAfee has designed and presented a series of seminars on innovations that are at the heart of the rapid expansion in electronic commerce, like public key cryptography. He holds dual M.S. degrees in mechanical engineering and management as well as a B.S. in mechanical engineering and a B.S. in French, all from MIT. Prior to his arrival at Harvard Business School, he worked as a consultant in operations management, advising clients in a range of industries from aerospace to consumer electronics, white goods, and OEM electronics.

Brian E. Mennecke is an Assistant Professor of Management Information Systems in the Department of Decision Sciences at East Carolina University. He is Past-President and cofounder of the GeoBusiness Association, the association that represents business professionals who develop, manage, or use geographic technologies. Professor Mennecke is currently studying the use of technologies like the Internet and geographic information systems in business and government. His other research interests include electronic commerce, electronic labor markets, data visualization, group decision making, and spatial data warehouses. He has been associated with several U.S. Department of Labor initiatives, such as America's Labor Market Information System, America's Job Bank, and America's Talent Bank. He has published articles in numerous academic and practitioner journals and has contributed a chapter to a leading book on group support systems. Professor Mennecke earned his Ph.D. in management information systems at Indiana University. He also holds master's degrees in geology and business from Miami University.

Richard L. Nolan, the William Barclay Harding Professor of Business Administration at the Harvard Business School, teaches M.B.A. courses on information strategy and management. Prior to joining the Harvard Business School faculty in 1991, he served fourteen years as chairman of Nolan, Norton & Co., a consulting company he cofounded in 1977 with David P. Norton. Now part of KPMG Peat Marwick, Nolan, Norton & Co. specializes in information technology management. Professor Nolan has published widely in the information technology and general management press, including the *Harvard Business Review* and *Sloan Management Review*. His most recent books are *Reengineering the Organi-*

338   *About the Contributors*

zation: Transforming to Compete in the Information Economy (with Donna B. Stoddard, Thomas H. Davenport, and Sirkka Jarvenpaa); *Creative Destruction: A Six-Stage Process for Transforming the Organization* (with David C. Croson); *Globalization, Technology, and Competition* (with Stephen P. Bradley and Jerry A. Hausman); and *Building the Information-Age Organization* (with James Cash, Robert Eccles, and Nitin Nohria). His Ph.D. is from the University of Washington.

PJ Santoro is the Director of Relationship/Target Marketing Services at Levi Strauss & Co. Since joining Levi Strauss & Co. in 1989, she has held various strategic marketing positions all of which have contributed to the Levi's® and Dockers® brands. In her current position she is responsible for developing and implementing Levi Strauss & Co.'s database marketing and targeted marketing technologies. Prior to joining Levi Strauss & Co., Ms. Santoro spent twelve years working for various advertising agencies on the West Coast in senior account management positions. Ms. Santoro has had articles published by *Business Geographics, Direct,* and *Marketing Weekly*. She has been a keynote speaker at the GIS in Business Conference, the Direct Marketing Association Annual Convention, and the Equifax/National Decision Systems Annual Conference. Ms. Santoro holds degrees in marketing and economics from Simmons College.

Linda J. Schuck is the Director of Brand Strategy and Communications Research at the Pacific Gas and Electric Company in San Francisco, California. From 1984 to 1996, she was a management consultant, specializing in marketing and strategic communications research in the energy industry. Prior to 1984, she served as the special counsel to the deputy secretary of the U.S. Department of Energy; as a Director of the Alliance to Save Energy; and as the Executive Director of the Stanford YWCA. Ms. Schuck has an M.B.A. from Stanford Graduate School of Business and a B.A. from Stanford University.

John J. Sviokla is an Associate Professor in the Managing Information Systems area at the Harvard Business School. Professor Sviokla's current work focuses on electronic commerce and knowledge management, in particular, how managers can use the power of technology to create value for customers and extract value through superior financial performance. With his colleague, Professor Jeffrey F. Rayport, he has collaborated on "Marketspace: The New Locus of Value Creation," in *Intelligent Environments*; "Managing in the Marketspace" and "Exploiting the Virtual Value Chain" in the *Harvard Business Review*; and a recent videotape on marketspace concepts. With another colleague, Professor Benson Shapiro, Sviokla has edited *Seeking Customers and Keeping Customers*. His publications also include numerous journal articles on expert systems. Professor Sviokla is on the editorial board of the *Journal of Electronic Commerce* and is an associate editor of *Organization Science*. Professor Sviokla consults with large and small firms and teaches regularly in the Harvard Business School. He received his B.A. from Harvard College and his M.B.A. and D.B.A. from Harvard University.

David M. Upton is an Associate Professor at the Harvard Business School, where he teaches the required first-year M.B.A. course in Technology and Operations Management. He is faculty chair of Harvard's executive course on Operations Strategy and Improvement and has taught in the International Senior Managers program and the China-based Managing Global Opportunities program. In 1996, Dr. Upton received the School's Apgar award for Innovation in Teaching. His current research focuses on the issue of improvement of flexibility in manufacturing companies. Dr. Upton has published many journal articles on manufacturing, most recently in *Management Science, Harvard Business Review, California Management Review* and the *Journal of Manufacturing Systems,* as well as the book *Strategic Operations: Building Competitive Advantage through Operating Capabilities* (1996), written with Robert Hayes and Gary Pisano. He graduated with Honors in engineering from King's College, Cambridge University and earned a Master's degree in manufacturing from the same institution. He completed his Ph.D. in industrial engineering at Purdue in computer integrated manufacturing (CIM) systems.

Gerald Zaltman is the Joseph C. Wilson Professor of Business Administration at the Harvard Business School and a member of Harvard University's interdisciplinary initiative, "Mind, Brain, and Behavior." Prior to arriving at Harvard, he held faculty appointments at the University of Pittsburgh and Northwestern University. His major research interests focus on buyer behavior and on how managers use information in learning about markets. He has developed a new market research tool (ZMET) which is now being used by major corporations for understanding the mental models underlying customer and manager thinking and behavior. Dr. Zaltman is author or co-author of fourteen books and editor or co-editor of twelve other books. He has published widely in journals, has contributed chapters to numerous books, and is a frequent presenter at national conferences. Dr. Zaltman received his Ph.D. in sociology from The Johns Hopkins University.